Co-Creation, Innovation and New Service Development

T0270857

Involving customers in the development and production of new services becomes a powerful force across many creative industries. Customers can directly supply the firm with innovative ideas, provide skilled labour, and act as a powerful force in marketing. Firms across the world, as they seek to innovate and to better respond to market needs, begin to recognize the benefits stemming from customers' involvement in their operations. Co-creation also becomes more prevalent as customers begin to expect it from firms—seeking to influence their favourite services or products, and to have them better tailored to their needs.

Nevertheless, empowering the customers and involving them in the internal affairs of a firm is both difficult and risky. Despite co-creation becoming increasingly important to firms, very few accounts of it exist and many firms fail. Therefore, to navigate those straits, and to reap the benefits of co-creation, requires knowledge and more complete understanding of socio-cultural forces underpinning it.

By studying a wide array of videogames firms in the USA and Europe, this book provides a unique insight into co-creation. It builds on the existing theories to provide a unified framework for understanding co-creation in creative industries and other sectors. It combines insights from the dynamics of customer communities with a firm's perspective on innovation management and organizational transformation.

The book offers highly detailed insights into the industry, which is at the forefront of co-creation. Furthermore, it sheds new light on the videogames firms and their operations and is therefore ideally designed for researchers, educators and students alike in the fields of knowledge management, innovation management, firm strategy, organization studies and creativity management.

Jedrzej Czarnota is a Research Analyst at Trilateral Research Ltd., UK.

Routledge Interpretive Marketing Research

Edited by
Stephen Brown
University of Ulster, Northern Ireland

For a full list of titles in this series, please visit www.routledge.com

Recent years have witnessed an 'interpretive turn' in marketing and consumer research. Methodologies from the humanities are taking their place alongside those drawn from the traditional social sciences.

Qualitative and literary modes of marketing discourse are growing in popularity. Art and aesthetics are increasingly firing the marketing imagination.

This series brings together the most innovative work in the burgeoning interpretive marketing research tradition. It ranges across the methodological spectrum from grounded theory to personal introspection, covers all aspects of the postmodern marketing 'mix', from advertising to product development, and embraces marketing's principal sub-disciplines.

Co-Creation, Innovation and New Service Development

The Case of the Videogames Industry

Jedrzej Czarnota

LONDON AND NEW YORK

First published 2018 by Routledge

2 Park Square, Milton Park, Abingdon, Oxfordshire OX14 4RN

52 Vanderbilt Avenue, New York, NY 10017

Routledge is an imprint of the Taylor & Francis Group, an informa business

First issued in paperback 2019

Library of Congress Cataloging-in-Publication Data
A catalog record for this book has been requested

ISBN: 978-1-138-63659-0 (hbk)
ISBN: 978-0-367-88695-0 (pbk)

Typeset in Sabon
by Apex CoVantage, LLC

To Marcus and my family

Contents

Figures and Tables

Figures

Tables

Acknowledgements

This book would have never happened if it wasn't for the help and insights of videogames developers in the USA and Europe. I wholeheartedly thank the staff of Obsidian Entertainment, with special thanks to Chris Avellone, Josh Sawyer, Feargus Urquhart and Adam Brennecke; the staff of Blizzard Entertainment, with special thanks to Steven Dowling; the staff and fans of CCP Games, with special thanks to Paul Elsy; the staff of Cloud Imperium Games and Foundry 42, with special thanks to Erin Roberts and Tom Johnson; the staff of 5th Planet Games, with special thanks to David Lease. I also sincerely thank the staff of inXile Entertainment, Deep Silver Volition, VMC, Born Ready Games, ArenaNet, Square Enix, Zenimax Online Studios, UKIE, Press Space PR and ICO Partners.

I also express my deepest gratitude to the professors and staff at Manchester Institute of Innovation Research, with special thanks to Maria Nedeva, Ian Miles, Thordis Sveinsdottir, Ronnie Ramlogan, and John Rigby. I also thank my University of Manchester friends Cameron Roberts, Robbie Watt and Franziska Drews.

Last but not least, I would like to thank my brother Tytus Czarnota for his timely support and help with editing and reviewing—I wouldn't have made it without you.

1 Introduction

Co-creation is becoming a practice of high importance. It accompanies the changes in economy, in which networks that exist both within and outside of organizations determine and generate value. In businesses, we observe the merging of processes that traditionally used to be separate, or even secret: production and use, marketing and consumption, innovation and experience. Co-creation is the key to understanding modern creative industries—it is the practice at the core of this dynamic.

Co-creation[1] is defined as a collaborative work between a consumer and a firm in an innovation practice, where a substantial component to the design, development, production, marketing or distribution of a new or existing service is contributed by a customer or customer communities (Roberts et al., 2014; Banks, 2013). It has become a widespread phenomenon, which reflects wider societal and economic changes in participatory culture (Hartley, 2008; Bruns, 2008), as value is increasingly co-created by both the firm and the customer (Hartley et al., 2012: 21). While this blurring of production and consumption practices is not a new phenomenon (Jenkins, 2009), it has become more salient in the context of digital technologies (Van der Graaf, 2009). This participatory turn in culture (OECD, 2007) is viewed as a logic that seems to favour new production-consumption configurations.

Firms have begun to realize the commercial potential of engaging customers in service development (Edwards et al., 2015). Nevertheless, it is a practice characterized by high uncertainty (Sakao et al., 2009; Lynn and Akgun, 1998; Knight, 1921), and for every firm mastering it, there are many others that fail spectacularly (Gebauer et al., 2013; Banks, 2009).

Co-creation, as it describes the dynamic of customer inputs to new service development, is a manifestation of the wider customer innovation phenomenon (Sundbo and Toivonen, 2011). In the light of scholarly works on customer innovation in technology-intensive industries (Füller et al., 2008; Baldwin et al., 2006; von Hippel, 2005; Franke and von Hippel, 2003; Luthje and Herstatt, 2004), there is a dearth of literature on how parallel practices occur in more experience-driven industries. With the associated rise in the importance of service-like dimensions of many products (Vargo and Lusch, 2004, 2008), and the role of customers in determining the value of these (Fisher and Smith, 2011; Grönroos, 2011; Echeverri and Skalen, 2011; Lusch and Vargo, 2006), it becomes important to study the customers' role in innovation in more experience-driven settings—such as the videogames industry. We also seek to apply some of the von Hippel's (2005) observations on lead user innovation to creative industries and experience services to provide practical lessons to managers on how to benefit from the creativity of the most talented customers.

Creative industries such as broadcasting, music, design and fashion are characterized by a large amount of continuous interaction between the firm and its customers, as well as the existence of networks of customers, where the value-ascribing decisions take place (Hartley et al., 2013; Potts, Cunningham et al., 2008, Potts, Hartley et al., 2008) by mechanisms such as word of mouth (Gebauer et al., 2013). Some works on the customers' input to the design of creative services exist already (Kohler, Füller, Matzler et al., 2011 and Kohler, Füller, Stieger and Matzler et al., 2011; Kohler et al., 2009; Füller and Matzler, 2007), but little attention is being paid to the firms themselves. To focus on the firm in the co-creation practice is the major goal of this work, as there is little research concerning the impact of co-creation on the firm—and how the practices of organizations are affected by it. At the same time, there is a wealth of literature proposing taxonomies, typologies, and other classifications of co-creation, depending on the role of the firm, duration, frequency, actors involved, stage in service development, locus of control and many others (O'Hern and Rindfleisch, 2010; O'Hern et al., 2011; Hoyer et al., 2010; Piller and Ihl, 2009; Piller et al., 2011; Frow et al., 2011). Existing work focuses on the practice itself, while the firm is black-boxed—we seek to shed light on the firm and its activities, thus being of use to businesses wishing to deploy co-creation in new service development (NSD) in creative industries. To that end, we need more empirical material and observations from firms which were successful at implementing co-creation, so the lessons from them can be transferred and applied to other companies.

Understanding how customer involvement works in the development of experiential services will show firms how to successfully tap into customer innovation. Furthermore, practical analysis of customer innovation in creative industries, where the 'content' of a service plays a significant role in determining market performance, is another core focus of this book.

Among creative industries, the videogames industry forms a particularly informative setting for a study of co-creation. Videogame firms are secretive and reluctant to share information about their own practices and operations, either with their peers or with researchers (Nardi, 2010; O'Donnell, 2014; Boellstorff et al., 2012). The videogames industry is also a young industry, in which production, innovation and marketing practices are still evolving in large leaps (Grantham and Kaplinsky, 2005). Many of the videogame developers are self-taught, and there are few higher education institutions that offer courses and degrees valued by industry practitioners. That's why the industry overall has a propensity to experiment with different new service development methodologies, including co-creation. Its companies are currently at the forefront of commercial application of co-creation, and other firms in creative industries can learn from their practices and copy some of them (or use them as a warning; see for example Banks, 2013).

In the videogames industry, socio-cultural effects of fandom and participation visibly overlap with market aspects of videogame development and marketing. Videogame customers actively shape their engagement with the service (Jäger et al., 2010). Videogame firms traditionally have also been close to their customers (King and Borland, 2014), and the industry has always been characterized by the close collaboration of both the makers, as well as players (Nardi, 2010). The clear distinction between videogame developers and customers has begun to emerge only in recent years, together with the spike in game production costs (Marchand and Hennig-Thurau, 2013; O'Donnell, 2012; Zackariasson and Wilson, 2012).[2]

Co-creation is surrounded by the uncertainty of using it as a viable business strategy. We don't know much about how co-creation practices should be structured in practice (Kohler, Füller, Matzler et al., 2011 and Kohler, Füller, Stieger and Matzler et al., 2011). We translate the potential locked in the cultural shifts such as prosumption (Ritzer and Jurgenson, 2010), playbour (Kücklich, 2005), Web 2.0 (O'Reilly, 2005) and user-generated content (Hartley et al., 2013) into firm practices and strategies. We highlight the pitfalls awaiting the firms, which are varied in their nature, and occur virtually in all sites of the firm (Miles and Green, 2008), service design areas (Voss and Zomerdjik, 2007), and stages of new service development (Piller et al., 2011; Hoyer et al., 2010). Understanding what they are, and more importantly, how to avoid them and succeed in co-creation, is the prime concern of this work. By identifying the main characteristics of a firm that influence co-creation practice, we enhance the existing managerial practice of involving customers as co-creators in NSD. This also assists in planning, or anticipating, the organizational changes accompanying co-creation—their scope, site within the organization, as well as their effect on NSD. It also helps in strategic planning of funding and revenue model within organizations—shedding light on their consequences.

This research unifies in a single analytical framework the effects of co-creation on both market performance as well as relationship with customers. It explains to managers how the marketing-driven decisions to co-create with customers may impact the firm's ability to develop its services, as well as affect the internal functioning of the organization. It also demonstrates the opposite—that having customers as participants in NSD must be managed not only for productivity, but also for its experience, in order not to cause heavy damage to the firm's relationship with customers (Gebauer et al., 2013). We explore the NSD dynamics in firms that have close links to customer communities, where innovation is influenced by communities of consumption (Jeppesen and Frederiksen, 2006).

Therefore, we seek to identify and understand the key organizational characteristics and arrangements that determine co-creation practice in firms. We also set out to enhance the understanding of the changes that co-creation has on the NSD and innovation. Finally, we investigate the way in which organizations assimilate the inputs from their customers, and how those ways are linked to both organizational characteristics, as well as co-creation's outcomes on the organizational level. Attention is devoted to the role of funding arrangements, crowdfunding in particular, as well as to the role of organizational culture in influencing a firm's propensity and style of co-creation (Naranjo-Valencia, 2011; Martins and Terblanche, 2003; Barney, 1986). We aim to enhance managers' understanding of co-creation and its role in firms, particularly in firms' NSD and innovation practices. From the stance of innovation management, we analyze the possibilities for innovation stemming from co-creation in creative industries. We uncover the effects of co-creation on firms' functioning related to NSD and innovation, as well as other aspects of a firm. We delve into organizational transformations and processes that need to be instituted by firms embracing customers as a source of innovation.

To achieve that, we analyze three elements of co-creation: firstly, the competences for co-creation on the side of the firm—the ability to assimilate and appropriate the inputs originating from the community of customers (Piller and Ihl, 2009; Yee, 2014; Füller, 2010; Burger-Helmchen and Cohendet, 2011); secondly, various patterns of interaction with the customers (Lettl, 2007) and establishing co-creative practice within a firm; thirdly, a firm's ability to maintain stable and positive relationship with its customers (Gebauer et al., 2013; Banks, 2013; Gummesson, 2002; Grönroos, 1994).

The form of co-creation can differ for various NSD projects conducted by a firm. A firm can decide to tap into customers' potential for co-creation to varying extents depending on its needs, competences and strategy (Teece, 2010; Rosenbloom and Christensen, 1994). In the case studies, we observe the practice of co-creation to be moderated by two factors: the funding arrangements and organizational culture. Funding arrangements are the first moderator (Ordanini et al., 2011; Hoyer et al., 2010). Of significance here is the phenomenon of crowdfunding (Belleflamme et al., 2014; Mollick, 2012). The second moderator is organizational culture (Naranjo-Valencia et al., 2011; Martins and Terblanche, 2003; Barney, 1986). It reflects the history of the firm (whose approaches to NSD and innovation were successful in the past), its strategic orientation (including also the stage at NSD; Cheng and Huizingh, 2014; Grant, 2010), and its employees' attitudes (meaning how employees view co-creating customers; Malaby, 2009).

We also investigate the way in which customer inputs contribute to a firm's co-creation practice, including innovation. While it is often seen as obvious that closer links to customers support successful innovation, there is reason to think that being too close to customers may impede radical innovation (Aoyama and Izushi, 2008; Christensen et al., 2005; Gruner and Hombug,

2000). Customer inputs typically involve incremental change, which is visible in the form of their inputs to firms' NSD and innovation, as they tend to fall along the existing trajectories of service development. Those inputs focus mostly on improvements on the propositions brought forward by the company and play a well-visible role in quality assurance as well as marketing. Such inputs take various channels in reaching organizations.

We set out to understand how the customers contribute to a firm's innovation practices in eight sites of an organization (Miles and Green, 2008). We clarify the issue of co-creation's relationship to radical innovation and incremental improvements (Kasmire et al., 2012). We investigate what is the form of customers' inputs that influence and are assimilated by the firm, seeking their locus in the domain of incremental, 'under-the-radar' contributions rather than break-through ideas reshaping and changing the nature of the firm's service offering. The third problem relates to the extent of co-creation occurring by the means of formal practices within an organization, as opposed to resulting from numerous and close interactions of employees with customers across the firm boundary (Cohendet and Simon, 2007; Van de Ven, 1993), akin to 'hidden innovation' described by Miles and Green (2008). We clarify the differences between formal and informal co-creation, as well as contextualize them within the issues of a firm's control over co-creation practice (O'Hern and Rindfleisch, 2010), changes to the organization (Voss and Zomerdijk, 2007; den Hertog, 2000) as well as the outcomes of that practice (Gustafsson et al., 2012).

We analyze the impact of co-creation on various aspects of a firm's functioning, as well as identify the main dimensions of its influence on a firm's practices. Co-creation has profound effects on organizations. They pertain to both market and socio-cultural dimensions (Banks and Potts, 2010; Potts, 2009; Potts, Cunningham et al., 2008, and Potts, Hartley et al., 2008), and influence a firm's back-office processes, revenue model, organizational culture, design of the service, as well as relationship between the firm and its customers (Miles and Green, 2008; Sundbo and Toivonen, 2011; Bengtsson and Ryzhkova, 2015). The main focus is on the firm's new service development and related innovation practices. We seek to understand how firms respond to the creative potential of their customers, and how their own internal functions and practices are adjusted to assimilate external inputs. We map these changes onto the eight sites of a firm (see Table 1.1).

We observe three case studies capturing various circumstances of co-creation, where the form of co-creation takes different shapes. They are linked to three ideal types of co-creation practice: structured, semi-structured and loose. Those firms in their practices differ in respect to the degree of formalization of the co-creation practice (where we identify formal versus informal co-creation), extent of organizational transformations associated with co-creation, as well as the role of customer inputs in NSD and marketing. We map the effect that co-creation has, in different circumstances of a firm's propensity and style, on NSD and innovation practices.

Table 1.1 Eight Sites of Co-Creation Outcomes (Including Innovation) Within Organizations

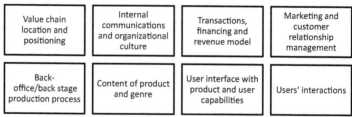

Value chain location and positioning	Internal communications and organizational culture	Transactions, financing and revenue model	Marketing and customer relationship management
Back-office/back stage production process	Content of product and genre	User interface with product and user capabilities	Users' interactions

Source: A Modification of Miles and Green (2008: 67)

Co-creation influences how services are developed and delivered; it also influences the content of those services, as well as transforms organizations that develop them. Those transformations are not always just the results of co-creation's adoption—often they are also organizational prerequisites for its successful use.

We observed how customer inputs are integrated with a firm's practices, as well as how a firm's practices are altered by the assimilation of customer inputs. We selected three major videogames firms: Obsidian Entertainment, CCP and Cloud Imperium Games, as well as a number of smaller firms, as the research site for data collection. The methods used were semi-structured interviews, site visits and online document analysis.

We identified four constructs: (1) competences for co-creation, (2) funding arrangements, (3) organizational culture, as well as (4) outcomes of co-creation. The 'competences for co-creation' informs the empirical investigation of particular characteristics of the firm that are conducive to co-creation and which aid its success, following on Piller and Ihl (2009) and Lettl (2007). It also guides our understanding of the integration of customers' inputs with the internal practices of the firm.[3]

The 'funding arrangements' explores the consequences of embracing crowdfunding as a way to finance NSD, affecting the relationship between the firm and its customers. It follows on the definitions of Belleflamme et al. (2014), Lehner (2012) and Ordanini et al. (2011). Crowdfunding is accompanied by customer empowerment in brand (or consumption) communities (Kozinets, 2007) and their gradual transformation into communities of creation (which generate ideas and provide feedback on firm's offerings; Jäger et al., 2010).

The 'organizational culture' pertains to the attitudes of the employees towards co-creation and externally developed ideas. They heavily influence the shape and presence of co-creation in any organization. Organizational culture is closely linked to organizational history (i.e., as an organization's capabilities depend on its cumulative historic activities, and a firm's success is dependent on its past activities; Cohen and Levinthal, 1990) and a firm's strategic orientation (Cheng and Huizingh, 2014). The 'organizational culture' construct is also of critical importance for rooting the analysis within the videogames industry and its idiosyncrasies of new service development. Following on the works of Martins and Terblanche (2003) and Naranjo-Valencia et al. (2011) we observe how organizational culture directly influences a firm's creativity and innovation strategy. Organizational culture is also linked to a firm's competences for co-creation, as they reside in the skills and attitudes of individual employees (Chatenier et al., 2010).

The 'outcomes of co-creation' reflect the effect that co-creation has on organizations, and aid in empirically describing which functions of the firm, stages of new service development, or dimensions of a service are affected by it. It also refers to the outcomes of co-creation that do not pertain to the firm alone, but to its relationship with the customers, their role in the development of firm's services, as well as roles that they can play in a firm's operations and value chain.

Co-creation involves various actors, both internal and external to the organization, both individuals and groups of individuals; even communities shape its dynamics. Various organizational departments become involved in this practice and are affected by its outcomes. It is a practice that depends on the firm strategy and on the culture and attitudes of individual employees. We must provide rich detail to understand co-creation, allowing for the explanation of its dynamics, actors, as well as relevance (to firms, their customers or industries at large).

Case Studies

In order to describe, analyze and understand the occurrence of co-creation within the videogames industry, as well as to map its impact on innovation in firms, we focus on three case studies. Each revolves around a major videogame studio in the USA or Europe. Its activities and co-creation are the focal point of each case.

The videogames industry can be divided into three large segments: personal computer (PC) games, console games (i.e., large-budget titles released on mainly Sony PlayStation and Microsoft Xbox) and mobile games. The degree of co-creation in those three segments varies significantly, mostly due to the high barriers of entry (easy accessing of videogame code is available only on the PC platform; similar manipulations of game code on console or mobile platform tend to be technically difficult and violate the license agreements). Those three platforms are also characterized by different patterns of use. PC games are regarded as the domain of the most demanding fans, who seek tailored and highly customizable game experiences. This is also the platform which is almost exclusively associated with modding (Nardi, 2010). Mobile platform games are considered to be catering predominantly to the casual or 'on the go' audiences, i.e., players who seek simple and undemanding games. Console games focus on the experiences that target large customer populations—for instance players who seek well-crafted and complete services that are simple to set up and enjoy (Zackariasson and Wilson, 2012).

We decided to focus on the firms developing videogames for the PC segment of the market, due to their association with modding (Nardi, 2010), age (PC games were the first games developed; King and Borland, 2014), close links between firms and their audiences (due to the fact that PC games are developed for niche audiences, or customers of particular taste and preference in gameplay; Pearce, 2009), association with crowdfunding (e.g. console games are too expensive to crowdfund; Marchand and Hennig-Thurau, 2013), as well as fast rate of innovation (due to lower development, production and distribution costs, there are many firms of all sizes releasing games on this platform, in numbers vastly exceeding, for example, console games). This is not to say that co-creation is absent from console or mobile segments of the videogames industry—although its practice, tools and competences might vary from what is described in this study. The lessons from this work have application to all segments and platforms of the videogames industry (and beyond it, in, for example, creative industries), as co-creation will have comparable effect on organizations regardless of their market. The operations of all videogame studios follow similar dynamics and structures (i.e., main functions, project management techniques, distribution channels, funding arrangements, etc.) as the videogames industry is fairly homogeneous.

Hence our data collection effort focused only on the PC games. Out of these, we identified the games which had a reputation for being developed together with the help from the customers. Of most interest here were the large MMO (massively multiplayer online) games, which, by their gameplay design and technology employed, are particularly prone to being co-created—a phenomenon observed already by Castronova (2005), Nardi (2010), Pearce (2009) and Boellstorff (2012). This is because MMO games have large and very active communities of players, and the firms interact with them frequently in order to make sure that the service meets their needs and expectations. Also of interest in this study were games that were crowdfunded. As the selection of cases was occurring largely in the mid-2013, there were still very few videogames that were funded that way. Obsidian Entertainment's *Pillars of Eternity*, inXile Entertainment's *Torment: Tides of Numenera*, as well as Cloud Imperium Games' *Star Citizen* were all financed using crowdfunding. As it is demonstrated in this study, crowdfunding creates the expectation of customers to participate in the internal works of the firm. The firms tend to meet that expectation by frequently releasing various reports to the crowdfunding customers, inviting them to the offices, granting them formal stake in the game development process and so on.

Various methods have been employed to provide a rich and insightful description of the co-creation practices of videogames firms. The data has been collected using a variety of methods: semi-structured interviews, participant observation, as well as documents and cultural artefacts. The description of co-creation, as well as its relationship to innovation, is approached from a variety of perspectives. Apart from the accounts from three major game development studios, each case study also involves the analysis of a few minor firms. Those firms are related to the core case firms by similarity of their operations. Their inclusion serves to deepen the understanding of some phenomena that were not in the first place explored or present in the main firm for each case study, as well as to view a certain aspect of co-creation in additional detail (firms have been selected basing on the replication logic; Yin, 2009). For those additional firms, data is more limited and usually comes from a single type of source—predominantly semi-structured interviews.

The cases differ in the relationship structure between the firm and customers, which then translates into three distinct types of co-creation. This relationship is described by the practice of integrating customer inputs with internal firm processes (in sites identified by Miles and Green, 2008, and Voss and Zomerdijk, 2007). This practice is influenced by competences for co-creation of a firm (Piller and Ihl, 2009; Lettl, 2007), absorptive capacity (Lichtenthaler and Lichtenthaler, 2009; Cohen and Levinthal, 1990), organizational culture (Naranjo-Valencia et al., 2011; Martins and Terblanche, 2003), presence of crowdfunding (Ordanini et al., 2011), as well as overall customer relationship management (Gebauer et al., 2013; Gummesson, 2002). The cases are on the spectrum of structured, semi-structured and unstructured co-creation.

The larger the amount of particular routines, processes, and systems that surround co-creation in a particular firm, the more structured its co-creation is. The employees know which channels to use when customers provide various inputs to service development, marketing, innovation or other functions of the firm; those are routine activities embedded in project management, team structure, and the way that people communicate within an organization. Furthermore, such practice of co-creation is accompanied by the presence of formal channels for the influx of ideas into the firm. Those channels for instance will take form of clearly formulated contests, volunteer programmes or democratic elections among the players, when participating customers know from the outset what kind of rewards or outcomes they can expect, what will happen with their ideas and so on.

At the opposite end of the spectrum is the unstructured co-creation practice. This approach means that the firm does not have any set practices for assimilating customer inputs, and that it processes them 'on the job' by the employees of the firm. It is down to the judgment of individual employees, and their relationship with particular members of the customer community, as to how co-creation practice is shaped. Moreover, there may be some processes that a firm deploys to assimilate customer inputs, but these are purely functional, incurring no obligations on the part of the firm for its customers. Customers may provide ideas to the firm, but they are promised nothing in return (contrary to parallel practices in structured co-creation).

Semi-structured co-creation practice is in-between structured and loose co-creation. It is characterized by the presence of both formal and informal practices for assimilating customer inputs, in roughly equal measure.

The three cases have been matched with those descriptions of ideal types of co-creation. Case Alpha, describing Obsidian Entertainment and other firms, is an example of structured co-creation. Case Beta, discussing CCP and related studios, is the case of semi-structured co-creation. Case Gamma, which focuses on Cloud Imperium Games, illustrates unstructured co-creation. We compare these three cases and thus three forms of co-creation. We use this comparison as a tool for better understanding the practice of co-creation in firms.

The three cases also differ in the strategic orientation of the firm (Cheng and Huizingh, 2014), funding arrangements (Ordanini et al., 2011), as well as stage in NSD (Hoyer et al., 2010). Main firms corresponding to each case are significantly different from one another, and at the same time sufficiently similar to each other as to allow for an analysis of their variations.[4] The differences in strategic orientation help to understand the importance of co-creation for organizations, and the degree of its formal integration with firm's practices (i.e., articulation as a part of the business model). Funding arrangements greatly alter the relationship between firms and their customers, empowering the latter—its presence or absence is a critical variable in determining the firm's propensity for and style of co-creation.

Case study firms differ in the dimension associated with organizational culture. The three main firms are active in similar sectors of the videogames industry (producing videogames of similar genres and for the same platform). Nevertheless, there are some interesting variations in their organizational culture (defined as their attitude towards co-creation and external sources of ideas and innovations, as well as the history of organization's successes and failures) that affect the role of co-creation in their innovation practices. Those differences allow us to focus on the importance of organizational culture as shaping co-creation. By selecting firms characterized by diverse cultures, we see how the attitudes of employees and organizational history (Cohen and Levinthal, 1990) contribute to adoption and successful retention of co-creation. It also accounts for the role of the relationship between individual employees and customers and the function of the 'hidden innovation' dynamics (Miles and Green, 2008) in co-creation.

The main firms selected for the purposes of the three case studies are respectively Obsidian Entertainment (located in California, USA), CCP (located in Iceland, as well as other locations worldwide), as well as Cloud Imperium Games (located in California, USA, as well as other locations worldwide, including Manchester, UK). All three main firms produce videogames in similar genres, for the same platform, consist of videogames industry veterans, are of similar size, as well as are located in the Western world (meaning North America and Western Europe). They are all characterized by the presence of devoted and highly skilled communities of customers. They also operate in market niches of comparable size and type. For a comparison of the firms see Table 1.2.

Table 1.2 Comparison of the Key Characteristics of the Main Three Firms Studied[5]

Case	Case Alpha	Case Beta	Case Gamma
Game genre	Role-playing, single player	Role-playing, online multiplayer	Role-playing, online multiplayer
Platform	Personal computer (Mac/Windows)	Personal computer (Mac/Windows)	Personal computer (Mac/Windows)
Size	Around 200 employees	Around 600 employees	Around 200 employees
Location/HQ	California, USA	Reykjavik, Iceland	California, USA

The three cases also include data from several other studios in Europe and the USA. These studios are inXile Entertainment, 5th Planet Games, Deep Silver Volition, Born Ready Games, ArenaNet and Zenimax Online Studios. We also collected data from a few firms positioned outside of the immediate scope of this study. Those are interviews with two videogames industry consulting firms (ICO Partners and Press Space PR), two videogame distribution firms (Valve Corporation and Square Enix Collective), as well as one trade association (UK Interactive Industry Association—UKIE).

Notes

1. As co-creation can also occur in the business-to-business context (i.e., between two firms) it is important to note that throughout this book, whenever we refer to co-creation, we mean customer co-creation (i.e., between a firm and its customers; Weber, 2011; Sanders and Stappers, 2008).
2. Today, there are relatively scarce academic sources discussing the internal functioning of videogame firms (examples here include Malaby, 2009; O'Donnell, 2014; Van der Graaf, 2012), and very few of these focus on business practices (Arakji and Lang, 2007; Grantham and Kaplinsky, 2005). The issues of access to firms are among the biggest obstacles to researching the videogames industry (Boellstorff et al., 2012; Nardi, 2010). Any empirical insights into the practices of videogame firms are a valuable addition to the knowledge. A detailed insight into that industry is a contribution to both innovation studies, as well as media studies.
3. In this study, the competences for co-creation embedded in a customer community are assumed to be constant across all cases (i.e., all videogame studios are assumed to be dealing with customer community of the same level of skill and affinity for co-creation). This does not affect our findings, while allowing to focus on the firm side of co-creation.
4. We adopted an approach of altering experimental conditions in cases (Yin, 2009). We chose subsequent cases for predicting similar results (a literal replication), with some degree of variance (stemming from the fact that they illustrate three different types of co-creation).
5. Firm size data obtained from LinkedIn on 03.09.2015.

References

Aoyama, Y., and Izushi, H., (2008). User-led innovation and the video game industry. IRP Conference, London, May 22–23, 2008.

Arakji, R.Y., and Lang, K.R., (2007). Digital consumer networks and producer-consumer collaboration: Innovation and product development in the video game industry. *Journal of Management Information Systems*, 24(2), pages 195–219.

Baldwin, C., Hienerth, C., and von Hippel, E., (2006). How user innovations become commercial products: A theoretical investigation and case study. *Research Policy*, 35(9), pages 1291–1313.

Banks, J., (2009). Co-creative expertise: Auran games and fury—a case study. *Media International Australia: Incorporating Culture and Policy*, 130(February), pages 77–89.

Banks, J., (2013). *Co-creating Videogames*. London: Bloomsbury Academic.

Banks, J., and Potts, J., (2010). Co-creating games: A co-evolutionary analysis. *New Media and Society*, 12(2), pages 252–270.

Barney, J.B., (1986). Organizational culture: Can it be a source of sustained competitive advantage? *The Academy of Management Review*, Vol. 11, No. 3, pages 656–665.

Belleflamme, P., Lambert, T., and Schwienbacher, A., (2014). Crowdfunding: Tapping the right crowd. *Journal of Business Venturing*, 29(5), pages 585–609.

Bengtsson, L., and Ryzhkova, N., (2015). Managing online user co-creation in service innovation. In: Agarwal, R., Selen, W., Roos, G., and Green, R., (eds). *The Handbook of Service Innovation*. London: Springer, pages 575–589.

Boellstorff, T., Nardi, B., Pearce, C., and Taylor, T.L., (2012). *Ethnography and Virtual Worlds*. Oxford: Princeton University Press.

Bruns, A., (2008). *Blogs, Wikipedia, Second Life and Beyond: From Production to Produsage*. New York: Peter Lang.

Burger-Helmchen, T., and Cohendet, P., (2011). User communities and social software in the video game industry. *Long Range Planning*, 44, pages 317–343.

Castronova, E., (2005). *Synthetic Worlds: The Business and Culture of Online Games*. Chicago and London: The University of Chicago Press.

Chatenier, E., Verstegen, J.A.A.M., Biemans, H.J.A., Mulder, M., and Omta, O.S.W.F., (2010). Identification of competencies for professionals in open innovation teams. *R&D Management*, 40(3), pages 271–280.

Cheng, C.C., and Huizingh, E.K., (2014). When is open innovation beneficial? The role of strategic orientation. *Journal of Product Innovation Management*, 31(6), pages 1235–1253.

Christensen, J.F., Olesen, M.H., and Kjær, J.S., (2005). The industrial dynamics of open innovation: Evidence from the transformation of consumer electronics. *Research Policy*, 34(10), pages 1533–1549.

Cohen, W.M., and Levinthal, D.A., (1990). Absorptive capacity: A new perspective on learning and innovation. *Administrative Science Quarterly*, Vol. 35, No. 1, pages 128–152.

Cohendet, P., and Simon, L., (2007). Playing across the playground: Paradoxes of knowledge creation in the videogame firm. *Journal of Organizational Behavior*, 28, pages 587–605.

den Hertog, P.D., (2000). Knowledge-intensive business services as co-producers of innovation. *International Journal of Innovation Management*, 4(4), pages 491–528.

Echeverri, P., and Skålén, P., (2011). Co-creation and co-destruction: A practice-theory based study of interactive value formation. *Marketing Theory*, 11(3), pages 351–373.

Edwards, M., Logue, D., and Schweitzer, J., (2015). Towards an understanding of open innovation in services: Beyond the firm and towards relational co-creation. In: Agarwal, R., Selen, W., Roos, G., and Green, R., (eds). *The Handbook of Service Innovation.* London: Springer London, pages 75–90.

Fisher, D., and Smith, S., (2011). Co-creation is chaotic: What it means for marketing when no one has control. *Marketing Theory*, 11(3), pages 325–350.

Franke, N., and von Hippel, E., (2003). Satisfying heterogeneous user needs via innovation toolkits: The case of Apache security software. *Research Policy*, 32(7), pages 1199–1215.

Frow, P., Payne, A., and Storbacka, K., (2011). Co-creation: A typology and conceptual framework. In: *Proceedings of ANZMAC* (November), pages 1–6.

Füller, J., (2010). Refining virtual co-creation from a consumer perspective. *California Management Review*, 52(2), pages 98–122.

Füller, J., and Matzler, K., (2007). Virtual product experience and customer participation—a chance for customer-centred, really new products. *Technovation*, 27(6), pages 378–387.

Füller, J., Matzler, K., and Hoppe, M., (2008). Brand community members as a source of innovation. *Journal of Product Innovation Management*, 25(6), pages 608–619.

Gebauer, J., Füller, J., and Pezzei, R., (2013). The dark and the bright side of co-creation: Triggers of member behaviour in online innovation communities. *Journal of Business Research*, 66, pages 1516–1527.

Grant, R.M., (2010). *Contemporary Strategy Analysis and Cases: Text and Cases.* Chichester, West Sussex: John Wiley & Sons.

Grantham, A., and Kaplinsky, R., (2005). Getting the measure of the electronic games industry: Developers and the management of innovation. *International Journal of Innovation Management*, 9(2), pages 183–213.

Grönroos, C., (1994). From marketing mix to relationship marketing: Towards a paradigm shift in marketing. *Management Decision*, 32(2), pages 4–20.

Grönroos, C., (2011). Value co-creation in service logic: A critical analysis. *Marketing Theory*, 11(3), pages 279–301.

Gruner, K.E., and Homburg, C., (2000). Does customer interaction enhance new product success? *Journal of Business Research*, 49(1), pages 1–14.

Gummesson, E., (2002). Relationship marketing in the new economy. *Journal of Relationship Marketing*, 1(1), pages 37–57.

Gustafsson, A., Kristensson, P., and Witell, L., (2012). Customer co-creation in service innovation: a matter of communication? *Journal of Service Management*, 23(3), pp. 311–327.

Hartley, J., (2008). *Television Truths.* Malden, MA: Wiley-Blackwell.

Hartley, J., Potts, J., Cunningham, S., Flew, T., Keane, M., and Banks, J., (2013). *Key Concepts in Creative Industries.* London: Sage.

Hartley, J., Potts, J., MacDonald, T., Erkunt, C., and Kufleitner, C., (2012). CCI creative city index. *Cultural Science Journal*, 5 (1–138).

Hoyer, W.D., Chandy, R., Dorotic, M., Krafft, M., and Singh, S.S., (2010). Consumer co-creation in new product development. *Journal of Service Research*, 13(3), pages 283–296.

Jäger, P., Haefliger, S., and von Krogh, G., (2010). A directing audience: How specialized feedback in virtual community of consumption stimulates new media production. ETH Zurich Working Paper.

Jenkins, H., (2009). What happened before YouTube. In: Burgess, J. and Green, J., (eds). *YouTube: Online Video and the Politics of Participatory Culture*. London: Polity Press, pages 109–125.

Jeppesen, L.B., and Frederiksen, L., (2006). Why do users contribute to firm-hosted user communities? The case of computer-controlled music instruments. *Organization Science*, 17(1), pages 45–63.

Kasmire, J., Korhonen, J.M., and Nikolic, I., (2012). How radical is a radical innovation? An outline for a computational approach. *Energy Procedia*, 20, pages 346–353.

King, B., and Borland, J., (2014). *Dungeons and Dreamers*. Carnegie Mellon University: ETC Press.

Knight, F.H., (1921). *Risk, Uncertainty, and Profit*. Boston, MA: Hart, Schaffner & Marx; Houghton Mifflin Co.

Kohler, T., Füller, J., Matzler, K., and Stieger, D., (2011). Co-creation in virtual worlds: The design of the user experience. *MIS Quarterly*, 35(3), pages 773–788.

Kohler, T., Füller, J., Stieger, D., and Matzler, K., (2011). Avatar-based innovation: Consequences of the virtual co-creation experience. *Computers in Human Behaviour*, 27, pages 160–168.

Kohler, T., Matzler, K., and Füller, J., (2009). Avatar-based innovation: Using virtual worlds for real-world innovation. *Technovation*, 29(6), pages 395–407.

Kozinets, R.V., (2007). Inno-tribes: Star Trek as Wikimedia. In: Cova, B., Kozinets, R., and Shankar, A., (eds). *Consumer Tribes*. Oxford: Elsevier.

Kücklich, J., (2005). Precarious playbour: Modders and the digital games industry. *The Fibreculture Journal*, 5. http://five.fibreculturejournal.org

Lehner, O.M., (2012). A literature review and research agenda for crowdfunding of social ventures. In: *2012 Research Colloquium on Social Entrepreneurship*, 16–19.07, SAID Business School.

Lettl, C., (2007). User involvement competence for radical innovation. *Journal of Engineering and Technology Management*, 24, pages 53–75.

Lichtenthaler, U., and Lichtenthaler, E., (2009). A capability-based framework for open innovation: Complementing absorptive capacity. *Journal of Management Studies*, 46(8), pages 1315–1338.

Lusch, R.F., and Vargo, S.L., (2006). Service-dominant logic: reactions, reflections and refinements. *Marketing Theory*, 6(3), pages 281–288.

Luthje, C., and Herstatt, C., (2004). The Lead User method: An outline of empirical findings and issues for future research. *R&D Management*, 34(5), pages 553–568.

Lynn, G.S., and Akgun, A.E., (1998). Innovation strategies under uncertainty: A contingency approach for new product development. *Engineering Management Journal*, 10(3), pages 11–18.

Malaby, T.M., (2009). *Making Virtual Worlds: Linden Lab and Second Life*. Ithaca and London: Cornell University Press.

Marchand, A., and Hennig-Thurau, T., (2013). Value creation in the video game industry: Industry economics, consumer benefits, and research opportunities. *Journal of Interactive Marketing*, 27(3), pages 141–157.

Martins, E.C., and Terblanche, F., (2003). Building organisational culture that stimulates creativity and innovation. *European Journal of Innovation Management*, 6(1), pages 64–74.

Miles, I., and Green, L., (2008). *Hidden Innovation in Creative Industries*. London: NESTA.

Mollick, E., (2012). The dynamics of crowdfunding: Determinants of success and failure. SSRN scholarly paper. Social Science Research Network, Rochester, NY.

Naranjo-Valencia, J.C., Jiménez-Jiménez, D., and Sanz-Valle, R., (2011). Innovation or imitation? The role of organizational culture. *Management Decision*, 49(1), pages 55–72.

Nardi, B.M., (2010). *My Life as a Night Elf Priest*. Ann Arbor: The University of Michigan Press and The University of Michigan Library.

O'Donnell, C., (2012). This is not a software industry. In: Zackariasson, P. and Wilson, T.L., (eds). *The Video Games Industry: Formation, Present State, and Future*. London and New York: Routledge.

O'Donnell, C., (2014). *Developer's Dilemma*. London, England: MIT Press.

OECD, (2007). *Annual Report*. Paris: OECD Publishing.

O'Hern, M.S., and Rindfleisch, A., (2010). Customer co-creation: A typology and research Agenda. In: Malhotra, N.K., (ed). *Review of Marketing Research*, 6, pages 84–106., Bigley: Emerald Books.

O'Hern, M.S., Rindfleisch, A., Antia, K.D., and Schweidel, D.A., (2011). The impact of user-generated content on product innovation. SSRN. http://ssrn.com/abstract=1843250 or http://dx.doi.org/10.2139/ssrn.1843250

O'Reilly, T., (2005). Spreading the knowledge of innovators. What is web, 2.

Ordanini, A., Miceli, L., Pizzetti, M., and Parasuraman, A., (2011). Crowd-funding: Transforming customers into investors through innovative service platforms. *Journal of Service Management*, 22(4), pages 443–470.

Pearce, C., (2009). *Communities of Play: Emergent Cultures in Multiplayer Games and Virtual Worlds*. Cambridge, MA and London, England: MIT Press.

Piller, F., and Ihl, C., (2009). *Open Innovation With Customers: Foundations, Competences and International Trends*. RWTH Aachen University.

Piller, F., Ihl, C., and Vossen, A., (2011). A typology of customer co-creation in the innovation process. In: Hanekop, H. and Wittke, V., (eds). *New Forms of Collaborative Innovation and Production on the Internet: An Interdisciplinary Perspective*. University of Goettingen.

Potts, J., (2009). Creative industries and innovation policy. *Innovation: Management, Policy and Practice*, 11(2), pages 138–147.

Potts, J., Hartley, J., Banks, J., Burgess, J., Cobcroft, R., Cunningham, S., and Montgomery, L., (2008). Consumer co-creation and situated creativity. *Industry and Innovation*, 15(5), pages 459–474.

Potts, J., Cunningham, S., Hartley, J., and Ormerod, P., (2008). Social network markets: A new definition of the creative industries. *Journal of Cultural Economics*, 32(3), pages 167–185.

Ritzer, G., and Jurgenson, N., (2010). Production, consumption, prosumption: The nature of capitalism in the age of the digital 'prosumer'. *Journal of Consumer Culture*, 10(1), pages 13–36.

Roberts, D., Hughes, M., and Kertbo, K., (2014). Exploring consumers' motivations to engage in innovation through co-creation activities. *European Journal of Marketing*, 38(½), pages 147–169.

Rosenbloom, R.S., and Christensen, C.M., (1994). Technological discontinuities, organizational capabilities, and strategic commitments. *Industrial and Corporate Change*, 3(3), pages 655–685.

Sakao, T., Panshef, V., and Dörsam, E., (2009). Addressing uncertainty of PSS for value-chain oriented service development. In: Sakao, T. and Lindahl,

M., (eds). *Introduction to Product/Service-System Design*. London: Springer, pages 137–157.

Sanders, E.B.N., and Stappers, P.J., (2008). Co-creation and the new landscapes of design. *CoDesign*, 4(1), pages 5–18.

Sundbo, J., and Toivonen, M., (eds). (2011). *User-B innovation in Services*. Cheltenham: Edward Elgar Publishing.

Teece, D.J., (2010). Business models, business strategy and innovation. *Long Range Planning*, 43(2), pages 172–194.

Van de Ven, A.H., (1993). A community perspective on the emergence of innovations. *Journal of Engineering and Technology Management*, 10(1), pages 23–51.

Van der Graaf, S., (2009). Designing for mod development: User creativity as product development strategy on the firm-hosted 3D software platform. Ph.D Dissertation, LSE.

Van der Graaf, S., (2012). Get organized at work! a look inside the game design process of valve and linden lab. *Bulletin of Science, Technology & Society*, pages 1–9, 0270467612469079.

Vargo, S.L., and Lusch, R.F., (2004). Evolving to a new dominant logic for marketing. *Journal of Marketing*, 68, pages 1–17.

Vargo, S.L., and Lusch, R.F., (2008). Service-dominant logic: Continuing the evolution. *Journal of the Academy of Marketing Science*, 36(1), pages 1–10.

Von Hippel, E., (2005). *Democratizing Innovation*. Cambridge, MA: MIT Press.

Voss, C., and Zomerdijk, L., (2007). Innovation in experimental services—an empirical view. In: DTI (ed). *Innovation in Services*. London: DTI, pages 97–134.

Weber, M., (2011). Customer co-creation in innovations: A protocol for innovating with end users. Doctoral thesis. Eindhoven University of Technology.

Yee, N., (2014). *The Proteus Paradox*. London: Yale University Press.

Yin, R.K., (2009). *Case Study Research. Design and Methods* (Fourth ed.). Thousand Oaks and New Delhi: Sage.

Zackariasson, P., and Wilson, T.L., (2012). *The Video Games Industry: Formation, Present State, and Future*. London and New York: Routledge.

2 Beyond State-of-the-Art in Co-Creation

Services are simultaneously product and process (De Jong and Vermeulen, 2003), and changes in them inherently involve innovation throughout the value chain (Chesbrough, 2011). Service innovation often coincides with new patterns of service content, distribution, client interaction, quality control and assurance and others (den Hertog, 2000). Miles and Green (2008) note that innovation in creative industries is not necessarily about the content, or the aesthetic dimension of the market offering (for example, 'content creativity' as defined by Handke, 2004, or 'aesthetic innovation' by Stoneman, 2007). Innovations in such settings can take place both in products, that are themselves largely aesthetic in nature, as well as in the functional dimensions of the industry's output. The innovation in the 'content' or 'aesthetic' dimensions of a service is the most visible for an external observer and from the perspective of a consumer in particular. Nevertheless, it is behind the stage (Grove et al., 1992) that the most important innovations take place—in the way that a service is designed, developed and delivered to the customers. Innovating in such highly malleable context is multi-dimensional, and applies to the service elements seen by the customer, but also to the processes and mechanisms within the firm that enable the staging of that experience in the first place.

Creative industries' outputs convey an idea, rather than playing a purely functional role of a purely economic good, and their value is usually overwhelmingly based on the experience that they help create, as well as their cultural meaning. They require consumers that can understand and process the information provided, and the consumers' experience of creative services is highly informed by their consumption of related works, prior knowledge and changing tastes (Hartley et al., 2013).

Innovation in Experiential Services

Voss and Zomerdijk (2007) suggest that there are five important design areas in which innovation may be created in experiential services: physical environment, service employees, service delivery process, fellow customers, as well as back-office support. The innovation in those five areas directly or indirectly contributes to a customer's experience. The areas are often referred to in theatrical terms, emphasizing that a service can be seen as a performance that involves a stage, actors, a script, an audience and a back stage area (Grove et al., 1992). In the case of videogames, these areas are synonymous with digital medium (software and the Internet), game developers, game design, fellow players and community members, as well as customer support and community management.

In Voss and Zomerdijk's (2007) understanding, back-office support is the back stage area of experiential design (c.f. Zomerdijk and de Vries, 2007), while front stage comprises physical environment, service employees and service delivery process. In the context of a videogames studio, the back stage area includes the design of the game itself, the code that defines it and gives it form, the writing, art direction, music and acting. Front stage in videogames is represented by community management, game experience, software interface, gameplay and other interactions (for example, with customer service). Worth noting here is that the customer experience is also influenced by fellow customers.

a. Physical environment is the setting in which a service is delivered or experience is created. In the case of videogames industry, it is environment created by digital technology (i.e., software) and the Internet. Environment is considered a key variable influencing customer perceptions and behaviour, and it performs different roles: accommodating customers and employees, guiding behavioural actions, and providing cues about the type of service to be expected. Sensory design is an important part of service environment. The Internet has its own culture and serves as a medium for forming of the communities of customers. Developers (i.e., service providers) must account for its idiosyncrasies when delivering videogames to their audiences. Phenomena such as fandom (Jenkins, REF) influence that dynamic.

b. Service employees and their attitudes towards customers (including the customers' role as co-creators) play a major role in influencing customer experience. Game developers determine the agency of players in the game and limit the scope of their ability to modify it, or to play outside of predefined patterns.

c. Service delivery process stands for a series of actions or events that take place to deliver the service, and in the context of the videogames industry it is the game design (i.e., the script, direction, interactivity and visual identity of a game). It is the script that defines the service performance and whether the customers will enjoy it. A videogame is designed by the studio employees before the customers interact with it. This is linked to management of start, end and peaks of the flow of service delivery process.

d. Fellow customers have a significant influence on a service experience alongside the service provider. Socializing and bonding with other customers can make an experience more enjoyable, as it is seen, for example, in the massively multiplayer online videogames. Creation of community around a product or service is one way to improve a service experience. Toxic community dynamics, such as abusive player groups (as it was the case in, for example, Riot Games' *League of Legends* and was a major problem to be tackled by the studio) can adversely and significantly affect the success of game as a service in the marketplace.

e. Back-office support denotes the plethora of processes that occur on the back stage and influence the front stage performance. Many service organizations, videogames firms included, have a considerable number of back-office employees who are vital to the customer experience (i.e., they design the tangible elements of a service, for example). The examples of such employees are staff in positions of customer service and community management. They are the 'back channel' that service customers take to access and influence the studio developers, or to resolve technical or administrative problems. According to Voss and Zomerdijk (2007), the main innovation related to back stage areas of service delivery involves connecting back-office employees to the front stage experience. Moreover, developers' interactions with customers in services can be another major factor influencing customer experience—although these interactions are fairly rare (although, as we observe in the case of CCP games, the emphasis on that type of interaction is growing in the videogames industry). Willingness to help customers, knowledge, and courtesy of employees and their ability to inspire trust, as well as caring and individualized attention the firm provides to its customers are main determinants of good customer interaction.

Voss and Zomerdijk (2007) note that the experiential service providers produce a continuous stream of innovations to improve elements of existing services. They also notice the role of customer insights (resulting from widely defined consumer research) as a driver of service innovation in experiential services. Miles and Green (2008) add that experiential innovations are typically driven by the customer rather than technology. Service experience concept must be developed and incorporated into service design deliberately and from the outset according to Fynes and Lally (2008), in order to deliver experiential components to customers.

Therefore, in the videogames industry and in creative industries overall, not only the content of the service or its aesthetic nature are the locus of potential innovation. More influential are the innovations on the strategic and organizational levels of firms. Those innovations are often spurred or reinforced by a firm's use of co-creation, as studios invite their customers to their marketing, development, and funding functions. Increasingly, there is no clearly identifiable point where the service producer's activity stops and the user's activity begins—due to high levels of co-creation of service products, as well as growing influence of fellow customers on service experience (den Hertog, 2000). In the chapters to come, we will explore and explain the impact that co-creation has on organizations and innovation in videogames industry.

Green et al. (2007) point out that in creative activities, there is much 'everyday problem solving' leading to a series of small innovations that shape the final creative product. They call it 'process innovation'; such 'on the job' innovation is for instance very common in many professional services.

This is likely the mechanism via which co-creation influences organizations and precipitates transformations in them: interactions with customers during co-creation introduce changes to the work routines and behaviours of employees (because co-creation is distinctly different from traditional, 'closed innovation' approaches to NSD), which then affect cumulatively higher levels of organizational structure (Edwards et al., 2015; Dahlander and Gann, 2010). According to Kuusisto (2008), it is often difficult to separate services from the actual service development. Hence, service innovation is intertwined with the actual service development process—an argument reinforcing co-creation as largely linked to hidden innovation (Miles and Green, 2008), occurring mostly on an 'on the job' basis.

Such 'on the job' innovation can also be labelled as ad hoc innovation. The concept of ad hoc innovation is useful when thinking of innovation in services: production, selling and innovation in services are merged together and occur simultaneously. It points towards the tendency of service innovation to occur organically, in the everyday practices of firm's employees, without any such activities being labelled as 'innovation'. An important locus of co-creation that we observe is in the informal interactions between individual employees and customers (so called dyadic interactions; Piller et al., 2011), which fit such organic occurrence of innovations. It is among the key messages of this work that co-creation will be very often co-located with such 'under the radar' innovation activities (very often incremental in nature), and as such the rich interactions across the organizational boundary (akin to open innovation) are a condition sine qua non for co-creation to occur.

User-Led Innovation in Services

From the models put forward by Voss and Zomerdijk (2007) and den Hertog (2000) it appears that the organizational aspects of service innovation (what happens 'back stage') is of paramount importance when thinking of service innovations. Such framework, linking innovation to specific business practices as well as adopting the perspective of the firm, is proposed by Miles and Green (2008: 67) as the 'Olympian model'. It identifies as much as 15 possible sites of innovation, a number that is relatively high and unwieldy for analytical purposes. We simplify this model to better match it with the notions of co-creating communities of customers, as well as more fully reconcile it with the nature of innovation in creative industries.[1] Also, many of the sites of innovation presented in the model become redundant once its application is narrowed down to the videogames industry, as it is the case in this study.

In the context of customer co-creation of experiential services in creative industries and in videogames industry, we refine the Olympian model to the following sites:

a. Value chain location and positioning (what parts of the service are being produced and processed by the firm, and what role is taken in terms of leadership; intellectual property);
b. Internal communications and organizational culture (management of human resources, work organization within the firm, knowledge management, individual interactions with customers, employees' attitudes);
c. Transactions, financing and revenue model (payment, raising finance, currencies and forms of exchanges);
d. Marketing and customer relationship management (communication with customers as collaborators, tools and techniques for managing those relationships; taking into account the interactive nature of creative services);
e. Back-office/back stage production process (design, scripting, prototyping, development of the tangible design of a service; heavily dependent on skilled labour, processes may be rendered visible as part of the consumer experience);
f. Content of product and genre (creation of new genres, reframing of familiar content within new context, novelty).

Furthermore, the above points can be divided into front stage, back stage and customer design areas, as they relate to the presence of co-creation in the development of an experiential service. These represent sites within firms which are the institutional context for co-creation—which enable the use of co-creation as part of firm's NSD effort (Figure 2.1). What is more, those sites are also the ones which are most transformed by co-creation over time, shifting away from the traditional models of service development (Edvardsson and Olsson, 1996) in creative industries (and the videogames industry in particular).

Successful service innovations are often not technology-based, but can depend on new organizational or managerial practices or marketing and distribution strategies (Preston et al., 2009). The nature of innovation in creative industries hinges on the division of labour and the creative tensions involved in the production of content, balancing technical and artistic sensibilities (Scarbrough et al., 2015; Panourgias et al., 2014; O'Donnell, 2014; Tschang, 2007). Preston et al. (2009) state that external market sources, such as customers and clients, are the strongest source of knowledge for innovation for companies in creative industries (followed by the intra-organizational sources of knowledge).

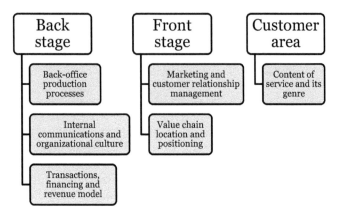

Figure 2.1 Diagram Representing the Eight Sites of Co-Creation Outcomes in Creative Firms

Furthermore, an often under-examined source of innovation is the horizontal networks of workers in a specific sector, particularly informal networks (also discussed by Cohendet and Simon, 2007). The role of trade shows, conferences, associations, informal ties, bulletin boards, websites and social networking sites is important to innovation in creative industries.[2]

In Miles (2008) we read that project management and on-the-job innovation are common ways of organizing service innovation. In much of the service sector, it is rare to find firms producing and employing specialized research and development (R&D). Where service innovation is formally organized, this tends to be through project-based teams, set up for the specific task at hand. This is in line with the phenomenon of 'hidden innovation' described in Miles and Green, 2008. Van der Graaf (2012) also illustrates it through the practices of Valve Corporation, a famously innovative firm within the videogames industry. Chathoth et al. (2013) describe it as interactive style. It characterizes firms which are very closely involved with their clients in the co-production of innovations (Chathoth et al., 2013).

Innovation activities are part of projects within organizations, but they can also be a part of other activities, for example, strategic planning, training or market development, taking place in operational areas and not in separate R&D departments (Voss and Zomerdijk, 2007). Investments in human resources are often a better indicator of innovativeness in service firms than R&D expenditure or performance. Innovations are often reflected in the increased knowledge and skills of service personnel (Sundbo and Toivonen, 2011). Therefore, innovation in services is difficult to measure because it is embedded in wider operational and organizational characteristics and frequently is incremental rather than radical (Voss and Zomerdijk, 2007).

The videogames development model corresponds to Päällysaho (2008). It contains milestones and phases in which a firm's NSD activities are different, as well as elements of task iteration (O'Donnell, 2014; Van der Graaf, 2012; Malaby, 2009; Tschang, 2007). Such experiential service development projects (Fynes and Lally, 2008) are often cross-functional, requiring contributions from people in operations, marketing, branding, business and technology, as it is demonstrated by the prevalence of, for example, multidisciplinary project teams in the videogames industry (O'Donnell, 2014; Van der Graaf, 2012). Furthermore, in organizations embracing such approach, the notion that creative ideas can come from anywhere and anyone in the firm—including customer communities—is emphasized. A great deal of innovation in experiential services is undertaken by people whose affiliation or job title does not refer to innovation at all. Some respondents in Voss and Zomerdijk (2007: 23) study even argued that having such a broad base for creativity was required to remain innovative. For these reasons, we adopt the innovation framings described above.

In experiential services in particular there is no discernible end result of consumption and production processes. The user[3] is an active party (Arvidsson, 2011). Therefore, the concept 'user-based service innovation' refers to the development of a new or modified service, or the conditions of its production, in a way which (Sundbo and Toivonen, 2011: 4)): (1) emphasizes the acquisition of deep and shared understanding of user needs, and actually utilizes this understanding in the development process, and/or (2) co-develops innovation together with users. This co-development may mean that users are original sources of innovation, partners in the innovation process, or developers of a launched novelty (Kuusisto, 2008).

The process of innovation, as well as the interaction between producers and users during it, cannot be viewed as a linear affair with a fuzzy front end (emphasizing creative problem solving) and systematic development (reflecting rational planning; Banks, 2013). Such linear approach, also tending to view customer involvement as occurring mostly in the fuzzy front end of the innovation process, does not match the reality of the videogames industry. Customer involvement occurs at all stages of NSD process, and pertains to numerous functions of the firm.

According to Päällysaho (2008), the interaction of the customer with the organization's business processes occurs in different ways, and is about both organizational innovation and about service innovation. Päällysaho (2008) also notices the need for the firm to be capable of training and guiding customers' participation in cases where the customer is used in the production system as a resource (which we refer to here as user involvement and integration competences). At the same time, customer disposition to participate in the innovation process and the diversity of customer demand may create uncertainty (Franklin et al., 2013)—which is both a cost and a risk of co-creation.

According to Matthing et al. (2004), customers' service ideas are highly innovative, in terms of originality and user value, but businesses do not implement them. This is due to the company's structures, processes and culture, which act to limit customer involvement in internal practices of a firm. Similarly, Magnusson (2009) and Magnusson et al. (2003) found that user-generated ideas are, on average, harder to convert into commercial services than ideas developed by professionals. As we see in data collected, users are often not aware of the working realities of firms, do not consider commercial feasibility of their contributions, or provide them using technology not used by the firm (also see Malaby, 2009). As a result, there are firms which solicit customer inputs not for their innovative value, but instead for the customer relationship benefits arising from such exchanges (Gustafsson et al., 2012; Grönroos, 1994). We observe that dynamic in empirical setting at Obsidian Entertainment (Case Alpha).

This exacerbates this research's focus on the specific competences and adaptations of organizations as prerequisites for successful co-creation. Lagrosen (2005) argues that customer involvement in NSD complicates the innovation process, and in Aoyama and Izushi (2008) we observe how it might be reasonable to exclude customers from the processes of developing fundamentally new services.

Ordinary customers need help, experience and time to meaningfully contribute to the development of new services and to be truly useful as NSD resources to firms. That requires both the competences on the part of the firm—both back stage and front stage (Voss and Zomerdijk, 2007). Customers need assignments that are meaningful and motivating (in different ways, depending on the customer and the nature of the task at hand; Füller, 2010). What motivates customers is different from employees' or managers' or studio owners' motivations, and effort and resources must be spent to understand them. This is in line with the empirical observations, which outline organizational difficulties in adopting co-creation, as well as transformative impact of co-creation on firms.

Furthermore, firms should be aware that developing an accurate understanding of user needs, and integrating customers in innovation, is not simple, or fast, or cheap (von Hippel, 2007, 2005)—instead, it requires appropriate competences and resources (Piller and Ihl, 2009). One response to that problem is the use of toolkits for user innovation, which improve customers' ability to innovate for themselves, allowing developing products via iterative trial-and-error (Päällysaho, 2008). Nevertheless, we demonstrate that such formal methods of co-creation are not the only ones deployed by the firms—for reasons associated with various competences of different firms, circumstances of funding and organizational culture, as well as the desired outcome of the co-creation process.

Organizational Culture

Organizational culture is a source of sustained competitive advantage (Barney, 1986) and is an important factor influencing the propensity and style of co-creation in firms (as well as its outcomes on innovation and NSD). It plays a significant role in influencing creativity and innovation within a firm

(Martins and Terblanche, 2003), including its approach towards the ideas or solutions generated outside of the firm boundaries (Chesbrough, 2011, 2006)—for instance in the customer communities.

Organizational culture supports or inhibits organizational innovative orientation (Naranjo-Valencia et al., 2011)—i.e., firm's understanding of the origin of innovative ideas and innovation-boosting activities. Malaby (2009) and Van der Graaf (2012) demonstrate similar findings in their works: open and accepting organizational cultures in firms enhance the communication with customers, influx of new ideas, and selection of best solutions, as well as contribute to the positive relationship with the customers. They also have a positive influence on promoting creativity and innovation. On the other hand, organizational culture which doesn't recognize customers as a source of valuable ideas, or as unaware of their own needs, will be less inclined to use co-creative practices in its NSD.

Organizational culture is often slow to change, and its transformations may also lead to changes in firm's competences (Chatenier et al., 2010). As they are a source of competitive advantage, they are closely linked to firm's dynamic capabilities (Teece, 2010, 2007; Teece and Pisano, 1994). The organization's historic activities and its past successes (and failures) also shape the organizational culture, in which employees will be predisposed towards some, and not other NSD approaches (Cohen and Levinthal, 1990). We see that very clearly in the case of Obsidian Entertainment (case study Alpha), which sticks to its 'true and tested' model of NSD even when in position to significantly open up its innovation activities to customers.

Firms also articulate their strategies on the management and leadership level by formulating organizational vision and mission, which can be customer- and market-oriented. We observe organizational culture as consisting of the following elements: strategic orientation (in the context of co-creation and using the customers as a resource in NSD and innovation; Chatenier et al., 2010), attitudes of employees, as well as organizational history (Cohen and Levinthal, 1990; see Figure 2.2).

Organizational culture consists of the values, norms, beliefs and hidden assumptions that organizational members have in common (Cameron and Quinn, 1999). These elements can either support or inhibit creativity

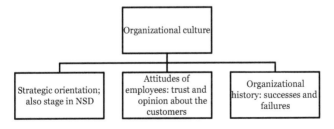

Figure 2.2 Diagram Displaying Three Constituents of Organizational Culture as Defined in This Study

and innovation in organizations (Martins and Terblanche, 2003). They also influence the relationships between the firm and the customers (Gummesson, 2002; Grönroos, 1994). Very often, in organizations with good customer relationship, we observe strong and numerous links between employees and individuals in the customers' community that cross the organizational boundary—becoming the setting of 'dyadic co-creation' (Cohendet and Simon, 2007; Piller et al., 2011).

Those links are not only a locus of knowledge and creativity exchanges, but they also are the driver of increasing alignment between the culture of the firm and culture of the customer community (Malaby, 2009). A match between those two is an asset for the firm, greatly enhancing customers' perceived fairness of the firm, as well as contributing to social network effects such as positive word of mouth and increased maximum willingness to pay (Gebauer et al., 2013). This is, for example, illustrated by the fact that hiring of employees from among the customer community increases that positive relationship by forming overlaps in the firm and customer culture (Bergstrom et al., 2013; Burger-Helmchen and Cohendet, 2011), as we observe in case study Beta (the practices of CCP).

Furthermore, the attitudes of individual game developers influence co-creation, thus playing a gatekeeping function to assimilating their inputs into NSD or innovation processes (Martins and Terblanche, 2003). The attitude of an individual employee affects the attitudes of fellow employees within a firm in a bottom-up dynamic. An opposite, top-down dynamic of organizational culture as established by firm management also exists, but we classify it as an element of firm strategy. We observe these dynamics in Case Gamma (Cloud Imperium Games).

Organizational cultures characterized by 'adhocracy' (i.e., innovation and solutions largely developed 'on the job', on a problem-by-problem basis) foster innovation strategies (Naranjo-Valencia et al., 2011), showing a link between informal forms of co-creation (occurring 'under the radar' of official classification as R&D for instance; Miles and Green, 2008) and a firm's propensity for innovation. An organization that favours risk taking by its employees, learning from mistakes, placing focus on the generation of high-quality ideas is more likely to engage in co-creation (which is largely seen as an experimental and risky approach, due to reliance on external and difficult to control resource of customer communities) than a risk-averse organization.

Martins and Terblanche (2003) underline the role of a firm's strategy in shaping the organizational culture—which includes other elements such as communication routines and attitudes of individual employees. Following on Cheng and Huizing's (2014), we define strategic orientation as the totality of a firm's decisions to create the proper and timely behaviours for the continuous superior performance of its business. Strategic orientation reflects how aggressively firms compete in the market and their willingness to explore and develop competences, products or markets. Most importantly, different strategic orientations involve different investments in organizational resources (for instance, 'crowd' can be seen as a resource used in open innovation or crowdfunding activities). Strategic orientations moderate the relation between co-creation and innovation performance because a firm's competitive advantage may rest on strategic orientations in utilizing distinctive innovation capabilities (Peteraf, 1993). Firm strategy also determines at the high level the extent of co-creation that an organization will engage in, as well as the managers' attitudes towards it. A company may seek competitive advantage by developing co-creation competences, and thus be invested in the notion of customer integration in its NSD and through the project routines of its employees, on all levels of organization.

There are also firm-level impediments and stimulators of co-creation to be considered by firms. Impediments include concerns about secrecy, ownership of intellectual property rights, information overload and development feasibility. Stimulators are linked to increasing the benefits to consumers from co-creation, and reducing the costs in terms of time, effort and foregone opportunities of co-creation activities (Hoyer et al., 2010). Depending on a firm's priorities and value proposition, it will weigh differently various impediments and stimulators.

Organizational history is defined as the track record of a firm's successes or failures with a particular approach to NSD (Gruner and Hombug, 2000). It can promote conservative behaviour, as it reflects the accumulated knowledge and competences of firm's employees in the light of the projects completed (and the market response to them; Banks, 2013). It is linked to how the firm functions and how it is organized (Van der Graaf, 2012). Overall, co-creation has a strong transformative effect on organizations, and many firms will resist co-creation because of the disruption to its existing practices and processes. This is particularly evident in the videogames industry, which largely suffers from the outdated service development methodologies (for example, illustrated by its adherence to antiquated project management techniques, c.f. Keith, 2010) and is slow to change its organizational structures (O'Donnel, 2014, 2012; Zackariasson and Wilson, 2012). As we see below, one of the videogames studios with the most innovative project management (and other organizational) practices, CCP described in Case Beta, is also correspondingly responsive and conducive to co-creation.

Analytical Framing of the Videogames Industry

Videogame studios delegate a significant part of their competences—production, accumulation and circulation of competitive knowledge—to diverse communities (Haefliger et al., 2010). These communities can be classified into two broad types. First, the videogames industry hires creators belonging to very diverse production communities or 'communities of specialists' (Cohendet and Simon, 2007): scriptwriters, game designers, 2D and 3D graphic artists, sound designers and software programmers. One of the main challenges for the managers of the firm is to align the functioning of these rather informal groups with the hierarchical structures of the organization (Tschang, 2007). Second is the increasing role played by the large communities of customers, and in particular their communities, in marketing and commercial performance of a game. As underlined by Jäger et al. (2010), virtual communities of consumption, such as brand communities, create value for studios by supporting their games, promoting the brand and spreading customer loyalty, or acting as a resource for ideas (Burger-Helmchen and Cohendet, 2011).

These two types of communities don't exist in separation from one another. Many game developers are also players; many players are developing their own videogames or are interested in the industry. In many events the two groups meet and talk, both on formal and informal (personal) levels. Cross-pollination of ideas is one example of a valuable process that occurs between these two groups, and which is valuable to be tapped into in co-creation. The videogames industry is shifting towards online content, customer interactivity and social gaming, where the joint effort of firms and communities creates value for the customer. Firms also utilize customer communities to create and appropriate value for themselves. In a creative industry such as videogames where managers must "analyse and address existing demand while at the same time using their imagination to extend and transform the market" (Lampel et al., 2000: 263), the relationship of a firm with its customers is a key success factor (Grönroos, 2011, 1994). Consequently, firms cultivate the relationship with customer communities as an important part of the industry's business model.

For many games (and multiplayer online games in particular) a significant part of the value is created by cognitive resources (the communities), which are not directly controlled by the firm. Studios can be seen as a nucleus of communities, whether internal to the firm (communities of production or of specialists) or external to the firm (communities of consumption or communities of users; Burger-Helmchen and Cohendet, 2011: 318). This is why we seek to better understand how firms tap into the communities of customers for inputs to NSD and for relationship building.

A reader might expect a high degree of similarity between the videogames industry and software (ICT) industry. Unfortunately, this is not the case. Comparing the videogames industry to software industries (O'Donnell, 2012) isn't easy. It is important to account for the videogames industry's idiosyncrasies in the context of rich and numerous links between firms, communities of customers, as well as videogames as socio-cultural objects. Videogame development is understood as a creative process involving numerous disciplines rooted in a particular culture producing creative, artistic and culturally important works (O'Donnell, 2012: 18), as opposed to traditional software development, which focuses almost exclusively on IT technology and the computer science domain.

According to Lampel et al. (2000), videogame developers are confronted with two problems: demand patterns that are highly unpredictable and production processes that are difficult to monitor and control due to their interdisciplinarity and task interdependencies. There are numerous accounts describing the difficulties in game development practice arising from the need to organize in a commercial production context creative inputs and individuals, who are by the very nature of their work resistant to organizational structures and management forms (Tschang, 2007; Van der Graaf, 2012). Many of the people working in videogames development are highly independent, creative and disinterested in rigid work routine. Furthermore, on the demand side in videogames industry, firms try to shape customer preferences by distribution, marketing and promotion—but shaping of customer tastes is difficult also due to the fact that tastes are part of a wider social and cultural matrix over which firms have little or no control (Lampel et al., 2000).

For the videogames industry at large, it is important to account for what Banks and Potts (2010), as well as Potts, Cunningham et al. (2008; Potts, Hartley et al., 2008) have identified as co-evolution of market and socio-cultural forces. What makes the videogames industry particularly interesting as a setting to study co-creation is its current state of flux (disequilibrium) that arises from various forms of networked creativity. This phenomenon, framed by Potts, Cunningham et al. (2008) as situated creativity, is viewed as an ongoing tension between economic evolution and socio-cultural evolution exemplified by the emergent phenomena of customer co-creation.

Co-creation is a disruptive force and has transformative implications on the relations between producers and consumers (as well as on each of these parties separately), as this research demonstrates (Banks and Deuze, 2009). OECD (2007) report suggests that more participatory media environment pushes changes in the creative industries towards models of 'decentralized creativity' and 'organizational innovation'.

At some point the creative industries will reach the point of equilibrium when current practices of networked creativity will solidify and form the dominant business model (Teece, 2010). Co-creation will likely become a permanent feature of creative industries' NSD overall, thanks to such developments as Web 2.0, structure of employment (i.e., freelancing) and innovative monetization and revenue models relying on audience engagement. That's why it is so important, at this moment in time, to better understand the implications of co-creation for firms, as well as best practices associated with innovating in the context of co-creation.

Videogames are seen as creative collaborative works that are infused with culture and its broad implications (O'Donnell, 2012: 19). Those cultural aspects infuse the very design, and thus key characteristics, of a game and its experience. This has been conceptualized as a three-part 'circuit of interactivity', by which culture, technology and marketing interact (Kline et al., 2003: 30–59).

Centrality of Networks in Creative Industries

Potts, Hartley et al. (2008) state that in creative industries demand and supply operate in complex social networks—contrary to the perspective of those industries as having creative inputs and producing intellectual property (IP) outputs. Complex social networks play significant coordination role in the videogames industry (Potts, Hartley et al., 2008). Also, the decisions to produce and consume are largely determined by the choice of others in a social network—a phenomenon enabled by the technological and communication affordances granted by Web 2.0 (O'Reilly, 2005).

This is often seen in the videogames industry where the reviews of fellow players, as well as seeing who consumes a particular game, determine an individual customer's decisions whether to buy that game as well. Phenomena such as word of mouth or popular culture are of great influence here (Gebauer et al., 2013). Many players buy and play the games that their friends and networks are also interested in.

As outlined also by Jenkins (2006), Banks (2013) and Banks and Humphreys (2008), the division between active producers and passive, consuming-only audiences is disappearing. The value chain cannot be seen as unidirectional, i.e., as flowing only from the firm to the customers. Experiential services, videogames included, where the role of customers in co-creation of value (according to service-dominant logic by Vargo and Lusch, 2004) and word of mouth are prominent, are an example of social network markets. In this understanding of videogames industry, the central node of analysis is the interaction between firms and the social network. 'Social' means the ability of one agent to connect to and interpret information generated by other agents, and to communicate in turn; and 'network' means that these are specific connections, often technologically enabled, and not an abstract aggregate group (Hoyer et al., 2010). Firm's employees belong to such social networks together with their customers, as shown above (Potts, Cunningham et al., 2008, Potts, Hartley et al., 2008).

Social network framing captures the features of organizations and institutions that characterize both the production of creative industries, as well as the processes by which consumers make choices (Potts, Hartley et al., 2008). The radical uncertainty of demand is emphasized as one of the defining characteristics of social networks and creative industries (Franklin et al., 2013). This framing also allows this research to integrate both the competences of community of customers for co-creation (Piller and Ihl, 2009), together with the competences of the firm in one framework. Nevertheless, only the competences existing within firms are of interest to this book, while the investigation of customers' competences for co-creation remains an avenue for future research.

Co-creation is a prime example of the conflation of the production and consumption decisions in a social network, in which the value of such co-creative actions is ultimately determined (Hartley et al., 2013). Adoption of such analytical frame further assists in the abandonment of the notion of one way flow of causation along value chain (Jenkins, 2009 and 2006). Identification of social networks as having a central role in NSD in creative firms is the theoretical foundation for the investigation of co-creation (von Hippel, 2007).

Co-Creation and Creative Industries

Aoyama and Izushi (2008) demonstrate that there are three major implications for the operations of firms from the empowered role of customers in NSD:

a.   Boundary between producers and consumers is redefined.
b.   Boundary between common property and private property is questioned.
c.   Potential customer involvement as co-creator at all stages of innovation process is foregrounded.

The sources of these changes are enabled by technological affordances, but also interrelated with and enhanced by other factors: economic, institutional and cultural. Furthermore, Van der Graaf (2009) shows that customers, in the case of freely shared developments, can outcompete closed-innovation firms due to their sharing of the best ideas and practices from across the innovating community. In such social networks, shared empathy spaces appear where critical knowledge is shared as part of a community of practice (Saur-Amaral et al., 2011; Saur-Amaral and Rego, 2010). That further underlines the significance of users as producers in the present-day economy and the waning significance of closed-innovation paradigms (Raasch and von Hippel, 2013; Prahalad and Ramaswamy, 2004).

We identify two major dichotomies in the definition of co-creation and contextualization within creative industries (Jenkins, 2006). Firstly, the opposition between firms that produce media (in the case of videogames industry those are game developers) and the communities of productive customers. The narratives of labour, exploitation and intellectual property accompany this discourse (as the notions of what constitutes 'play' and 'labour' in the setting of co-creation changes; Grimes, 2006; Humphreys et al., 2005; Humphreys, 2007; 2005a and b). Secondly, there is the dichotomy between co-creation as belonging to either the market (i.e., economic) or cultural domain. Co-creation is a phenomenon that accompanies forms of participation in cultural production first and foremost, and relies on social and psychological effects related to fandom and intrinsic motivations (Jenkins, 2009; Füller, 2010). Banks and Potts (2010) demonstrate that co-creation exists in both of these domains at once, and that they are integrated together via the mechanisms of multiple games and social network markets.

According to Roberts et al. (2014), customer co-creation is defined as collaborative work between a consumer and a firm in an innovation process, whereby the consumer and firm engage (to varying degrees) in the activity of co-ideation, co-design and co-development of new products or services (Prahalad and Ramaswamy, 2004). It refers to a process where more than one person is involved, which results in a service that none of the creators could achieve alone (Sanders and Stappers, 2008). Customer co-creation is the collaboration between firms and customers to create value together, rather than by the firm alone (Prahalad and Krishnan, 2008). The co-creation experience is the basis of unique value for each individual (Weber, 2011), which underlines the social nature of this phenomenon.

In part, co-creation is a specific form of user contribution whereby 'active' as opposed to 'passive' consumers participate with the firm and voluntarily contribute input (be that knowledge, informed opinions, experience or resources) into an innovation process (Cook, 2008), the outcome of which is better and more market-focused innovation. Co-creation is defined as a process occurring at all stages of the new service development process, as well as after the service is launched in the marketplace. According to Weber (2011: 104): "it is neither the transfer nor outsourcing of activities to customers, nor a marginal customization of products and services". Co-creation is different from crowdsourcing (Saur-Amaral et al., 2011), as it implies less control of the firm over the task definition and scope of proposed solutions from the crowd (the users). Co-creation also focuses more on the ongoing individual exchanges with lead users (von Hippel, 2005), who define problems and may lead the company through articulating their needs and proposing innovations. Crowdsourcing on the other hand delegates a pre-defined task to the community, strictly follows a firm's practices, and expects the submissions which are on-topic (akin to contest entries). Crowdsourcing exerts much less pressure on a firm's organizational structures, culture and NSD practices as compared to co-creation, which by definition is more disruptive to the firm's functioning (but also holds more NSD and innovative potential, as it taps into lead users' and customers' need-related knowledge).

The following definition of co-creation captures the role of co-creation in the practices of videogames firms, and underlines the importance of customer inputs in co-creation practice (Roberts et al., 2014; Banks, 2013: 1):

> Co-creation is defined as a collaborative work between a consumer and a firm in an innovation process, where a non-trivial component to the design, development, production, marketing or distribution of a new or existing service is contributed by a customer, or customer communities.

Still, this definition does not account for the full extent of the process—as co-creation has a profound effect on organizations which embrace it. The statement "non-trivial component to the design, development, production, marketing or distribution" (Banks, 2013: 1) underplays the significance of the transformative effect of co-creation on firms and their services. The changes to all of those categories result from profound changes to the firm itself: its culture, practices, routines and others. Thus the component being the subject of co-creation cannot be just 'non-trivial'—instead, more emphasis needs to be placed on co-creation as a meaningful exchange between customers and the firm.

Co-creation challenges the existing power structures of companies that are built on hierarchy and control—it requires that control be relinquished and given to customers (Sanders and Stappers, 2008). This is also in line with Prahalad and Ramaswamy (2004), who argue that value is increasingly co-created by both firm and the customer. Commons-based forms of peer production are no longer marginal cultural or economic activities, but are moving from the periphery to the core of contemporary economies (Benkler, 2006).

Scholarly perspectives on user-created content and its circulation within social networks generally fall along classical development versus dependency theories (Banks and Deuze, 2009). Development focuses on customer empowerment and recognition of fandom, while more sceptical dependency describes the unequal power relationships that remain between a handful of media corporations and the multitude of consumers. Various authors such as Jenkins (2006, 2009), Bruns (2008) and Benkler (2006) tend to focus on the democratizing potential of this increased user participation, although they adopt various perspectives on the phenomenon.

The literature on contestations of control over the process of co-creation often omits the agency of the customers themselves in the shaping of this process (O'Hern and Rindfleisch, 2010; Bonsu and Darmody, 2008). Co-creating consumers are not some hapless starry-eyed participants who have no idea that firms are benefitting from their work (c.f. Wexler, 2011; Kline et al., 2003). Not only that—customers do benefit from freely revealing their work in that context, in line with discussion on user innovation phenomena, having more products or services tailored to their needs and tastes (von Hippel, 2005, 2007). There are also other benefits to customers from that process: membership in social groups, elicitation of feelings of belonging and peer acceptance, development of self-identity, reputation building, business opportunities, altruism and many others (Nardi, 2010; Füller, 2010; Pearce, 2009; Castronova, 2005). Finally, it is precisely though these commercial networks that both consumers and media professionals explore the possibilities for participatory empowerment and emancipation (Hartley, 2008).

Origins of Co-Creation

Ind and Coates (2013: 91) see co-creation as having emerged due to the coincidence of several developments: the mainstream adoption of Internet technologies, the orientation towards services and experiences, a more open approach to innovation, and the growth of social, collaboration and customization technologies. Customers can collaborate with one another to meet their needs for socialization and meaning making. Ind and Coates (2013) highlight that firms should influence the process of co-creation not from a position of dominance, but that of equality. Such an attitude is framed as 'power with'—a jointly developed, co-active, and not coercive, power (Ind and Coates, 2013).

Nonaka and Hirotaka (1995) note that customers have always been linked through social interaction. While an organization may believe it controls the meaning of its brands, it can be argued that brand meanings are co-created by consumers and other stakeholders and are dialogic (Ind and Coates, 2013). This is reflected by the industrial move of the recent years towards constructing brand meanings beyond the walls of the organization, and is reflected by the emergence of consumer brand communities (Fournier and Lee, 2009)—which can be seen as the precursor of communities of lead users, which von Hippel (2005) identifies as critical to co-creation in NSD. Ind and Coates (2013) further state that the emergence of co-creation is linked to the focus on services, because it is the service experience that matters to customers (Saarijärvi, 2012; Saarijärvi et al., 2013).

For Hoyer et al. (2010), co-creation is linked to the sense of 'empowerment'—i.e., the customers' desire for a greater role in exchanges with companies, and in value creation. This in turn is seen as an important manifestation of customer engagement behaviour (van Doorn et al., 2010). Hoyer et al. (2010: 283) focus on customer co-creation in new service development (NSD), where they define it as a "collaborative NSD activity in which consumers actively contribute and select various elements of new product offering", allowing consumers to take an active and central role as participants in the NSD process.

Those definitions are similar to the ones proposed by O'Hern and Rindfleisch (2010), who argue that co-creation is a collaborative NSD activity in which customers actively contribute and/or select the content of new product offering. Customer co-creation is seen as involving two key processes: (1) contribution (that is, submitting content), and (2) selection (choosing which of these submissions will be retained). In this understanding, co-creation is a response to the condition of information asymmetry (von Hippel, 2005), when the customers mostly have the information about their needs and the firm has the information about the possible solutions.

Customer needs are often idiosyncratic and tacit in nature and, hence, hard to measure and implement. Customers have deep and complex ('high fidelity') needs; however, traditional market research methods often provide managers with only a cursory ('low fidelity') signal of what customers want or need, which then leads to their misinformed decisions about new services (von Hippel, 2005). Co-creation is seen as a solution to that problem. This is coupled with the cultural development of consumers' growing suspicion and distrust of marketing communications (Darke and Ritchie, 2007), as well as their heightened activism (O'Hern and Rindfleisch, 2010).

This is particularly visible in the videogames industry, where the most impactful channels of marketing are now players broadcasting from their own bedrooms, unaffiliated with any firm. Customers are also less fulfilled by the consumption act itself. Co-creation is seen as an alternative to the traditional NSD paradigm. Hence the act of co-creation with customers, apart from the NSD potential, also can carry the benefits to the relationship between firm and its customers (Gustafsson et al., 2012).

Crowdsourcing and Open Innovation

Co-creation is a democratic process in innovation, one allowing firms to benefit from their customers' knowledge and skills. Co-creation gives customers the power to actively influence services used by them. Prahalad and Ramaswamy (2004: 8) define co-creation as being about joint problem definition and solving. As mentioned in Ind and Coates (2013), it is about 'power with' the customers, and not just unilaterally tapping the customers' skills and knowledge by the firm (such a process in literature is framed as crowdsourcing; Belleflamme et al., 2014; Ordanini et al., 2011; Mollick, 2012).

Crowdsourcing is a framing of the co-creative dynamic that occurs between firms and customers, which is reflected by the following integrated crowdsourcing definition (Estelles-Arolas et al., 2012: 197):

> Crowdsourcing is a type of participative online activity in which . . . a company proposes to a group of individuals of varying knowledge, heterogeneity, and number, via a flexible open call, the voluntary undertaking of a task. The undertaking of the task, of variable complexity and modularity, and in which the crowd should participate bringing their work, money, knowledge and/or experience, always entails a mutual benefit. The user will receive the satisfaction of a given type of need, be it economic, social recognition, self-esteem, or the development of individual skills, while the crowdsourcer will obtain and utilize to their advantage what the user has brought to the venture, whose form will depend on the type of activity undertaken.

It is not only the benefit that is mutual. This definition does not take into account the following: (1) the customers establish their power of influencing the product or service being developed by the firm; (2) a by-product of such 'undertaking of the task' is the formation of complex relationship between firm and the customers, as well as among the customers, and the strengthening of the communities of customers; (3) crowdsourcer not only obtains advantages from the process, as it involves significant restructuring of the way in which a firm functions, and there are numerous risks associated with that process.

Customers who decide to devote their time, energy and effort to co-create are not unaware participants of some sleek labour exploitation scheme. They have their own agenda on one hand (reflected by their various motivations to engage in co-creation processes), and on the other the communities that they form in the process hold real power both in the relationship with the firm itself, but also in influencing the market (by mechanisms such as word of mouth; Gebauer et al., 2013; Bonsu and Darmody, 2008; Arvidsson, 2011).

In the current economy, characterized by participatory culture, Web 2.0 dynamics and open source movements (OECD, 2007), it is difficult to tap into the customer community for a single project without considering the impact that it has on the formation of those communities. They in turn put pressure and affect the firm in various ways (both on the organizational, cultural, as well as on the market levels). The community is reactive to such mechanisms (Wexler, 2011), and their buy-in is critical to crowdsourcing success. For some, a crowdsourcing firm may be an instrumental user of the value conferred by calling, filtering and managing the customer community (Jenkins, 2009). This view, however, is not corresponding to reality. Customers demand an active stake in the development of the brands that they love, and simple framing of some nebulous 'crowd' which has no dynamics, motivations, organization or influence does not apply (Jenkins, 2009, 2006).

Co-creation, which accounts for that bidirectional dynamic between firms and customers, is a more realistic framework for describing firms' accessing the resource of customers' creativity. This is reflected by Prahalad and Ramaswamy (2004: 12), who describe the transformation of the relationship between firms and consumers as part of co-creation:

- from one way, firm to consumer, controlled by the firm;
- to two-way, consumer to firm and consumer to consumer dynamic.

The market itself is also seen as a forum for co-creation. Consumers can initiate a dialogue among themselves, just as well as among themselves and the firm. This is also reflected in Gummesson (2002), who describes the shift in marketing paradigm to total relationship marketing, relying on the firm's meaningful interactions with customers.

Co-creation fits within the general boundaries of the open innovation paradigm, as the latter is a broad concept that comes in many different forms (Huizingh, 2011). Following on Chesbrough (2011, 2006), co-creation shares open innovation's underpinning tenets of opening the firm up to the ideas and concepts from outside its immediate environment. It is impossible for a single firm to have all the knowledge and skills in-house. Open innovation is "the use of purposive inflows and outflows of knowledge to accelerate internal innovation, and expand the markets for external use of innovation" (Chesbrough, 2006: 1). Closed innovation is an internally focused logic, while open innovation combines internal and external ideas to create more value for the firm (Chesbrough, 2006; Hau and Kim, 2011).

Typologies of Co-Creation

Co-creation exists in a variety of contexts—at all stages of new service development, long after a service launch on the market, between a variety of actors (for example, different departments of a firm can get involved in co-creation, different segments of the customer community, etc.). It also exists in a plethora of forms: from simple contests, voting mechanisms and feedback-giving activity, to the production of assets and sitting on customer-elected advisory councils. The literature on co-creation reflects this. A number of typologies of co-creation have emerged. O'Hern and Rindfleisch (2010) state that developing a new service entails two essential activities: (1) the contribution of novel concepts and ideas, and (2) the selection of which specific concepts and ideas should be pursued. Firms can release control of either contributions made to the NSD process and/or the selection of these contributions, thus engaging in co-creation. We observe this dynamic throughout all case studies discussed in the chapters below. The basis for this typology is consequently formed by the degree of customer autonomy across these two activities. Implicit in this model is the power of the firm in the co-creation mechanics—it is the firm's decision whether to open the contribution activity to its customers, as well as the firm's decision whether to involve customers in deciding which of those inputs become new service features. This model sits well with the theoretical underpinnings of this study, demonstrating the rationale for focusing on the firm as the dominant actor in co-creation.

Similarly, O'Hern et al. (2011) discuss the impact of user-generated content (UGC) on service innovation, focusing on its role as a form of consumer-to-developer communication that facilitates innovation. The authors identify two types of UGC (i.e., contributions that reflect customer ideas and contributions that contain customer-generated solutions). They also highlight UGC's impact on two possible innovation outcomes (product improvement and market response). This typology builds on the notion that successful innovation depends upon sourcing novel ideas and solutions directly from the customers and integrating these contributions with the internal efforts of the development team (Bhalla, 2010; von Hippel, 2005).

Information-centric UGC represents customers' communicating how well a given service performs and satisfies their need. This type of UGC provides ideas to the service development team, who decides which of these ideas will get implemented. Conversely, solution-centric UGC occurs when users themselves modify an existing service to better suit their needs. That division could also be seen as underpinning co-creation for relationship (in the case of idea-centric inputs) and co-creation for NSD (for solution-centric inputs).

The work of O'Hern et al. (2011) is interesting as it demonstrates that in some cases, user contributions may actually be a detriment to a firm's innovation activities. Their findings suggest that while idea-centric UGC enhances market response (for example, number of downloads of a software), solution-centric UGC hinders service improvement (for example, number of code commits in open source software). This is in line with the empirical findings presented in the chapters to follow, which reflect the disruptive effects that co-creation can have on organizations and their processes, as well as on the large amount of useless and low-quality inputs that vast numbers of users are providing in their communications with firms.

A corresponding dichotomy is observed in Witell et al. (2011), who distinguish two types of co-creation: co-creation for use and co-creation for others. The two processes differ in their orientation: co-creation for use is performed by a specific customer for their own benefit, while co-creation for others is to be used by fellow customers. While the aim of co-creation for use is to enjoy the service development process and its outcome (pointing towards co-creation experience, Kohler et al., 2011a and b; Verhagen et al., 2011), co-creation for others aims to provide an idea, share knowledge or participate in the development of a service that can be of value to other customers. This dichotomy is also congruent with the theories outlining the motivations of co-creating customers (intrinsic versus extrinsic for instance; c.f. Füller, 2010), as well as various types co-creation activities underpinned by those motivations. It is also aligned with the observations of Gustafsson et al. (2012), pointing towards the possibility of both relationship- and NSD-related outcomes of co-creation.

Such dichotomy is also reflected in Piller et al. (2011), who identify dyadic co-creation and networked co-creation. In the former, co-creation takes place between a firm and one customer at a time. In the latter, co-creation exists in the context of networks of customers who collaborate among themselves as well as with the firm. This dyadic co-creation points towards the role of interactions between individuals for co-creation, and those interactions' role in transforming organizations in the presence of co-creation. We observe it in detail in Case Alpha (the practices of Obsidian Entertainment). Networked co-creation highlights the role of customer relationship and flexible project management, and Case Gamma (Cloud Imperium Games) offers particularly interesting insights into it.

Füller and Matzler (2007) identify four forms of virtual customer integration, which explains how customer inputs are integrated with NSD. It outlines two dimensions: level of integration, describing how actively customers engage in NSD, ranging from passive to active, as well as continuity, which deals with the frequency customers are integrated into NSD. That frequency varies from one-time integration, to continuous interaction during the entire NSD project or several such projects over multiple tasks. These two dimensions also seem to reflect the dual nature of co-creation outcomes: for relationship (relating to 'continuity'), as well as for NSD (relating to 'level of integration').

Piller and Ihl (2009), Hoyer et al. (2010) and Piller et al. (2011) base their typology of co-creation on the stage of NSD when the customer integration takes place (early or late, where early means in the front stages of NSD, i.e., idea generation and concept development, and where late denotes the back-end of NSD, i.e., service design and testing). Degree of co-creation is understood as a function of the scope of activities across service development stages, as well as intensity of those activities. Co-creation occurring at the front end of the NSD is characterized by generation of novel concepts and selection of specific ideas to be pursued further. Co-creation at the rear end of NSD is about improving existing solutions, testing them in various technical or use scenarios, and ensuring positive service experience. Examples of co-creation at early stages include cases Alpha and Gamma, while late-stage co-creation is documented in Case Beta. This framework exposes the root of O'Hern and Rindfleisch's (2010) typology of co-creation, as it focuses on the freedom of collaboration between customers and the firm—which often decreases as the NSD progresses. Piller et al. (2011) build and strengthen the understanding of co-creation as a power tension and imbalance between firm and the communities of customers when it comes to deciding what kind of ideas and solutions (following on O'Hern et al., 2011) become integrated with the service in development. Late in the NSD process, customer inputs need to be more concrete and elaborated in order to be of value to the firm. A higher degree of collaboration often requires a more structured approach for the interaction with the customers. Piller et al. (2011) mention the high cost of the co-creative processes at this stage—as the firm needs to combine need information (which is highly sticky with the customers; von Hippel, 2005) from the customer domain with their own solution information (which, in turn, is sticky on the side of the firm; von Hippel, 2005). Because of that, exchanges between parties here tend to be tedious and accompanied by high transaction costs. This contributes to the point made by Gebauer et al. (2013) and Payne et al. (2009), who stress the importance of structuring of the co-creation experience so that it is positive to the participating customers. That's also why, in the late stages of NSD, customers' inputs are subjected to intensive selection by the firm. Firms structure co-creation with customers to invite only such inputs which fit well with existing service development trajectories (e.g., elaborate on existing ideas instead of proposing constantly new ones).

Dynamic Capabilities

Firms compete on the basis of competences and capabilities (Tushman and Anderson, 1986; Nelson and Winter, 1982; Pavitt, 1990; Cohen and Levinthal, 1990). External and internal environments of a firm are dynamic. As the external environment of the firm is changing, so must its internal processes and characteristics. We are currently observing such changes in creative industries and economy. They are focused around the production-consumption relationship between firms and customers.

Following on the work of Teece (2007), Eisenhardt and Martin (2000) and Teece and Pisano (1994), dynamic capabilities form a starting point for the analysis of service innovation in firms. Dynamic capabilities capture the firm's ability to adapt to changing customer and technological opportunities. Following on Teece (2007: 1319), "dynamic capabilities can be disaggregated into the capacity (1) to sense and shape opportunities and threats, (2) to seize opportunities, and (3) to maintain competitiveness through enhancing, combining, protecting and reconfiguring the business enterprise's intangible and tangible assets".

In that respect, the firm's ability to co-create with its customers is a reflection of those dynamic capabilities. Co-creation requires a firm to respond to changing conditions of the marketplace, as precipitated by the socio-cultural shifts (Bruns, 2008; Jenkins, 2006). New models of participation of customers in the service experience (which is also expanding and being redefined), and customers' interest in getting involved in firm's processes, form such a change. Co-creation is challenging for the firms which have been successful in the past using traditional, 'closed innovation' NSD paradigms (Dahlander and Gann 2010; Cohen and Levinthal, 1990). Dynamic capabilities reflect a firm's willingness to evolve its innovation practices successfully in the light of a changing external environment, and the ability to implement NSD and innovation practices that embrace customers' active role in that process.

Despite the fact that firms engaging in both internal and external sourcing of knowledge exhibit better innovation performance than firms relying only on one or the other (Cassiman and Veugelers, 2006), empowering users with tools and technologies has significant effects on the firm's capabilities. This is because firms have to adapt to a new way of dealing with users and user knowledge (Ogawa and Piller, 2006; Prahalad and Ramaswamy, 2004), as it is also demonstrated in this work.

In firms deciding to pursue co-creation in their innovation processes, necessary reconfiguration of existing capabilities and development of new capabilities do not come for free. Bengtsson and Ryzhkova (2015) state that firms must understand the costs and risks of dynamic service innovation capabilities, and have a balanced view of these tools. Dynamic capabilities that allow firms to successfully adopt co-creation are reflected by the competences for co-creation present within a firm. Those competences ensure that the firm is capable of taking advantage of the new customer-firm dynamic in the development of its services. They are a sum of skills, attitudes and abilities present in the co-creation firm (Chatenier et al., 2010). We now turn to discuss them in detail.

Competences for Co-Creation

Organizational competences are knowledge, skills, management practices and routines acquired over time and difficult to replicate (Trott, 2005; Danneels,

2000). They are embedded in the tacit knowledge and organizational routines of a firm (Prahalad and Hamel, 1994). Competences reflect a firm's ability to use its assets to perform value-creating activities. In co-creation, the focus is on the customer community as such an asset. Therefore, we identify competences for co-creation, which describe a firm's ability to harness that asset in NSD.

Piller and Ihl (2009) state that co-creation can only be successful if the involved partners (meaning the firm and the communities of its customers) have sufficient and symmetric degrees of both motivation and competence. The co-creation competences of the firm are described here. The model presented by Piller and Ihl (2009) also reflects the role of the stage in NSD on co-creation.

Piller and Ihl (2009) identify three competences for co-creation on the firm side of the process. Those are disclosure competence, appropriation competence, as well as integration competence. These competences can also be thought of in a process-like manner: first, firms need to disclose their problem in order to establish an interaction with customers; secondly, firms need to be able to capture and protect the knowledge co-produced with customers; third, firms need to assimilate and integrate new knowledge co-produced with customers into their own NSD process. The model proposed by Piller and Ihl (2009) is complemented by the work of Lettl (2007), who identifies user involvement competence[4] in relation to NSD. The integrated model of firms' co-creation competences is presented in Figure 2.3.

We will now discuss the four competences for co-creation in detail. User involvement competence allows firms to systematically involve customers in the innovation process. It comprises a firm's ability to manage the community of its creative customers (lead users; von Hippel, 2005) and direct their efforts to be productive for the firm. It is different from, for example, integration competence, as the latter emphasizes a firm's ability to integrate what the customer community produced into its routines and project management practices. We distinguish two dimensions of user involvement competence. First, firms need to know which customers are capable of providing valuable inputs in innovation projects, which means awareness of NSD-contributing customer characteristics. It allows firms to segment capable customers according to distinct activities in the NSD. Second, the firm needs to know what interaction patters with customers will be most

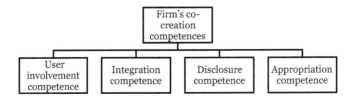

Figure 2.3 Diagram Representing Four Co-Creation Competences, Combining the Models of Piller and Ihl (2009) and Lettl (2007)

productive in NSD. This dimension contains variables like the personal level of interaction, the number of customers, the temporary extent of interaction, and the network competence[5] of the customer interaction personnel (Lettl, 2007). This competence therefore strictly determines the co-creative interface between firm and the customer communities, and the firm's ability to structure that interface (and, in the long run, the relationship) for efficient co-creation (i.e., bidirectional flow of ideas, inputs, suggestions and communication at large between firm and customers). As such, it complements the more inward, organization-focused competences described by Piller and Ihl (2009), as well as allows relating those to co-creation competences characterizing customer community.

Integration competence describes a firm's ability to integrate the inputs from customers with their project management routines, service development pipelines, communications and similar functions. It also captures the firm employees' skills in reviewing and processing these inputs, and developing working relationships with customers. This competence also determines the firm's ability to choose the appropriate co-creation approach for its needs, so that the customer inputs are as undisruptive for the organization as possible.

Disclosure competence reflects a firm's skill in recognizing the weaker aspects of the service being developed, articulating the problem, and making it known to the community of customers. It also includes firm's ability to divulge enough information (i.e., about the videogames source code, or engine, or internal project routines and deadlines) to allow customers to productively contribute and without endangering the company's trade secrets, IP and other confidential information. This aspect of co-creation resembles crowdsourcing to an extent—where the task parameters are set and the customers are expected to provide inputs in compliance with them. On the other hand, customers often won't be waiting for the firm to communicate that to them—instead, customers will just contribute to those aspects of the service which they consider most interesting or in need of improvement. The firm and their customers may differ in that opinion, especially since customers are not privy to the internal development constraints and decisions, which may limit the scope for the implementable solutions. Disclosure competence will therefore also involve the ability to assess such situations and lead to the firm either rejecting customers' inputs or modifying the NSD activities.

Appropriation competence captures a firm's capacity to assimilate and legally protect the inputs that co-creating customers provide it with. It is also linked to being able to attract co-creating customers (and lead users among them in particular) to contribute to their, and not their competitors', services. The lead users in the co-creating customer community can provide firms with highly innovative ideas or solutions, often departing from the existing service development trajectories of the firm. The firm must have the ability to judge such inputs on the basis of their merits and without falling into the 'not invented here' syndrome. This is a difficult task, because switching to such ideas bears a high sunk cost and overall increases the risk for the firm. Appropriation competence also includes a firm's ability to find a legal solution that allows it to commercialize customers' inputs (with their consent and ethically) in a streamlined fashion (i.e., without causing delays to the NSD work). For instance, inXile Entertainment demonstrates a strong appropriation competence in that sphere—we discuss their case in detail later in this work.

Those competences are visible when investigating a firm's aptitude for identifying and solving co-creation challenges. One of the most recognized cases in the academic literature on co-creating customers is the Dell *IdeaStorm* community, where customers could submit, vote and comment on ideas (Gangi et al., 2010). Gangi et al. (2010) identified four key challenges to customer co-creation which demonstrate some problems that co-creating organizations encounter:[6]

a. Understanding the ideas posted (i.e., organization facing difficulty implementing ideas due to lack of understanding among the idea contributor, other customers and the organization itself)—a problem which would be addressed by firm's appropriation competence.
b. Identifying the best ideas (i.e., organization facing difficulty identifying the most promising ideas contributed by customers)—corresponding to a firm's user involvement competence.
c. Balancing the needs of transparency with the community against disclosure to competitors (i.e., organization facing difficulty balancing information disclosure to customer community members against disclosure to competitors, who were assumed to have been listening in on the exchanges of ideas)—reflected in a firm's disclosure competence.
d. Sustaining the community (i.e., organization facing difficulty maintaining customer engagement within the community and the continued contribution of new ideas to improve its product and service portfolios; Gangi et al., 2010)—addressed by user involvement competence.

All of those challenges are discussed by Hoyer et al. (2010) as costs and risks associated with co-creation. As their result, new strategies for the role of customers in NSD had to be developed to effectively solve them. Gangi et al. (2010) list recommendations for overcoming the challenges of implementing customer communities in a firm's operations—as they are tackled by a firm's co-creation competences. These recommendations: creation of a toolkit, strategic positioning of key personnel, engaging lead users (von Hippel, 2005), promoting self-governance, responding quickly and asking questions, making customer votes count, and presenting the firm's progress clearly and openly to the community. The authors also draw the attention to the fact that if a community of co-creating customers is poorly managed, it becomes a waste of resources and can disenfranchise customers. Note, that focus is again on the customer-facing co-creation competences, and little attention is directed to internal processes of the firm—a gap in knowledge that we are addressing here.

Dahlander and Magnusson (2008) expand on the user involvement and integration competences. Co-creation practice includes: (1) accessing customer communities to extend the resource base; (2) aligning the firm's strategy with that of the community, and (3) assimilating the work developed within communities in order to integrate and share results. This corresponds to user involvement (accessing and aligning) and integration competences (assimilating; Piller and Ihl, 2009; Lettl, 2007) in the following way:

> Accessing (user involvement competence) corresponds to the capacity to capture the production held by the community. Firms use two major tactics to access developments in communities to extend their resource base: (1) establishing new communities to attract outsiders to work in the firm's area, and (2) identifying and using developments in existing communities.

Aligning (user involvement competence) refers to the existence of common goals between the strategy of the firm and the goal or ambition of the community (which change depending on the community type—Burger-Helmchen and Cohendet, 2011).

Assimilating (integration competence) corresponds to the integration capabilities of the firm, its absorptive capacity (Lichtenthaler and Lichtenthaler, 2009; Zahra and George, 2002), utilization or reutilization that can be made by the firm of the outputs or resources of the communities. By harnessing different types of communities (developer, player and tester type in cognitive customer communities), or helping their establishment, firms structure a portfolio of resources (Burger-Helmchen and Cohendet, 2011).

Balancing the Benefits and Costs of Co-Creation

When customer communities participate in co-creation, the positive outcomes of that process are not guaranteed (Edwards et al., 2015). A firm may enjoy valuable inputs to its NSD and improvements to its customer relationships. On the other hand, customers organize themselves, which means that a firm is dealing with an external organization that can amplify problems (O'Mahony and Ferraro, 2007). Co-creation can backfire, lead to disruptions in NSD, negative marketing, and in extreme cases to the failure and bankruptcy of the firm.

Hoyer et al. (2010) outline positive and negative outcomes of co-creation (which also change in different stages of NSD[7]). Positive outcomes of co-creation include cost reduction, increased effectiveness of products/services, relationship building potential (Whitla, 2009), reduction of market uncertainties, identification of future needs Füller and Matzler (2007), greater variety of ideas (Saur-Amaral, 2012), accessing new potential customers (Whitla, 2009), increased customer retention, as well as broader decision basis by parallel testing and more product alternatives. Saur-Amaral (2012) notices two types of benefits to the process of involving customers: NSD-related and market-related. This supports the dichotomy of co-creation for NSD, and co-creation for relationship (or marketing-focused). In the former category, Saur-Amaral (2012) identifies such benefits as problem identification, idea generation and problem solving. In the latter, these are advertising and promotion activities, opening markets and creating new market share. Later we explore these outcomes as the two possible and non-exclusive categories of co-creation results.

Negative outcomes on the other hand are associated with diminished control over strategic planning, increased complexity of managing the firm's objectives, complexity of managing mis-performance and selection of consumers' ideas, intellectual property problems (Bach et al., 2008), disturbance of internal processes, niche market orientation (needs and ideas articulated by participating customers may be specific and not transferable to a larger target group), as well as the lack of secrecy protecting from competitors. Enkel et al. (2005) expand the list of negative co-creation outcomes: the company's loss of know-how to the customer, the company's dependence on customers, the company being limited to only incremental innovations, serving a niche market only, dependence on customers' demands or personality, as well as misunderstandings between customers and employees.[8] Co-creation needs to be attuned to company's goals and support its competences in the first place, as well as its expected benefits must be balanced against its costs (Füller and Matzler, 2007).

These lists of outcomes demonstrate the breadth of strategic considerations that a firm must make before embarking on co-creation, as well as the profound impact that co-creation has on numerous departments within a firm. The latter has been demonstrated by Miles and Green (2008: 66), where innovations are linked to specific business processes in creative industries. Co-creation therefore is framed as a high-level strategic choice that significantly influences firms.

A firm's explicit strategic orientation towards customer involvement in NSD enhances the effectiveness of co-creation (Cheng and Huizingh, 2014). Furthermore, some strategic orientations are more conducive to co-creation than others (Martins and Terblanche, 2003; Naranjo-Valencia et al., 2011). Cheng and Huizingh (2014) review three such orientations: entrepreneurial, market and resource orientation. Entrepreneurial orientation, which is associated with a firm's proactive stance toward market opportunities, tolerance of risk, openness to innovative ideas, and active and intensive support of the innovation process, is most positively related to the innovation performance stemming from co-creation. This implies that firms wishing to benefit most from co-creation with their customers need to integrate co-creation into their strategic and long-range planning, as well as decisively embrace it as a source of value and innovation. Conversely, firms that remain undecided as to the role of co-creation in their strategy have a harder time unlocking its full potential. As mentioned above, firms may use co-creation for customer-firm NSD or relationship gains (Whitla, 2009). Entrepreneurial strategic orientation could promote co-creation for NSD inputs, while market and resource orientations could be favouring co-creation for relationship benefits.

Customer Communities and Co-Creation

For the purposes of this study, the definition of a community is that of a network, in active collaboration with the firm, where customers voluntarily and freely develop and share their innovation-conducive knowledge with other community members (Hau and Kim, 2011: 957). This is because customers can be considered genuine experts in the field and their communities are a valuable source of skills to the firm. Nevertheless, those communities are very diverse. Different types of communities bring the firm different advantages and require different configurations of competencies to maintain these advantages (Burger-Helmchen and Cohendet, 2011; Piller and Ihl, 2009; Lettl, 2007). This is seconded by Bitner et al. (1997), who identify customers' role as a productive resource, contributors to quality, as well as competitors to the service organization. Furthermore, these roles are not mutually exclusive; we see various sub-segments of the community of customers emerging.

According to von Hippel (2005: 96), a customer community is defined as "the nodes consisting of individuals or firms interconnected by information transfer links which may involve face-to-face, electronic, or other communications". Von Hippel (2001) views the incentive to voluntarily reveal innovation-conducive knowledge as an important condition of customer communities. Customer communities are believed to be the strategic resources that cannot easily be imitated by competitors (Jeppesen and Frederiksen, 2006). Pisano and Verganti (2008: 81) describe a customer community as "a network where any [customer] can propose problems, offer solutions and decide which solutions to use". Füller et al. (2008) define customer community as a place where customers actively discuss ideas, offer solutions, elaborate and test them, or give their opinions. Following on Burger-Helmchen and Cohendet (2011), a community is a "unit of competence" (Wenger et al., 2002) that attracts passionate people willing to focus their cognitive work on the specific domain of knowledge of the community. A community can be broadly defined as a "gathering of individuals who accept to exchange voluntarily and on a regular basis about a common interest or objective in a given field of knowledge" (Amin and Cohendet, 2004).

Members of a given community share knowledge on an informal basis, and respect the social norms of their community that in turn drive their behaviour and beliefs. Hau and Kim (2011) see three commonalities of any customer community: innovation-conducive knowledge sharing, network based on user interaction, as well as the existence of an active collaborative relationship with the firm. As a firm increasingly delegates parts of its competencies to customer communities, a progressive 'division of knowledge' comes into play: a firm has to manage its relationships with increasingly specialized communities. Consequently, each specialized community requires a specific mode of management from the firm to harness the community to serve the functioning of the firm. In response to that, firms develop competences for co-creation, which allow them to tap into the communities' creativity, and which are the focus of our discussion here.

In a community, customers can participate in the firm's entire value chain process, from innovation to service distribution and beyond. In a customer community, users not only share their ideas, information and knowledge about the firm's service, but also interact to improve it. Its members create a pool of collective knowledge based on their interaction with the service, and this knowledge is sticky with this community (von Hippel, 2005, 2007). Such a pool of sticky and collective knowledge can be an efficient and effective external knowledge source of a firm's innovations (Hau and Kim, 2011). Customers inspire, assist and collaborate with each other in innovation process (Van der Graaf, 2009). Customer-led innovation increasingly involves peer-to-peer interactions and communal efforts among customers (Aoyama and Izushi, 2008). These interactive dynamics of communities are very well illustrated by, for example, case study Beta (the practices of CCP).

Von Hippel (2005) argues that customers engage in innovations if their use benefits exceed their costs. Customers tend to innovate because they seek to satisfy their own needs. As we see in Füller (2010), their motives can also be mapped along the intrinsic-extrinsic spectrum, where enjoyment, learning and the process of participation lay on the intrinsic side, and firm and peer recognition and career development belong to the extrinsic end of spectrum. Customers are sovereign and rational, capable of deciding whether they want to get involved with a specific firm (Alford, 2002). Social, cultural, moral and political values influence both individual consumers and consumer groups (Banks and Potts, 2010) in their collaborations with firms. There is also the importance of elaborating information on customer needs into shared understanding within an organization. In order to be applicable, customer information has to be structured, elaborated, interpreted and shared within the organization—underlining the importance of disclosure, appropriation and integration competences for co-creation (Piller and Ihl, 2009).

There are many reasons for which customers co-create services. From the free revealing of innovations among lead users as observed by von Hippel (2005), via the free provision of one's labour in open source software communities (von Krogh and von Hippel, 2006), to modding specifically rooted in the videogames industry (Nardi, 2010; Van der Graaf, 2009; Jeppesen and Molin, 2003)—the customers have always seemed to be driven by a compelling set of motivations, even when the firm did nothing to incentivize its customers. Besides, customer communities are not uniform entities, and the sub-segments of those communities have different motivations, as well as interests and skills to engage in co-creation in varying aspects of the service, and to various extents. Skilful and knowledgeable recruitment of customers' creativity is the cornerstone of successful co-creation.

This demonstrates the heterogeneity of co-creating communities of customers, and the differences not only in their motivations, but also in their capacity to co-create, and to provide the innovative and valuable inputs to firms. Füller (2010) notes that customers engage in virtual co-creation for several reasons: curiosity, dissatisfaction with existing services, intrinsic interest in innovation, to gain knowledge, to show ideas, or to get monetary rewards. In order to create vibrant co-creation platforms, the needs of the heterogeneous user groups—experience-oriented as well as goal-oriented ones—have to be addressed.

Differences in customer motivations for co-creation also persist across the three forms of co-creation identified by Roberts et al. (2014): independent innovating, joint innovation and direct collaboration with the firm. To motivate consumers to engage in any form of value co-creation then requires the firm to create situations in which consumers are informed of opportunities to co-create (disclosure competence). Consumers must also believe that the firm is genuine about its involvement (in line with Gebauer et al., 2013 and their customer-perceived procedural justice). Consumer cynicism is one of the major dangers—goal and value incongruence can cause breakdowns in relationships between firms and consumers (few meaningful outputs will emerge as the goals of the firm strike as overtly self-centred). Management of those challenges, as well as the ability to understand customers' motivations in a particular setting, are parts of a firm's user integration competence (Lettl, 2007).

A number of successful co-creating firms rely on customer communities to provide inputs to service development over a prolonged period, implying a shift from owning important resources to coordinating them (Dahlander and Magnusson, 2008). Nevertheless, firms never rely exclusively or fully on the inputs from their customers—instead, they use them to supplement NSD activities. They also tap into co-creation for benefits other than those pertaining directly to NSD.

Co-creation is a frequent, bidirectional and face-to-face communication process based on four dimensions of communication: frequency, direction, modality and content (Gustafsson et al., 2012). Those dimensions result in an interactive communication climate that is more or less conducive to the learning, sharing and understanding of customer needs (Amin and Cohendet, 2004). Frequent, bidirectional, face-to-face and active communication is likely to enable trust and high-quality information exchange about customers' needs, which in turn is instrumental for successful co-creation, as we see in all cases studied.

The communication process, and therefore co-creation, is different for radical innovations than for incremental innovations (Kasmire et al., 2012). Companies must apply different communication strategies in co-creation depending on the degree of innovativeness of a service under development. From a managerial perspective, it is beneficial when working with incremental innovation to spend time with customers and to become immersed in the customers' context as much as possible. Frequency, direction and content of communication with customers affect it positively, meaning that firms should communicate with customers often, in a democratic manner, as well as focus on specific types of content of that communication (Gustafsson et al., 2012). A majority of firms engaging in co-creation will be focusing on incremental innovation—and we also observe that in the case studies. CCP and CIG (cases Beta and Gamma) in particular demonstrate how regular and rich exchanges with customers build a sense of community stretching across the firm-customer divide. Customers incessantly riff and build on the firm's ideas, modify them, and propose new ideas and solutions to the firm based on what has already been implemented in the game.

On the other hand, when co-creating radical innovations, companies should communicate with their customers frequently as well, although should not be bothered by the customers' suggestions for the features of the new offering (which is also in line with the notion that customers have trouble radically innovating as they create solutions based on their previous experiences of usage of different services; Gustafsson et al., 2012). We did not observe that dynamic in the cases studied here, but Aoyama and Izushi (2008) provide a rich account of how Nintendo managed its customer community and their suggestions during the development of Nintendo Wii. That console was a radical innovation, and Nintendo encountered resistance to its innovations from customers (and the most loyal customers in particular). In order to realize their vision, Nintendo decided not to listen to the customers who wished the new Nintendo console to simply be an improved version of the previous one (i.e., incremental innovation). Later, Nintendo Wii was a great success in the marketplace, and this demonstrates von Hippel's (2005) warning that in co-creation customers usually desire more of what they know and have problems envisioning radically innovative solutions.

For various types of co-creating customers, different methods of tapping into their use information are necessary (von Hippel, 2005). Firms differ in their ability to identify those types, and to deploy appropriate methods—which feeds into the argument about competences for co-creation (user involvement competence in particular, Lettl, 2007). Customers also change over time with regard to knowledge, skills and motivations to co-create; that change results from their evolving experiences and changes in needs, wants and preferences (Magnusson, 2009; Bayus, 2013). Edvardsson et al. (2012) make a recommendation to interact with customers on the basis of duplex, dialog-based methods. That means allowing feedback to and from customers, and facilitating their learning (also organizational learning from and with customers). This frames co-creation as a process, co-located with individual interactions between employees and customers across the firm boundary (Cohendet and Simon, 2007).

Co-Creation Experience

The design of co-creation experience has been the focus of several academic journal articles (Verhagen et al., 2011; Payne et al., 2009; Füller and Matzler, 2007). According to some, it is an extension of the brand experience (Payne et al., 2009), while for the others a successful co-creation experience is a prerequisite for attracting and motivating appropriate types of innovative consumers (Kohler et al., 2011a, b). Considering the form of co-creation experience has become a major concern, as it influences not only the quality of contributions, but also the perceptions of the brand and the attitude of the customer community (Ebner et al., 2009). Positive co-creation experience, i.e., one that results in satisfaction, stimulates customer loyalty and recommendation behaviour—both of which are highly prized by the firms in creative industries (Verhagen et al., 2011).

Customer communities also have their dark side, as demonstrated by Gebauer et al. (2013). The quality of ideas provided by co-creating communities is not the only thing that firms need to be aware of. As customers form networked communities, they can influence the perceptions of services in the market, significantly affecting their commercial performance by word of mouth (WOM) and maximum willingness to pay (WTP). In particular, perceived injustice as well as dissatisfaction with a company's actions and offerings may unleash customer misbehaviour: complaining, boycotting, fraud and abuse of employees. These behaviours may result in negative brand perceptions for customers, stress and job dissatisfaction for employees, financial damages, and a loss of reputation for firms.

Managing co-creation in communities is a challenging task that resembles a multi-user dialog—it is important to consider not only the interactions between the company and the participants but also interactions among the participants (Pearce, 2009; Aoyama and Izushi, 2008; Boellstorff, 2008). It represents another challenge for a company seeking to integrate customers as participants in NSD. Commonly agreed norms and values between the firm and customers are required (Malaby, 2009; Taylor, 2006a, b). Interestingly, both positive and negative actions of the innovation community members stem from their feelings of affiliation and commitment. Without emotional investment in co-creation, community members would be taking no positive or negative actions whatsoever (Gebauer et al., 2013).

Co-creation experience is the content of participation in co-creation. Experience is a complex interplay of situations, individuals and the system over time, and designers of the virtual co-creation do not control all aspects of that experience. Understood this way, users in co-creation processes always have an experience—whether good or bad (Kohler et al., 2011a)—and they share their opinions of it through their social network. Firms go to great lengths to ensure that not only their products or services, but also their general communication and interactions with customers are branded and convey the emotions and aesthetics of their offerings. Customers are always engaged with the brand (Kohler et al., 2011b; Kohler et al., 2009).

Therefore, Kohler et al. (2011b) advocate inviting customers to co-create the content they wish to experience. The collective sharing of experiences by co-creating customers induces a sense of community. Following on Yee (2014, 2007), if the experience fulfils participants' hedonic needs, the efforts involved in a co-creation system are no longer considered work (shifting to 'playbour' and 'prosumption'; Ritzer and Jurgenson, 2010; Kücklich, 2005). Kohler et al. (2011a) and Payne et al. (2009) stress the interaction experience as a motivator to join and enjoy co-creation projects, as well as regard it as critical for inspiring consumers to make creative contributions.

Creating a compelling experience is linked to the state of flow—a term introduced by Csikszentmihalyi (1991) to describe a highly enjoyable and rewarding 'optimal' experience, in which challenge and skills match (a similar term is 'jouissance', Kohler et al., 2011a). A compelling experience leads to increased persistence and interest in further co-creation activities. It also positively influences participants' attitudes. Hence Kohler et al. (2011a) see the success of co-creation as stemming from the firm's ability to aggregate, retain and encourage customers to make contributions—in other words, to stage a positive co-creation experience. Füller and Matzler (2007) also point out that virtual interaction has to meet not only producers' but also customers' expectations in order to get high-quality inputs to NSD. Not only lead users (von Hippel, 2005) are able to deliver inputs, but a wide range of customers assume different roles and are capable of providing various contributions (Burger-Helmchen and Cohendet, 2011).

The co-creation experience impacts the success of co-creation as an innovation strategy. It attracts customers, influences the quality of the ideas, as well as impacts the effects such as word of mouth and willingness to pay. Co-creation experience is linked to and informs the experience of the service. The staging of the right co-creation experience is enabled by the competences for co-creation embedded in a firm (Piller and Ihl, 2009). Designing that experience is among the chief tools at a firm's disposal. Below we compare the differences in co-creation experience staged by firms in three case studies, and corresponding innovation strategies. As customers become more engaged with the service, they interact more among themselves as well as with the firm. These interactions form the space in which co-creation plays out, extending the experience of a service.

Definition of Co-Creation

Elaborating on the work of Banks (2013), we propose the following working definition of co-creation:

Co-creation is such transformative practice of a firm, when collaborative work between a consumer, or customer communities, and the firm takes place, entailing a meaningful exchange that influences the innovation, design, development, production, marketing or distribution of a new or existing service, transforming the 'back-end' processes of the firm, as well as rendering accessible some functions of the firm so far unavailable to the customers.

The 'meaningful exchange' differs for the type of actor involved. For the firm, it pertains to accessing customers' need-related knowledge (von Hippel, 2005), using customer labour through interacting with communities (Kücklich, 2005; Castronova, 2005), tapping into the customers as an investor (Ordanini et al., 2011), as well as benefitting from positive word of mouth (Franklin et al., 2013; Gebauer et al., 2013). On the other hand, for customers the 'meaningful exchange' will correspond to their motivations for co-creating and participation—both intrinsic and extrinsic (Roberts et al., 2014; Füller, 2010), as well as will meet their desires for participation in culture and influencing the organization (Banks, 2013; Hartley et al., 2013; Jenkins, 2009, 2006).

At the same time, co-creation must be framed as a deeply transformative practice for firms. Linking to the works of Voss and Zomerdijk (2007), den Hertog (2000), Sundbo and Toivonen (2011), Kuusisto (2008) and Päällysaho (2008), it demonstrates how the processes that were the sole domain of the firm become visible to the customers (migrating from 'back-office' to 'front office' for instance) and can be influenced by them. This is also underlined by Miles and Green (2008), who describe the innovation sites all across the creative firm. With co-creation related to hidden innovation, as well as the role of organizational culture in co-creation practice, co-creation must be understood for its transformative influence on firms.

This definition best fits exploring co-creative practices of videogames firms. It emphasizes the understanding of the organizational transformations as the key to framing co-creation. It differentiates co-creation from, for example, open innovation in general (Chesbrough, 2011; Christensen et al., 2005) or crowdsourcing (Estelles-Arolas et al., 2012). For the former, it frames with more specific detail the phenomenon itself, instead of focusing on general mapping of the source of ideas and their crossing of organizational boundary, and a description of firm strategy. For the latter, it demarcates itself by placing the emphasis on the organizational transformation, which is largely absent in crowdsourcing (which constitutes an open call for submissions, closely controlled and curated by the firm; Estelles-Arolas et al., 2012).

This definition also clearly captures the differences between co-creation and peer production (Van der Graaf, 2009; Benkler, 2006) or open source movement (von Krogh and von Hippel, 2006). Co-creation is a practice undertaken by the firms, and for anything to be identified as co-creation, a business actor who plays the role of coordinator of external competences must be present. Co-creation has its roots in the labour of the customer community, spans the boundary of the firm, as well as transforms the organization by questioning the traditional separation between its internal functions (so far unavailable to customers) and external functions (into which the customers traditionally have had an input; Miles and Green, 2008; den Hertog, 2000).

Therefore, it is a unique practice. It exists in all three of those areas (Voss and Zomerdijk's back office, front office, as well as customer interaction areas; 2007), while crowdsourcing omits the back office, and peer production largely excludes corporate actors from the equation altogether (and open innovation describes only a general corporate paradigm of sourcing ideas and solutions). Co-creation, as framed in the definition above, also captures the role of customers in the internal processes of the firm, such as innovation and new service development (NSD). It also offers a better understanding of hidden innovation.

The Videogames Industry

The videogames industry develops software running on various digital devices: personal computers, dedicated game consoles, mobile phones and tablets. Videogames consist of software code, script (determining the rules of the game, as well as its premise), artwork and music. They belong to a large number of genres: racing, shooting, strategy, role-playing, as well as simulator games. Videogames studios vary greatly in their size (from one-man operations, to organizations with a few thousand employees). Studios are also often specialized in developing videogames in a particular genre. Videogames are distributed to customers by the means of physical (discs) and digital (downloads) channels.

Some videogames command a large fan following. Their players form communities where various game-related topics are discussed. Players develop social bonds, band together in guilds or clans, help one another with various game-related problems, as well as compete against each other. Those communities are an important asset to videogames firms, as they ensure continued sales, both for the existing as well as upcoming videogames, as well as reduce demand uncertainty (Franklin et al., 2013). They can also be an asset during videogame development.[9]

The videogames industry also includes other actors apart from studios and customer communities (such as publishers, middleware developers, platform owners), but they do not engage in co-creation with customers (Broekhuizen et al., 2013). This is because they are located upstream in the value chain (i.e., rarely interacting directly with the players), and it is the videogames studios themselves who are their customers. Predominantly, it is videogames firms who design the gameplay, build the underlying software, create art and compose the music, as well as coordinate the work process and ensure problem-free functioning of the finished game (Scarbrough et al., 2015; O'Donnell, 2014; Van der Graaf, 2012; Malaby, 2009). Videogame studios have the most to gain from learning about co-creation.

Videogame firms will retain their central position in relation to the communities of customers. They play a coordinative role in various production-related activities, and have numerous functions that could not be outsourced to the community of customers. Nevertheless, players' desire to influence NSD has been encroaching upon the firms with increasing force in the recent years. The control over creative agency (O'Hern and Rindfleisch, 2010) can be ceded to customers to varying degree depending on the competences and culture of a firm. Still, the firm's role as the coordinator of customers' competences and architect of the systems for customers' creativity will remain undisputed in the foreseeable future (Boellstorff, 2012; Malaby, 2009; O'Hern et al., 2011; Piller and Ihl, 2009). Still, customers can actively seek and adopt strategic positions in the official production space (Hills, 2002), as they no longer abide by the formal separation between producers and consumers (Banks, 2013). Jenkins (2006) and Van der Graaf (2009) see media users as pursuing complex and contradictory alliances and suggest that fans seek to open and explore possibilities for participatory alliances within these commercial networks.

Game development is a highly coordinated and complex activity (Van der Graaf, 2012; Tschang, 2007) performed by expert groups (Panourgias et al., 2014; Scarbrough et al., 2015). Game design for instance is a centralized process, requiring skills which are tacit and thus difficult to pass on to others (or learn in formal education; O'Donnell, 2014). There are many terms in the practice of game developers that denote bad design, which vastly reduces the quality of any game—such as 'feature creep' or 'kitchen-sink design' (Schell, 2008; Koster, 2005). Attempting to outsource portions of game design could result in a game that is unplayable. The same applies to other aspects of game development—for example, to writing of the software code governing how the game functions, or creation of the high-level game art, setting the mood and feel of the game (Hight and Novak, 2008). Without the nexus of the firm and its role of coordinating customers' competences (c.f. O'Hern and Rindfleisch, 2010), co-creation would quickly descend into a chaotic and unstructured process, unable to produce any type of media that would be competitive in the market economy (Banks (2013). Moreover, the ownership of intellectual property resulting from co-creation remains an unregulated issue which sits uneasily with current framings of copyright and plagiarism (Humphreys, 2007, 2005a; Grimes, 2006). Since IP is an important asset to a creative firm, any risk or uncertainty associated with it is avoided. Firms can't be vulnerable to lawsuits over commercial use of a valuable element of IP which might have been ideated by a customer.

Videogame Firms

Game development is a complex process. It requires technical, as well as artistic expertise, and skilful coordination of those two in the conditions of demand-driven marketplace (O'Donnell, 2014). In the videogames industry, this means bringing together large numbers of specialists in completely different fields. This has caused the development costs to soar, as the customers expect the highest standard of graphics, complexity and connectivity of videogames. Still, it is player experience (as mediated by a videogame's software) that is the focus in videogame NSD (O'Donnell, 2012). Hence videogames are deeply experiential products (c.f., Saarijärvi et al., 2013; Saarijärvi, 2012; Vargo and Lusch, 2004). A videogame's value is heavily influenced by the opinions of peers in social network (Gebauer et al., 2013; Banks and Potts, 2010; Potts, Cunningham et al., 2008, Potts, Hartley et al., 2008). Services such as Metacritic or Amazon reviews, which aggregate users' opinions, are important quality signals. The market demand, and thus commercial success, for any particular title is difficult to predict (Tschang, 2007; Franklin et al., 2013).

Videogame development is creative in its nature (Van der Graaf, 2012; Tschang, 2007; Cohendet and Simon, 2007). It resists framing into prescribed routines. On top of that, the videogames industry is highly secretive about its practices, as well as shows little institutional memory (O'Donnell, 2014). The state of flux, which characterizes the mode of functioning of the videogames firms, is linked not only to the process and organization, but to the relative youth of the industry (O'Donnell, 2014). Reporting on the practices of videogames industry is further complicated by the reluctance of game developers and other firms within the industry (such as publishers) to grant access to researchers (Nardi, 2010: 35).

In the context of videogame development practices, any type of deviation from the true-and-tested methods of game development add to the already high uncertainty (Sakao et al., 2009; Knight, 1921). Co-creation is seen as requiring new organizational routines and processes that are not proven, as well as it is equated with investment in an external resource which essentially cannot be controlled ('the crowd'). Managing the inputs from the customers and assimilating them into the game development processes is seen as a difficult and disruptive task. The game development professionals are reluctant to process customers' ideas, as that requires a change in their role within the studio—from the makers of content, who can "simply go in their hole and make some stuff" (O'Donnell, 2014: 52), to curators of external ideas and inputs. The fears for the stability of their employment and becoming obsolete accompany this (Wexler, 2011).

A videogame development project can be divided into three major functions: programming, art and design (Hight and Novak, 2008; Irish, 2005; Bethke, 2003). Employees working in these respective disciplines are highly specialized professionals whose work is coordinated and brought together by producers and project managers. Communication and coordination between those specializations pose one of the main challenges to successful game development. Co-creative inputs from customers fit uneasily within these disciplines (customer inputs often concern numerous issues at once, falling into remit of different teams within the studio). This further increases the firm's reluctance to accept them, as they are disruptive to established methods of game development and require interdisciplinary teams to process them (and not many videogame firms function like that—one notable exception is CCP described in Case Beta).

Still, recent trends in the videogame development practice enable the rise of such interdisciplinary teams, as well as industry professionals, who in their skillset combine two or three of those disparate disciplines (for example, tools engineers and technical artists; O'Donnell, 2014). Some firms do embrace them, thus opening the doors to sustainable capitalization on co-creation in their practices. They embrace co-creation, purposefully departing from more traditional approaches to game development, experimenting with their team composition, project management timelines, revenue streams, as well as degree of player involvement in internal affairs of the firm. Those studios integrate those processes deeply into their own practices and operations, becoming unique actors within the industry. This is also a method of achieving sustainable competitive advantage over other firms in their sector. We focus on such firms (for example, CCP and Cloud Imperium Games in Cases Beta and Gamma), just as we describe more traditional types of firms that have only adopted co-creation out of necessity and as an add-on to their proven game development practices, normally in the wake of crowdfunding (such as Obsidian Entertainment in Case Alpha). Consequently, we observe three distinct styles of co-creation in videogames firms, occurring on the structured, semi-structured and unstructured spectrum, as well as for relationship or NSD purposes.

Player Communities

The roots of the videogames industry are related to the notions of fandom and participation (Pearce, 2009). Gaming as an activity stems from niche forms of interests and accompanying closely-knit communities (for example, the original MUD communities; King and Borland, 2014; Boellstorff, 2012). In the environment of online videogames, emotional and social bonds unique to play form. They are equally authentic as the bonds that humans form in the offline lives (Pearce, 2009).

Only recently we observe rapid expansion of videogames into the mainstream mass market, and the drive of the industry to market its products to diverse demographics (Zackariasson and Wilson, 2012; Marchand and Hennig-Thurau, 2013). In its wake, gaming as a cultural activity has been losing its niche character. Social groups associated with gaming have been gradually expanding. Gaming is no longer popularly perceived as something that only socially awkward, white, teenage middle-class boys do (Pearce, 2009). As a result, gameplay is no longer synonymous with belonging to a community of players. Being a member of such communities has become optional; a domain of only the most involved and engaged customers (Burger-Helmchen and Cohendet, 2011). Some videogames lend themselves to the growth of player communities better than the others. Certain videogames are single-player experiences by design; others rely on the social dynamics, interactions and cooperation between players for their core functionality (the latter are characterized by closer integration of social elements into gameplay, and tend to promote better organized—but also often firm-controlled—player communities).

'Indie' Developers and Crowdfunding

The most visible manifestation of increasing involvement of players and their communities in the videogames industry is the phenomenon of crowd-funding (Belleflamme et al., 2014; Mollick, 2012; Lehner, 2012). Enabled by such platforms as Kickstarter[10] and Indiegogo,[11] and boosted by recent technological developments, it has taken the industry by storm, enabling the development of numerous innovative services (Howe, 2008). It allows the community members to take on the role of videogame producers, funding their development, marketing and other aspects. According to Ordanini et al. (2011), crowdfunding is an initiative undertaken to raise money for a new project by collecting small to medium-size investments from several other people. In the case of the videogames industry, those donations are predominantly small (for the case of Obsidian Entertainment described in this work, the overwhelming majority of crowdfunding customers contributed less than 70 USD to a project). The donors do not receive any financial benefits from contributing, such as equity in the firm or share of the revenues.[12]

Crowdfunding, on the highest level of analysis, has led to the major change in the videogames industry manifested by the mass appearance of small, independent game development studios, called 'indies'. Those indie game developers, which are firms normally consisting of just a few employees (many of them are single-man enterprises), take advantage of the facilitated communication between themselves and their customers offered by Web 2.0. Because of the limited budget, indie studios cannot develop photorealistic graphics or complex videogames that would captivate the mass market, just like the big-budget videogames do. Instead, those small developers seek to attract a market niche by offering products that are unique. Due to the inherent nostalgia as well as heightened artistic dimension of indie videogames, as well as tapping of indie developers into their own social network to advertise their productions, it is common for indie videogames to have a following of dedicated customers. This forms what Ordanini et al. (2011) call a brand community, or a community of consumption (Jäger et al., 2010). Such community consists of customers who are deeply involved with a brand that offers then symbolic benefits, can develop "a common understanding of a shared identity" (Muniz and O'Guinn, 2001: 413) and actively engage in activities such as new service development, quality reassurance, experience sharing, and joint consumption (Ordanini et al., 2011: 447; c.f. consumer tribes in Kozinets, 2007).[13]

Brand communities are one of the most important resources for those small studios, which are often composed of relatively inexperienced game developers. Brand community members are typically motivated by fun, learning, identification and status, especially when the activity is shared through social networks (Bagozzi and Dholakia, 2006). Online, they generate "a process of collective value creation" (Schau et al., 2009: 30)—facilitated by the community of customers, which often includes experienced consumers (customers with high product competence; Lettl, 2007), as well as game developers already established in the industry (Cohendet and Simon, 2007; Van de Ven, 1993). Such community can provide suggestions, feedback, help with some activities (such a testing)—overall be an asset of considerable importance to the small indie team.

Brand community can be tapped into as a source of funding, but also for information, knowledge and labour as the primary resources (Chathoth et al., 2013; Arvidsson, 2011; Fang, 2008). In crowdfunding, the consumer's monetary funds and project-screening capabilities represent important resources that a firm can tap into (Ordanini et al., 2011). The motivations of customers involved in crowdfunding relate to the feeling of being at least partially responsible for the project's success (desire for patronage) as well as being a part of a communal social initiative (desire for social participation; Etgar, 2008).

We recognize the similarities between crowdfunding behaviour, user-led innovation (von Hippel, 2005) and co-creation (Roberts et al., 2014; Füller, 2010). Still, it is not only the indie studios that take advantage of crowdfunding. Major videogame studios that are characterized by a strong customer following (a result from having released at least one product that had proven to be a success, at least in the socio-cultural dimension) have been turning to crowdfunding as well. We discuss a few such firms in detail: apart from aforementioned Obsidian Entertainment, those will be inXile Entertainment and Born Ready Games (as well as, to some extent, Cloud Imperium Games). Crowdfunding as a strategic decision heavily influences a firm's propensity for co-creation, elevating the status and role of community of customers in relation to the firm (and empowering the customers). The dynamics of interaction between those two parties are significantly affected in the wake of such arrangement, and have significant implications for the firm.

Modding—A Precursor to Co-Creation

In one of the most popular MMO videogames of all time, World of Warcraft (Blizzard Entertainment, 2004), many technically savvy players are engaged in modding (Davidovici-Nora, 2009; Jeppesen and Molin, 2003). Modding captures the dynamics of the customer community that also pertain to the phenomenon of co-creation (Arakji and Lang, 2007; Van der Graaf, 2009). In its essence, modding is a modification of videogame by its users in order to add new functionality to it (a functionality which was not included in the original, officially released title). These modifications (mods) are created by players who enjoy the videogames and generate ideas for customizing gameplay, seeking to explore new directions and to deepen their connection to the game (Nardi, 2010). This is very much in line with the observations of user-innovators by von Hippel (2005), as well as the motivations for co-creating customers (Füller, 2010), which have very much to do with the intrinsic, altruistic motivations related to learning, as well as internalized extrinsic motivators having to do with peer recognition and social standing.

Following on Van der Graaf (2009) and Sotamaa (2004), firms regard mod development as attractive sources for free brand creation, extensions of the game's shelf life, increased loyalty, innovation and recruitment (Kücklich, 2005; West and Gallagher, 2006). As such, modding can be viewed as a form of co-creation, albeit a limited one. It mostly pertains just to the content of the service offered by the firm, as well as to the customer interface with it (Miles and Green, 2008). Modding does not occur on the level of NSD in a firm; instead it affects the customer experience of a service. It constitutes inputs to the front stage area of experiential service design (Voss and Zomerdijk, 2007). A firm's NSD processes are not affected by modding—which is contrary to co-creation. Communities of modders have been around the videogames industry for a long time (Arakji and Lang, 2007), but they exist in separation from the game development firm. They are either not supported by the game developer, or supported by very few and select employees of the firm, who tend to do that in their free time (illustrated by Obsidian Entertainment's practices on Neverwinter Nights 2). This is again contrary to co-creation, which requires thorough integration across the firm NSD practices, and strategic and organizational change within the videogames studio.

Impact of Co-Creation in the Videogames Industry

There are many dynamics and characteristics of the videogames industry that influence co-creation. In the context of game development, co-creation is not an easy NSD approach to embrace, as it brings many new challenges that can be disruptive to the already precarious practices of firms. Studios work within tight budgets, in conditions of demand uncertainty (Franklin et al., 2013), and need to continuously manage their complex relationships with customers (Gustafsson et al., 2012; Grönroos, 2011, 1994).

Those customers form distinctive communities, engage in emergent behaviour that sometimes comes to game-breaking, are vocal, and their opinions exist in the context of social network markets (Potts, Hartley et al., 2008). The appearance and success of such phenomena as crowdfunding, as well as the rise of indie game developers and their capitalization on market niches, further empower the customers in their interactions with studios (Bonsu and Darmody, 2008). Videogames themselves are experiential services where the aesthetic impressions of an individual matter (Verhagen et al., 2011; Pine and Gilmore, 1998) and contribute to the creation of value (Saarijärvi et al., 2013; Vargo and Lusch, 2004, 2008).

Co-creation is not new for the videogames industry. It has its roots in historic dynamics between the studios and their customers (King and Borland, 2014). Phenomena such as modding (Nardi, 2010; Van der Graaf, 2009), fandom and participatory culture (Jenkins, 2009 and 2006), as well as the role of customers as co-producers of services as exemplified in MMO videogames, have paved the way for co-creation as a viable game production practice. Despite the advent of high-definition consoles in the first decade of 21st century, and associated entrance of gaming into the mainstream culture, this industry retains its power to create experiences that promote the development of emotional bonds between customers and videogames that they play. Very often, as demonstrated by Pearce (2009), this bond plays out not only in-game, but spills over to other media and forms of communication, for example, to Internet forums and fan events. Firms in the videogame industry have taken note of the power of those phenomena, and their recent interest in harnessing co-creation for creation of value in their business practices reflects that awareness.

In co-creation it is the firm who bears the risk of the process (Gebauer et al., 2013; Banks, 2009). It is also the firm who needs to find the application and means of assimilating customer inputs internally (Zahra and George, 2002; Hoyer et al., 2010). The firm needs to understand and manage (by developing new competences; Piller and Ihl, 2009) the ebbs and flows of the resource 'crowd'—remaining ever outside of the reach of traditional management tools. It is these and other considerations that solidify the focus of this study on the firm's role in co-creation, together with its characteristics.

Notes

1. Green et al. (2007) propose a 'diamond' framework for capturing the six dimensions of innovation in the creative industries. These consist of technology and process of production, as well as cultural product (i.e., the product that carries the cultural meanings and information content), cultural concept (i.e., the information content of the product, such as characters or narratives), user interface (i.e., how the customer interacts with the product to gain the experience), and

delivery (i.e., how the product is made accessible to customers). This framework is merged with the observations of Miles and Green (2008) to generate the conceptual framework.

2. The videogames industry is characterized by abundance of trade shows, conferences, professional bodies, special interests groups (SIGs) and other similar initiatives.

3. In this text, the term 'user', 'consumer' or 'customer' refers to a person who applies the end result of the innovation process in practice and benefits from it due to the new value included; it does not denote a corporate entity.

4. The term *user* involvement competence is used throughout this work. We did not replace the word *user* with *customer*, choosing to adhere to the original wording of Lettl (2007).

5. Network competence denotes the employees' ability to build, manage and exploit social networks for value-adding purposes.

6. Problems linked to integration competence aren't present above due to the little focus in the literature on organizational aspects of co-creation. This is a gap which this book is addressing.

7. For example, in idea generation and service development stages, positive outcomes are the same as for the co-creation process overall, while risks and costs are centred around provision of incentives for more and better ideas from customers, challenges in recognizing potentially successful ideas from numerous customer inputs (Saur-Amaral, 2012), as well as managing customer expectations and relationships (Gebauer et al., 2013; Gummesson, 2002). In testing and post-launch, risks and costs involve challenges in managing potentially negative word of mouth, while positive outcomes include increased likelihood of success and faster diffusion (as services match customers' needs better), savings on marketing expenses (greater customer enthusiasm and word-of-mouth effects), savings on customer education and other support activities, as well as early warning of potential issues with the new service.

8. Further reflecting on the differences between NSD stages, Bayus (2013) identified the fluctuations of community members' ability to come up with innovative ideas over time. He identifies one additional challenge to firms co-creating services with their customers: maintaining an ongoing supply of quality ideas from the customer community over time is problematic, as the quality tends to decrease. The firm's ability to overcome those challenges is an aspect of disclosure competence for co-creation (Piller and Ihl, 2009). It hinges on the organizational ability to provide the customers with enough material and information so that meaningful co-creation can sustainably be taking place and new customers are attracted to contribute to it.

9. We consider the communities of customers as one of the actors in the videogames industry, influencing it through the mechanisms of social network markets and situated creativity (Potts, Cunningham et al., 2008; Potts, Hartley et al., 2008). They are framed not as passive consumers of media content, but instead as their co-creators (Banks and Humphreys, 2008; Jenkins, 2006, 2009; Hills, 2002).

10. www.kickstarter.com [accessed on 14.09.2015]

11. www.indiegogo.com [accessed on 14.09.2015]

12. Crowdfunding 'backers' (as they are called by game developers) are motivated by non-economic benefits. Their actions in supporting projects match donor behaviour (Cermak et al., 1994), which suggests that they are motivated by self-esteem, public recognition, satisfaction of expressing gratitude for one's own wellbeing, and relief from feelings of guilt and obligation (White and Peloza, 2009). This is highlighted by the role of crowds in trying to sustain small projects having a social meaning (Ordanini et al., 2011).

13. Ordanini et al. (2011) identify two distinct traits of customers who are likely to participate in crowdfunding initiatives in the videogames industry (which are

characterized by a 'donor' type of behaviour): innovative orientation (stimulating the desire to try new modes of interacting with firms and other consumers), and social identification with the content, cause or project selected for funding (sparking the desire to be a part of the initiative).

References

Alford, J., (2002). Why do public-sector clients coproduce? Toward a contingency theory. *Administration & Society*, 34(1), pages 32–56.

Amin, A., and Cohendet, P., (2004). *Architectures of Knowledge: Firms, Capabilities and Communities*. Oxford University Press.

Aoyama, Y., and Izushi, H., (2008). User-led innovation and the video game industry. IRP Conference, London, May 22–23, 2008.

Arakji, R.Y., and Lang, K.R., (2007). Digital consumer networks and producer-consumer collaboration: Innovation and product development in the video game industry. *Journal of Management Information Systems*, 24(2), pages 195–219.

Arvidsson, A., (2011). Ethics and value in customer co-production. *Marketing Theory*, 11(3), pages 261–278.

Bach, L., Cohendet, P., Penin, J., and Simon, L., (2008). IPR and "open creativity": The cases of videogames and of the music industry: The Creative Industries and Intellectual Property. DIME–London conference, May 22–23, 2008.

Bagozzi, R.P., and Dholakia, U.M., (2006). Open source software user communities: A study of participation in Linux user groups. *Management Science*, 52(7), pages 1099–1115.

Banks, J., (2009). Co-creative expertise: Auran games and Fury—a case study. *Media International Australia: Incorporating Culture and Policy*, 130(February), pages 77–89.

Banks, J., (2013). *Co-creating Videogames*. London: Bloomsbury Academic.

Banks, J., and Deuze, M., (2009). Co-creative labour. *International Journal of Cultural Studies*, 12(5), pages 419–431.

Banks, J., and Humphreys, S., (2008). The labour of user co—creators: Emergent social network markets? *Convergence: The International Journal of Research into New Media Technologies*, 14(4), pages 401–418.

Banks, J., and Potts, J., (2010). Co-creating games: A co-evolutionary analysis. *New Media and Society*, 12(2), pages 252–270.

Barney, J.B., (1986). Organizational culture: Can it be a source of sustained competitive advantage? *The Academy of Management Review*, 11(3), pages 656–665.

Bayus, B.L., (2013). Crowdsourcing new product ideas over time: An analysis of the Dell IdeaStorm community. *Management Science*, 59(1), pages 226–244.

Belleflamme, P., Lambert, T., and Schwienbacher, A., (2014). Crowdfunding: Tapping the right crowd. *Journal of Business Venturing*, 29(5), pages 585–609.

Bengtsson, L., and Ryzhkova, N., (2015). Managing online User co-creation in service innovation. In: Agarwal, R., Selen, W., Roos, G., and Green, R., (eds). *The Handbook of Service Innovation*. London: Springer, pages 575–589.

Benkler, Y., (2006). *The Wealth of Networks*. Yale: Yale University Press.

Bergstrom, K., Carter, M., Woodford, D., and Paul, C., (2013). Constructing the ideal EVE Online player. In: *Proceedings of DiGRA 2013: DeFragging Game Studies*. Atlanta.

Bethke, E., (2003). *Game Development and Production*. Plano, TX: Wordware Publishing, Inc.

Bhalla, G., (2010). *Collaboration and Co-Creation: New Platforms for Marketing and Innovation*. New York: Springer.

Bitner, M.J., Faranda, W.T., Hubbert, A.R., and Zeithaml, V.A., (1997). Customer contributions and roles in service delivery. *International Journal of Service Industry Management*, 8(3), pages 193–205.

Boellstorff, T., (2008). *Coming of Age in Second Life: An Anthropologist Explores the Virtually Human*. Princeton and Oxford: Princeton University Press.

Boellstorff, T., Nardi, B., Pearce, C., and Taylor, T.L., (2012). *Ethnography and Virtual Worlds*. Oxford: Princeton University Press.

Bonsu, S.K., and Darmody, A., (2008). Co-creating second life market—consumer cooperation in contemporary economy. *Journal of Macromarketing*, 28(4), pages 355–368.

Broekhuizen, T.L., Lampel, J., and Rietveld, J., (2013). New horizons or a strategic mirage? Artist-led-distribution versus alliance strategy in the video game industry. *Research Policy*, 42(4), pages 954–964.

Bruns, A., (2008). *Blogs, Wikipedia, Second Life and Beyond: From Production to Produsage*. New York: Peter Lang.

Burger-Helmchen, T., and Cohendet, P., (2011). User communities and social software in the video game industry. *Long Range Planning*, 44, pages 317–343.

Cameron, K.S., and Quinn, R.E., (1999). *Diagnosing and Changing Organisational Culture*. Reading: Addison-Wesley.

Cassiman, B., and Veugelers, R., (2006). In search of complementarity in innovation strategy: Internal R&D and external knowledge acquisition. *Management Science*, 52(1), pages 68–82.

Castronova, E., (2005). *Synthetic Worlds: The Business and Culture of Online Games*. Chicago and London: The University of Chicago Press.

Cermak, D.S.P., File, K.M., and Prince, R.A., (1994). A benefit segmentation of the major donor market. *Journal of Business Research*, 29(2), pages 121–30.

Chatenier, E., Verstegen, J.A.A.M., Biemans, H.J.A., Mulder, M., and Omta, O.S.W.F., (2010). Identification of competencies for professionals in open innovation teams. *R&D Management*, 40(3), pages 271–280.

Chathoth, P., Altinay, L., Harrington, R.J., Okumus, F., and Chan, E.S.W., (2013). Co-production versus co-creation: A process based continuum in the hotel service context. *International Journal of Hospitality Management*, 32, pages 11–20.

Cheng, C.C., and Huizingh, E.K., (2014). When is open innovation beneficial? The role of strategic orientation. *Journal of Product Innovation Management*, 31(6), pages 1235–1253.

Chesbrough, H.W., (2006). *Open Innovation: The New Imperative for Creating and Profiting From Technology*. Cambridge, MA: Harvard Business Press.

Chesbrough, H.W., (2011). Bringing open innovation to services. *MIT Sloan Management Review*, 52(2), 85–90.

Christensen, J.F., Olesen, M.H., and Kjær, J.S., (2005). The industrial dynamics of open innovation: Evidence from the transformation of consumer electronics. *Research Policy*, 34(10), pages 1533–1549.

Cohen, W.M., and Levinthal, D.A., (1990). Absorptive capacity: A new perspective on learning and innovation. *Administrative Science Quarterly*, Vol. 35, No. 1, pages 128–152.

Cohendet, P., and Simon, L., (2007). Playing across the playground: Paradoxes of knowledge creation in the videogame firm. *Journal of Organizational Behavior*, 28, pages 587–605.

Cook, S., (2008). The contribution revolution. *Harvard Business Review*, 86(October), pages 60–69.

Csikszentmihalyi, M., (1991). *Flow: The Psychology of Optimal Experience* (Vol. 41). New York: HarperPerennial.

Dahlander, L., and Gann, D.M., (2010). How open is innovation? *Research Policy*, 39(6), pages 699–709.

Dahlander, L., and Magnusson, M., (2008). How do firms make use of open source communities? *Long Range Planning*, 41, pages 629–649.

Danneels, E., (2000). The dynamics of product innovation and firm competences. *Academy of Management Proceedings*, 2000(1), pages D1-D6.

Darke, P.R., and Ritchie, R.J.B., (2007). The defensive consumer: Advertising deception, defensive processing, and distrust. *Journal of Marketing Research*, 44(1) (February), pages 114–127.

Davidovici-Nora, M., (2009). The dynamics of co-creation in the video game industry: The case of World of Warcraft. *Communications & Strategies*, 73, pages 43–66.

De Jong, J.P., and Vermeulen, P.A., (2003). Organizing successful new service development: A literature review. *Management Decision*, 41(9), pages 844–858.

den Hertog, P.D., (2000). Knowledge-intensive business services as co-producers of innovation. *International Journal of Innovation Management*, 4(04), pages 491–528.

Ebner, W., Leimeister, J.M., and Krcmar, H., (2009). Community engineering for innovations: The ideas competition as a method to nurture a virtual community for innovations. *R&D Management*, 39(4), pages 342–356.

Edvardsson, B., Kristensson, P., Magnusson, P., and Sundström, E., (2012). Customer integration within service development—a review of methods and an analysis of insitu and exsitu contributions. *Technovation*, 32(7), pages 419–429.

Edvardsson, B., and Olsson, J., (1996). Key concepts for new service development. *Service Industries Journal*, 16(2), pages 140–64.

Edwards, M., Logue, D., and Schweitzer, J., (2015). Towards an understanding of open innovation in services: Beyond the firm and towards relational co-creation. In: Agarwal, R., Selen, W., Roos, G., and Green, R., (eds). *The Handbook of Service Innovation*. London: Springer London, pages 75–90.

Eisenhardt, K.M., and Martin, J.A., (2000). Dynamic capabilities: What are they? *Strategic Management Journal*, Vol. 21, pages 1105–1121.

Enkel, E., Kausch, C., and Gassmann, O., (2005). Managing the risk of customer integration. *European Management Journal*, 23(2), pages 203–213.

Estelles-Arolas, E., and Gonzales-Ladron-de-Guevara, F., (2012). Towards an integrated crowdsourcing definition. *Journal of Information Science*, 38(2), pages 189–200.

Etgar, M., (2008). A descriptive model of the consumer co-production process. *Journal of the Academy of Marketing Science*, 36(1), pages 97–108.

Fang, E., (2008). Customer participation and the trade-off between new product innovativeness and speed to market. *Journal of Marketing*, 72(4), pages 90–101.

Fournier, S., and Lee, L., (2009). Getting brand communities right. *Harvard Business Review*, 87(4), pages 105–112.

Franklin, M., Searle, N., Stoyanova, D., and Townley, B., (2013). Innovation in the application of digital tools for managing uncertainty: The case of UK independent film. *Creativity and Innovation Management*, 22(3), pages 320–333.

Füller, J., (2010). Refining virtual co-creation from a consumer perspective. *California Management Review*, 52(2), pages 98–122.

Füller, J., (2010). Refining virtual co-creation from a consumer perspective. *California Management Review*, 52(2), pages 98–122.

Füller, J., and Matzler, K., (2007). Virtual product experience and customer participation—a chance for customer-centred, really new products. *Technovation*, 27(6), pages 378–387.

Füller, J., Matzler, K., and Hoppe, M., (2008). Brand community members as a source of innovation. *Journal of Product Innovation Management*, 25(6), pages 608–619.

Fynes, B., and Lally, A.M., (2008). Innovation in services: From service concepts to service experiences. In: Hefley, B. and Murphy, W., (eds). *Service Science, Management and Engineering: Education for the 21st Century*. New York: Springer Science & Business Media, pages 329–333.

Gangi, P.M., Wasko, M.M., and Hooker, R.E., (2010). Getting customers' ideas to work for you: Learning from Dell how to succeed with online user innovation communities. *MIS Quarterly Executive*, 9(4), pages 213–228.

Gebauer, J., Füller, J., and Pezzei, R., (2013). The dark and the bright side of co-creation: Triggers of member behaviour in online innovation communities. *Journal of Business Research*, 66, pages 1516–1527.

Green, L., Miles, I., and Rutter, J., (2007). *Hidden Innovation in the Creative Industries*. London: NESTA Working Paper.

Grimes, S.M., (2006). Online multiplayer games: A virtual space for intellectual property debates? *New Media & Society*, 8(6), pages 969–990.

Grönroos, C., (1994). From marketing mix to relationship marketing: Towards a paradigm shift in marketing. *Management Decision*, 32(2), pages 4–20.

Grönroos, C., (2011). Value co-creation in service logic: A critical analysis. *Marketing Theory*, 11(3), pages 279–301.

Grove, S.J., Fisk, R.P., and Bitner, M.J., (1992). Dramatizing the service experience: A managerial approach. *Advances in Services Marketing and Management*, 1, pages 91–121.

Gruner, K.E., and Homburg, C., (2000). Does customer interaction enhance new product success? *Journal of Business Research*, 49(1), pages 1–14.

Gummesson, E., (2002). Relationship marketing in the new economy. *Journal of Relationship Marketing*, 1(1), pages 37–57.

Gustafsson, A., Kristensson, P., and Witell, L., (2012). Customer co-creation in service innovation: A matter of communication? *Journal of Service Management*, 23(3), pages 311–327.

Haefliger, S., Jäger, P., and von Krogh, G., (2010). Under the radar: Industry entry by user entrepreneurs. *Research Policy*, 39(9), pages 1198–1213.

Handke, C., (2004). Defining creative industries by comparing the creation of novelty. In the workshop Creative Industries–a measure of urban development, WIWIPOL and FOKUS, Vienna.

Hartley, J., (2008). *Television Truths*. Malden, MA: Wiley-Blackwell.

Hartley, J., Potts, J., Cunningham, S., Flew, T., Keane, M., and Banks, J., (2013). *Key Concepts in Creative Industries*. London: Sage.

Hau, Y.S., and Kim, Y.G., (2011). Why would online gamers share their innovation-conducive knowledge in the online game user community? Integrating individual motivations and social capital perspectives. *Computers in Human Behavior*, 27(2), pages 956–970.

Hight, J., and Novak, J., (2008). *Game Development Essentials: Game Project Management*. Clifton Park, NY: Delmar.

Hills, M., (2002). *Fan Cultures*. London: Routledge.

Howe, J., (2008). *Crowdsourcing: Why the Power of the Crowd Is Driving the Future of Business*. New York: Crown Business.

Hoyer, W.D., Chandy, R., Dorotic, M., Krafft, M., and Singh, S.S., (2010). Consumer co-creation in new product development. *Journal of Service Research*, 13(3), pages 283–296.

Huizingh, E.K., (2011). Open innovation: State of the art and future perspectives. *Technovation*, 31(1), pages 2–9.

Humphreys, S., (2005a). Productive users, intellectual property and governance: The challenges of computer games. *Media and Arts Law Review*, 10(4), pages 299–310.

Humphreys, S., (2005b). Productive players: Online computer games' challenge to conventional media forms. *Communication and Critical/Cultural Studies*, 2(1), pages 36–50.

Humphreys, S., (2007). You're in our world now: Ownership and access in the proprietary community of an MMOG. In: Sugumaran, V., (eds). *Intelligent Information Technologies: Concepts, Methodologies, Tools, and Applications*. Hershey, PA: Information Science Reference (IGI Global), pages 2058–2072.

Humphreys, S., Fitzgerald, B.F., Banks, J.A., and Suzor, N.P., (2005). Fan based production for computer games: User led innovation, the 'drift of value' and the negotiation of intellectual property rights. *Media International Australia Incorporating Culture and Policy: Quarterly Journal of Media Research and Resources*, 114, pages 16–29.

Ind, N., and Coates, N., (2013). The meanings of co-creation. *European Business Review*, 25(1), pages 86–95.

Irish, D., (2005). *The Game Producer's Handbook*. Boston, MA: Course Technology.

Jäger, P., Haefliger, S., and von Krogh, G., (2010). A directing audience: How specialized feedback in virtual community of consumption stimulates new media production. ETH Zurich Working Paper.

Jenkins, H., (2006). *Convergence Culture: Where Old and New Media Collide*. New York: New York University Press.

Jenkins, H., (2009). What happened before YouTube. In: Burgess, J. and Green, J., (eds). *YouTube: Online Video and the Politics of Participatory Culture*. London: Polity Press, pages 109–125.

Jeppesen, L.B., and Frederiksen, L., (2006). Why do users contribute to firm-hosted user communities? The case of computer-controlled music instruments. *Organization Science*, 17(1), pages 45–63.

Jeppesen, L.B., and Molin, M., (2003). Consumers as co-developers: Learning and innovation outside the firm. *Technology Analysis & Strategic Management*, 15(3), pages 363–383.

Kasmire, J., Korhonen, J.M., and Nikolic, I., (2012). How radical is a radical innovation? An outline for a computational approach. *Energy Procedia*, 20, pages 346–353.

Keith, C., (2010). *Agile Game Development With Scrum*. Upper Saddle River, NJ: Addison-Wesley.

King, B., and Borland, J., (2014). *Dungeons and Dreamers*. Carnegie Mellon University: ETC Press.

Kline, S., Dyer-Witherford, N., and De Peuter, G., (2003). *Digital Play: The Interaction of Technology, Culture and Marketing*. Montreal: McGill-Queen's University Press.

Knight, F.H., (1921). *Risk, Uncertainty, and Profit*. Boston, MA: Hart, Schaffner & Marx; Houghton Mifflin Co.

Kohler, T., Füller, J., Matzler, K., and Stieger, D., (2011b). Co-creation in virtual worlds: The design of the user experience. *MIS Quarterly*, 35(3), pages 773–788.

Kohler, T., Füller, J., Stieger, D., and Matzler, K., (2011a). Avatar-based innovation: Consequences of the virtual co-creation experience. *Computers in Human Behaviour*, 27, pages 160–168.

Kohler, T., Matzler, K., and Füller, J., (2009). Avatar-based innovation: Using virtual worlds for real-world innovation. *Technovation*, 29(6), pages 395–407.

Koster, R., (2005). *A Theory of Fun for Game Design*. Sebastopol, CA: Paraglyph Press.

Kozinets, R.V., (2007). Inno-tribes: Star Trek as Wikimedia. In: Cova, B., Kozinets, R., and Shankar, A., (eds). *Consumer Tribes*. New York: Routledge.

Kücklich, J., (2005). Precarious playbour: Modders and the digital games industry. *The Fibreculture Journal*, 5. http://five.fibreculturejournal.org

Kuusisto, A., (2008). Customer roles in business service production-implications for involving the customer in service innovation. In: Kuusisto, A. and Päällysaho, S., (ed). *Customer Role in Service Production and Innovation—Looking for Directions for Future Research*. Lappeenranta University of Technology, Faculty of Technology Management Research Report.

Lagrosen, S., (2005). Customer involvement in new product development: A relationship marketing perspective. *European Journal of Innovation Management*, 8(4), pages 424–436.

Lampel, J., Lant, T., and Shamsie, J., (2000). Balancing act: Learning from organizing practices in cultural industries. *Organization Science*, 11(3), pages 263–269.

Lehner, O.M., (2012). A literature review and research agenda for crowdfunding of social ventures. In: *2012 Research Cooloquium on Social Entrepreneurship*, 16–19.07, SAID Business School.

Lettl, C., (2007). User involvement competence for radical innovation. *Journal of Engineering and Technology Management*, 24, pages 53–75.

Lichtenthaler, U., and Lichtenthaler, E., (2009). A capability-based framework for open innovation: Complementing absorptive capacity. *Journal of Management Studies*, 46(8), pages 1315–1338.

Magnusson, P., Matthing, J., and Kristensson, P., (2003). Managing user involvement in service innovation. *Journal of Service Research*, 6(2), pages 111–24.

Magnusson, P.R., (2009). Exploring the contributions of involving ordinary users in ideation of technology-based services. *Journal of Product Innovation Management*, 26(5), pages 578–593.

Malaby, T.M., (2009). *Making Virtual Worlds: Linden Lab and Second Life*. Ithaca and London: Cornell University Press.

Marchand, A., and Hennig-Thurau, T., (2013). Value creation in the video game industry: Industry economics, consumer benefits, and research opportunities. *Journal of Interactive Marketing*, 27(3), pages 141–157.

Martins, E.C., and Terblanche, F., (2003). Building organisational culture that stimulates creativity and innovation. *European Journal of Innovation Management*, 6(1), pages 64–74.

Matthing, J., Sanden, B., and Edvardsson, B., (2004). New service development: Learning from and with customers. *International Journal of Service Industry Management*, 15(5), pages 479–498.

Miles, I., (2008). Patterns of innovation in service industries. *IBM Systems Journal*, 47(1), pages 115–128.

Miles, I., and Green, L., (2008). *Hidden Innovation in Creative Industries*. London: NESTA.

Mollick, E., (2012). The dynamics of crowdfunding: Determinants of success and failure. SSRN scholarly paper. Social Science Research Network, Rochester, NY.

Muniz, A.M., Jr., and O'Guinn, T.C., (2001). Brand community. *Journal of Consumer Research*, 27(4), pages 412–432.

Naranjo-Valencia, J.C., Jiménez-Jiménez, D., and Sanz-Valle, R., (2011). Innovation or imitation? The role of organizational culture. *Management Decision*, 49(1), pages 55–72.

Nardi, B.M., (2010). *My Life as a Night Elf Priest*. Ann Arbor: The University of Michigan Press and The University of Michigan Library.

Nelson, R.R., and Winter, S.G., (1982). The Schumpeterian tradeoff revisited. *The American Economic Review*, 72(1), pages 114–132.

Nonaka, I., and Hirotaka, T., (1995). *The Knowledge-Creating Company: How Japanese Companies Create the Dynamics of Innovation*. Oxford University Press.

O'Donnell, C., (2012). This is not a software industry. In: Zackariasson, P. and Wilson, T.L., (eds). *The Video Games Industry: Formation, Present State, and Future*. London and New York: Routledge.

O'Donnell, C., (2014). *Developer's Dilemma*. London, England: MIT Press.

OECD, (2007). *Annual Report*. Paris: OECD Publishing.

Ogawa, S., and Piller, F.T., (2006). Reducing the risks of new product development. *MIT Sloan Management Review*, 47(2), page 65.

O'Hern, M.S., and Rindfleisch, A., (2010). Customer co-creation: A typology and research Agenda. In: Malhotra, N.K., (ed). *Review of Marketing Research*, 6, pages 84–106, Bigley: Emerald Books.

O'Hern, M.S., Rindfleisch, A., Antia, K.D., and Schweidel, D.A., (2011). The impact of user-generated content on product innovation. SSRN. http://ssrn.com/abstract=1843250 or http://dx.doi.org/10.2139/ssrn.1843250

O'Mahony, S., and Ferraro, F., (2007). The emergence of governance in an open source community. *Academy of Management Journal*, 50(5), pages 1079–1106.

Ordanini, A., Miceli, L., Pizzetti, M., and Parasuraman, A., (2011). Crowd-funding: Transforming customers into investors through innovative service platforms. *Journal of Service Management*, 22(4), pages 443–470.

O'Reilly, T., (2005). Spreading the knowledge of innovators. What is web, 2.

Päällysaho, S., (2008). Customer interaction in service innovations: A review of literature. In: Kuusisto, A., and Päällysaho, S., (eds). *Customer Role in Service Production and Innovation–Looking for Directions for Future Research*. Lappeenranta University of Technology, Faculty of Technology Management Research Report, 195.

Panourgias, N.S., Nandhakumar, J., and Scarbrough, H., (2014). Entanglements of creative agency and digital technology: A sociomaterial study of computer game development. *Technological Forecasting and Social Change*, 83, pages 111–126.

Pavitt, K., (1990). What we know about the strategic management of technology. *California Management Review*, 32(3), pages 17–26.

Payne, A., Storbacka, K., Frow, P., and Knox, S., (2009). Co-creating brands: Diagnosing and designing the relationship experience. *Journal of Business Research*, 62(3), pages 379–389.

Pearce, C., (2009). *Communities of Play: Emergent Cultures in Multiplayer Games and Virtual Worlds*. Cambridge, MA and London, England: MIT Press.

Peteraf, M.A., (1993). The cornerstones of competitive advantage: A resource-based view. *Strategic Management Journal*, 14(3), 179–191.

Piller, F., and Ihl, C., (2009). *Open Innovation With Customers: Foundations, Competences and International Trends*. RWTH Aachen University.

Piller, F., Ihl, C., and Vossen, A., (2011). A typology of customer co-creation in the innovation process. In: Hanekop, H. and Wittke, V., (eds). *New Forms of Collaborative Innovation and Production on the Internet: An Interdisciplinary Perspective*. University of Goettingen.

Pine, J., and Gilmore, J.H., (1998). Welcome to the experience economy. *Harvard Business Review*, (July–August), pages 97–105.

Pisano, G.P., and Verganti, R., (2008). Which kind of collaboration is right for you. *Harvard Business Review*, 86(12), pages 78–86.

Potts, J., (2009). Creative industries and innovation policy. *Innovation: Management, Policy and Practice*, 11(2), pages 138–147.

Potts, J., Cunningham, S., Hartley, J., and Ormerod, P., (2008). Social network markets: A new definition of the creative industries. *Journal of Cultural Economics*, 32(3), pages 167–185.

Potts, J., Hartley, J., Banks, J., Burgess, J., Cobcroft, R., Cunningham, S., and Montgomery, L., (2008). Consumer co-creation and situated creativity. *Industry and Innovation*, 15(5), pages 459–474.

Prahalad, C.K., and Hamel, G., (1994). Strategy as a field of study: Why search for a new paradigm? *Strategic Management Journal*, 15(S2), pages 5–16.

Prahalad, C.K., and Krishnan, M.S., (2008). *The New Age of Innovation. Driving Co-created Value Through Global Networks*. New York: McGraw-Hill.

Prahalad, C.K., and Ramaswamy, V., (2004). Co-creation experiences: The next practice in value creation. *Journal of Interactive Marketing*, 18(3), pages 5–14.

Preston, P., Kerr, A., and Cawley, A., (2009). Innovation and knowledge in the digital media sector: An information economy approach. *Information, Communication & Society*, 12(7), pages 994–1014.

Raasch, C., and von Hippel, E., (2013). Innovation process benefits: The journey as reward. *MIT Sloan Review*, 55(1), pages 33–39.

Ritzer, G., and Jurgenson, N., (2010). Production, consumption, prosumption: The nature of capitalism in the age of the digital 'prosumer'. *Journal of Consumer Culture*, 10(1), pages 13–36.

Roberts, D., Hughes, M., and Kertbo, K., (2014). Exploring consumers' motivations to engage in innovation through co-creation activities. *European Journal of Marketing*, 38(½), pages 147–169.

Saarijärvi, H., (2012). The mechanisms of value co-creation. *Journal of Strategic Marketing*, 20(5), pages 381–391.

Saarijärvi, H., Kannan, P.K., and Kuusela, H., (2013). Value co-creation: Theoretical approaches and practical implications. *European Business Review*, 25(1), pages 6–19.

Sakao, T., Panshef, V., and Dörsam, E., (2009). Addressing uncertainty of PSS for value-chain oriented service development. In: Sakao, T. and Lindahl, M., (eds). *Introduction to Product/Service-System Design*. London: Springer, pages 137–157.

Sanders, E.B.N., and Stappers, P.J., (2008). Co-creation and the new landscapes of design. *CoDesign*, 4(1), pages 5–18.

Saur-Amaral, I., (2012). Wisdom-of-the-crowds to enhance innovation: A conceptual framework. ISPIM Conference Proceedings 1–7. Barcelona, Spain, 17–20.06.2012.

Saur-Amaral, I., Nugroho, J., and Rego, A., (2011). Innov@tion intelligence: Advances in understanding knowledge sourcing in social networks. The Proceedings of the XXII ISPIM Conference in Hamburg, Germany, 12–15, June 2011. ISBN 978-952-265-092-4.

Saur-Amaral, I., and Rego, A., (2010). Innovation intelligence: Crowdsourcing in a social network. *International Journal of Technology Intelligence and Planning*, 6(3), pages 288–299.

Scarbrough, H., Panourgias, N.S., and Nandhakumar, J., (2015). Developing a relational view of the organizing role of objects: A study of the innovation process in computer games. *Organization Studies*, 36(2), pages 197–220.

Schau, H.J., Muniz, A.M., Jr., and Arnould, E.J., (2009). How brand community practices create value, *Journal of Marketing*, 73(5), pages 30–51.

Schell, J., (2008). *The Art of Game Design: A Book of Lenses*. Boca Raton, FL: CRC Press.

Sotamaa, O., (2004). Playing it my way? Mapping the modder agency. *In Internet Research Conference*, 5, pages 19–22.

Stoneman, P., (2007). *An Introduction to the Definition and Measurement of Soft Innovation*. London: NESTA.

Sundbo, J., and Toivonen, M., (eds). (2011). *User-Based Innovation in Services*. Cheltenham: Edward Elgar Publishing.

Taylor, T.L., (2006a). *Play Between Worlds: Exploring Online Game Culture*. Cambridge, MA: MIT Press.

Taylor, T.L., (2006b). Beyond management: Considering participatory design and governance in player culture. *First Monday*, special issue, 7(September). http://firstmonday.org/issues/issue11_9/taylor/index.html.

Teece, D.J., (2007). Explicating dynamic capabilities: The nature and microfoundations of (sustainable) enterprise performance. *Strategic Management Journal*, 28(13), pages 1319–1350.

Teece, D.J., (2010). Business models, business strategy and innovation. *Long Range Planning*, 43(2), pages 172–194.

Teece, D.J., and Pisano, G., (1994). The dynamic capabilities of firms: An introduction. *Industrial and Corporate Change*, 3(3), pages 537–556.

Trott, P., (2005). *Innovation Management and New Product Development*. Harlow, Essex: Pearson Education.

Tschang, F.T., (2007). Balancing the tensions between rationalization and creativity in the video games industry. *Organization Science*, 18(6), pages 989–1005.

Tushman, M.L., and Anderson, P., (1986). Technological discontinuities and organizational environments. *Administrative Science Quarterly*, Vol. 31, No. 3, pages 439–465.

Van de Ven, A.H., (1993). A community perspective on the emergence of innovations. *Journal of Engineering and Technology Management*, 10(1), pages 23–51.

Van der Graaf, S., (2009). Designing for mod development: user creativity as product development strategy on the firm-hosted 3D software platform. Ph.D Dissertation, LSE.

Van der Graaf, S., (2012). Get organized at work! A look inside the game design process of valve and linden lab. *Bulletin of Science, Technology & Society*, pages 1–9, 0270467612469079.

van Doorn, J., Lemon, K.N., Mittal, V., Nass, S., Pick, D., Pirner, P., and Verhoef, P., (2010). Customer engagement behavior: theoretical foundations and research directions. *Journal of Service Research*, 13(3), pages 253–266.

Vargo, S.L., and Lusch, R.F., (2004). Evolving to a new dominant logic for marketing. *Journal of Marketing*, 68, pages 1–17.

Vargo, S.L., and Lusch, R.F., (2008). Service-dominant logic: Continuing the evolution. *Journal of the Academy of Marketing Science*, 36(1), pages 1–10.

Verhagen, T., Feldberg, F., van den Hooff, B., Meents, S., and Merikivi, J., (2011). Satisfaction with virtual worlds: An integrated model of experiential value. *Information & Management*, 48(6), pages 201–207.

Von Hippel, E., (2001). Learning from open-source software. *MIT Sloan Management Review*, 42(4), pages 82–86.

Von Hippel, E., (2005). *Democratizing Innovation*. Cambridge, MA: MIT Press.

Von Hippel, E., (2007). Horizontal innovation networks—by and for users. *Industrial and Corporate Change*, 16(2), pages 293–315.

Von Krogh, G., and von Hippel, E., (2006). The promise of research on open source software. *Management Science*, 52(7), pages 975–983.

Voss, C., and Zomerdijk, L., (2007). Innovation in experimental services—an empirical view. In: DTI (ed). *Innovation in Services*. London: DTI, pages 97–134.

Weber, M., (2011). Customer co-creation in innovations: A protocol for innovating with end users. Doctoral thesis, Eindhoven University of Technology.

Wenger, E., McDermott, R.A., and Snyder, W., (2002). *Cultivating Communities of Practice: A Guide to Managing Knowledge*. Cambridge, MA: Harvard Business School Press.

West, J., and Gallagher, S., (2006). Challenges of open innovation: the paradox of firm investment in open-source software. *R&D Management*, 36(3), pages 319–331.

Wexler, M.N., (2011). Reconfiguring the sociology of the crowd: Exploring crowdsourcing. *International Journal of Sociology and Social Policy*, 31, pages 6–20.

White, K., and Peloza, J., (2009). Self-benefit versus other-benefit marketing appeals: Their effectiveness in generating charitable support. *Journal of Marketing*, 73(4), pages 109–124.

Whitla, P., (2009). Crowdsourcing and its application in marketing activities. *Contemporary Management Research*, 5(1), pages 15–28.

Witell, L., Kristensson, P., Gustafsson, A., and Löfgren, M., (2011). Idea generation: Customer co-creation versus traditional market research techniques. *Journal of Service Management*, 22(2), pages 140–159.

Yee, N., (2007). Motivations of play in online games. *Journal of Cyber Psychology and Behaviour*, 9, pages 772–775.

Yee, N., (2014). *The Proteus Paradox*. London: Yale University Press.

Zackariasson, P., and Wilson, T.L., (2012). *The Video Games Industry: Formation, Present State, and Future*. London and New York: Routledge.

Zahra, S.A., and George, G., (2002). Absorptive capacity: A review, reconceptualization, and extension. *Academy of Management Review*, 27(2), pages 185–203.

Zomerdijk, L.G., and de Vries, J., (2007). Structuring front office and back office work in service delivery systems: An empirical study of three design decisions. *International Journal of Operations & Production Management*, 27(1), pages 108–131.

3   Observing the Videogames Industry

By framing videogames as experiential services, it is possible to analytically reconcile the rich and detailed contributions of ethnographic and anthropological studies (conducted by authors such as Nardi, 2010; Pearce, 2009; Boellstorff, 2012; Taylor, 2006; Castronova, 2005; Rowlands, 2012; Yee, 2014; and others) that describe the individual's and community's engagement and deeply personal interaction with videogames, with videogames as an artefact produced and offered by firms. We can account for the market forces that shape videogames, together with the social, psychological and deeply subjective experiences that videogames elicit (in the social and cultural spheres). When discussing NSD in the videogames industry, various analyses include different functions of the firm. They list service development (programming, art direction, design and sound), as well as marketing and public relations, customer service and quality assurance, distribution, human resources and administration functions (O'Donnell, 2014; Banks, 2013; Van der Graaf, 2012; Cohendet and Simon, 2007; Malaby, 2009; Tschang, 2007 and 2005). Creativity management, networks existing inside and outside of the firm, and the culture of a studio all influence the practice of game development. We investigate various functions of firms as co-creation seeps into organizations via different channels, many of which are informal. The data presented here reflects that richness of co-creation's influences on organizations. We use the model of eight sites of innovation within firms in creative industries (see Figure 2.2; Miles and Green, 2008). Not all sites pertain strictly to intra-organizational characteristics of a firm. Some of them describe the characteristics of the service itself, or users' interactions with it. Still, data demonstrates that a lot of co-creation-related activity occurs in those sites as well (as they often are the platforms for negotiation of access, empowerment and player roles).

Case Alpha

Obsidian Entertainment (OE) embraced its community as a source of funding and support as an early adopter. Together with several other studios, such as Double Fine Adventure and inXile Entertainment, they discovered the customer community's potential in realizing market offerings. The production of OE's game *Pillars of Eternity* (2015) was accompanied by a successful crowdfunding campaign which raised 4.2 million USD.

Prior to that, OE had explored more traditional means of obtaining funds to develop *Pillars of Eternity*—without any luck, as the producer firms (i.e., firms that normally fund the cost of the development of a new game in exchange for a share in revenues, or intellectual property developed during production, or other types of benefits; O'Donnell, 2014) regarded this type of a game as not having a market large enough. In other words, the game could have never been produced if it was not for the funds raised for its development via Kickstarter, a major crowdfunding platform on the Internet. Furthermore, a successful crowdfunding campaign could not have taken place if it weren't for several factors, prime of which was the presence and involvement of a strong and loyal community of OE's customers and fans of their previous productions.

Obsidian Entertainment has long specialized in the production of story-driven, immersive role-playing videogames (RPGs).[1] This type of videogame has always been well represented within the videogames industry, and there is a connection between classical pen-and-paper RPGs (such as the *Dungeons and Dragons* system developed by Gary Gygax and Dave Arneson in 1974) and the first videogames, and thus the advent of the videogames industry in its early days (King and Borland, 2014; Boellstorff, 2012; Nardi, 2010). Some of the games developed in the nineties of the 20th century are today considered as classics, with titles such as *Ultima*, *Diablo*, *Fallout*, *Baldur's Gate*, *Planescape: Torment* and *Icewind Dale*. Those were deeply interactive, graphically advanced and innovative videogames that garnered a large fan following (for instance, *Baldur's Gate* and *Icewind Dale* were remastered and re-released in 2012 and 2014 by Overhaul Games and Beamdog, and *Planescape: Torment* in 2017). Those videogames have set the standards for the whole RPG genre of videogames, and newly released RPGs cannot avoid comparisons to them.

Many of those videogames were made in the studio called Black Isle. Black Isle ceased to exist in December 2003. Following its dissolution, many former employees of Black Isle Studios established Obsidian Entertainment. It has retained its expertise and capability to make RPGs, and those types of videogames have become the focus of its development efforts. Today, Obsidian Entertainment remains both a spiritual as well as factual successor to Black Isle's accomplishments. Since Black Isle's disappearance, the studio has managed to continue making RPGs. OE has also retained, as well as further developed, its brand name together with the loyalty and following of the community of fans and engaged players. Even though their productions until *Pillars of Eternity* (started production in 2012) did not involve players as co-creators of videogames, some of their titles (with the best example of *Neverwinter Nights* 2) have enabled extensive modding, and have become very popular among the modding communities.

As the videogames industry has been growing in the last years (Marchand and Hennig-Thurau, 2013; Zackariasson and Wilson, 2012), expanding its reach to new technological platforms as well as appealing to broadened audiences and demographics, RPG videogames in their classical formula have become too risky to produce. That is due to their cost and length of development, as well as the relatively niche and small audience. As the result, classical role-playing videogames have ceased to be made, leaving a market vacuum. Communities of loyal and involved customers had to turn to other genres, or to rely on the efforts of modders in adding unofficial content to the old titles.

In 2012 some firms within the videogames industry realized the potential of devoted customer communities when coupled with the affordances of crowdfunding (interviews with Square Enix Collective, 2014). Crowdfunding of the development of RPG videogames would allow for bypassing the main obstacle to their production (i.e., the publishers not willing to finance the development of these types of videogames). Necessary funds would be obtained directly from the communities of customers, which—despite their position as niches within the now huge videogames industry—were still large enough to fund the development of complex and technologically advanced videogames. This effect was further reinforced by the fact, that it would be the original makers of the nineties' classical titles who would be asking for those funds, therefore acting as guarantors of their quality and their relevance to those classics. This is illustrated by a quote from the interviews with OE (2013):

> We knew that customers were out there, and there was no other way to get the game made for them than to do a Kickstarter [campaign]. [The current financing options are] publisher money, your own money, or crowdsourcing. People have tried debt financing, film financing etc., but those are not popular. [Those who tried couldn't] get certain types of games made. From that perspective, our customers are a resource—because we know they are out there and want our game.

Obsidian Entertainment was among the wave of established studios and well-recognized names in 2012 and early 2013 that managed to obtain sizable amounts for the development of their 'nostalgia-fuelled' titles. The other firm being discussed in this case, inXile Entrainment, was another such studio, as well as Cloud Imperium Games discussed in Case Gamma. For those firms, it was the time when the community of customers was first formally used as a resource for game development. The description of these first cases of crowdfunding and its relationship to co-creation and customer communities is one of the focal points of this book.

This case study illustrates co-creation mainly for customer-firm relationship gains. The firm doesn't prioritize customers' inputs to NSD; instead it focuses its co-creative efforts on building closer ties to the community of its customers (field notes from Dragon*Con, 2013). OE operates within a market niche, exacerbating strengthened impact of social network mechanisms such as word of mouth and customers' willingness to pay. A community of customers is a long-term resource for a firm—not just on a single project, but in a sustainable capacity (interviews with OE, 2013):

> On the business side: the more you engage with your customers as a resource, the more inclined they are to speak well of you, to buy your next game, tell about you to their friends . . . They become a long-term resource for us.

This is related to OE's competences for co-creation—OE balances customers' expectations against its internal game development processes.

Crowdfunding campaigns give players a strong sense of empowerment and many new avenues to discuss videogames with game developers (interviews with Press Space PR, 2013). At OE, design ideas came from the players who have exceeded a certain pledge threshold and were rewarded by the ability to provide design suggestions to the developers (analysis of OE's website, 2014). The financial involvement of customers was followed by their deeper integration with game development at OE (field notes from OE, 2014):

> [Deeper interaction takes place due] to several reasons, chief of which are the obligations incurred by OE during its crowdfunding campaign—promising some backers the ability to have their ideas taken on during development, or simply having an engaged community of customers who wish to be a part of the game development process, and to have an 'insider's look' into what is going on at OE.
>
> In meetings at OE, which are attended by employees from various functions and disciplines of the firm (production, programming, sound, art, etc.), customers' inputs are labelled as originating from the community and discussed alongside the ideas generated internally.

Furthermore, customers were used as a source of funds even after the initial campaign on Kickstarter had ended (analysis of OE's website, 2014). The OE's management considered its crowdfunding customers as publishers to some extent, updating them regularly about the game development. This is reflected in the following quote (interviews with OE, 2013): "OE should keep players informed about what is being done on Pillars of Eternity. Similar conversations are normally held with publishers". Such a dynamic between the firm and the community called for a close relationship between those two parties—and thus development of user involvement competence at OE. "Positive relationship served to increase the influx of monies from crowdfunding campaign, sustain customers' interest about game's development, as well as to help spread positive word of mouth throughout the social network of players and potential new players", we read in the field notes from Game Connection (2014). Granting players an insight into the internal workings of a firm, as well as enabling them to provide feedback, acted as a mechanism for enhancing customers' satisfaction with the game, as well as provided them with exciting co-creation experience (interviews with Press Space PR, 2013).

OE also saw the community of engaged players as a resource in game design and as a sounding board for various decisions taken during production (field notes from OE, 2014). Customers helped OE by validating the trajectories of game production, although their function was purely advisory, resembling a focus group approach. This points to the presence of integration competence at OE. According to the interviews with OE (2013):

> If we can't convince the players about something, maybe that idea is not feasible. That's the way that we think and use our players. We are also making videogames for niches—players are experts in playing videogames, as OE hasn't been exposed to as many videogames as players (especially when seen as a collective group).

OE's customers are strongly opinionated and seek involvement in the decision-making during production (field notes from Dragon*Con, 2013). We can also see that in the interviews with OE (2013):

> Making of a niche game is very different from making a mass-market game. When it comes to releasing huge games such as *Call of Duty*, I need to keep the giant group of people progressing from game to game, so I need to listen to either marketing department or some key customers. When we make our [Obsidian Entertainment's] games, we make them in different ways. We involve many of our players, as they are a unique audience, strongly opinionated and liking to dabble in the specifics.

This has benefits to the studio, which can glean marketing insights from its key customers. The customers are also willing to perform testing and quality assurance (QA) duties at later stages of game development process. This shows OE's awareness of the potential uses of its customers in NSD for their numbers. In the field notes from OE (2014):

> Examples of direct customer involvement in game development were game testing and asset production.[2] For *Pillars of Eternity* (2015), it was mostly the players exceeding certain crowdfunding threshold, who could design an element of the game (in return for their financial contribution).

To many firms in the videogames industry, the big tests conducted with the help of the players (i.e., the stress tests) are seen as providing the best value from customer engagement (field notes from GDC, 2014). Customers' involvement in them enables testing across thousands of systems (software and hardware configurations). Most importantly, it is rare for companies such as OE to have that kind of scope in-house (interviews with Valve Corporation, 2014). OE, and other videogame firms, identified customer involvement in quality assurance as an important element of relationship building and making better videogames overall. OE management regarded customer involvement as allowing their audiences to better understand what the studio does and why—deepening OE's relationship with the players, but also establishing closer fit to the market (pointing to OE's user involvement competence; Lettl, 2007).

Those points demonstrate the co-creation's role in enhancing the customer-firm relationship. Improved relationship with the customers often results in positive marketing (through positive word of mouth), service development (through providing feedback by customers to the game developers) and funding effects (field notes from OE, 2014). This relates to the usefulness of receiving customers' participation in NSD as described von Hippel (2005). Some customers have the need-related knowledge, and firms can access that knowledge through co-creation without transferring it across the customer-firm boundary (which is a costly and difficult process). Interestingly, von Hippel (2005) also describes the innovation-generating functions of the co-creating customers. Conversely, OE employees did not view customers as a reliable source of creative or innovative inputs. OE chose to retain the maximum of the traditional model of closed game development in the wake of its successful crowdfunding campaign. OE involved customers in the game development mostly for the purposes of public relations management, as well as fulfilling the firm's obligations incurred during the crowdfunding campaign (interviews with OE, 2013): "Outside of our backer stuff we don't have people on our project who are directly contributing from the community".

Co-creation is a problematic activity for studios because of how different it is from traditional game development practices. OE also has a long history and tradition of making successful games—since 2003 the studio has been developing its best practices. This adds to this firm's reluctance to depart from its established 'closed' game development paradigms, and slows down its adoption of co-creation throughout the organization. Furthermore, as we see in the field notes from OE (2014):

> There are logistic difficulties in incorporating inputs from players into the game. They are often related with community's ideas being unfeasible for production. Engaging customers as a marketing resource is easier, as it does not require changes in the essential [NSD] functions of a firm.

This demonstrates that competences for co-creation carry over from other, related activities performed by the firm—such as allowing modding of its games. OE could embrace co-creation in the wake of crowdfunding because of the competences it already had developed while engaging with customer community as modders to *Neverwinter Nights 2*. OE already had good understanding of creative customers' needs and knew how to structure their interaction with them (analysis of OE web forums, 2014).

The reluctance of OE toward integration of customers in NSD and the firm's entrenchment in more traditional, retrospective models of production and community management are best contrasted with the practices of inXile Entertainment (XE), a sister company to OE. Some of the developments of XE have been also co-authored by OE (for example, *Wasteland 2*), and some key staff from OE has also been involved in helping XE with their other projects. inXile Entertainment has, similarly to OE, successfully crowdfunded two projects that are classical RPGs—gathering 7.2 million USD for both projects combined from the customer community. Nevertheless, XE embraced more experimental and open approach to using player inputs and co-creation in general.

XE tapped into the community of its customers in three ways. First of all, it had a formalized system for 'crowdvoting' (Saur-Amaral, 2012), where the customers as a collective could let the firm know about their preferences regarding a particular aspect of the game—for instance, whether the combat system is 'real-time with active pause', or 'turn-based' (field notes from XE, 2014). Secondly, the employees of the firm had a system for letting the community know about their opinion about customers' creative inputs on forums (including their suggestions and feedback; analysis of XE website, 2014):

> A variety of labels such as 'seen', 'considering', 'tell us more', 'will do' and 'won't do' is in use. The forums themselves are called UserVoice, further underlining the role of customers in influencing the development decisions made by the firm. This forum is available only to the backers of the project, and is not accessible by the general public.

The team at XE asked questions on these forums to collect the customers' opinions about various aspects of the game. This is illustrated by the following quote (interviews with XE, 2013):

> Perhaps the greatest value added by the community is not the ideas themselves, but the discussion itself. If you don't have that discussion with your co-workers, then your community, among other things, can provide you with that discussion (and with the benefit of knowing other mind-sets).

Thirdly, due to the fact that one of the XE projects was being developed in a publicly available and easy to use software system (called 'Unity'), the customers had been invited to directly submit ready-made graphical assets to the firm. Using an online marketplace 'Unity Asset Store', the players were developing and then (if their work met the studio's standards of quality) selling their creations to XE. That created not only an environment of selecting high-quality work to be incorporated into the final game, but also automatically resolved any IP issues (as the Unity Asset Store allows selling game assets, which means clear transfer of the use license from the seller to the buyer). That approach resembled crowdsourcing to a great extent, as XE released the guidelines of what the assets should be like, what their technical parameters should be, as well as how they should comply with the artistic vision and feel of the game.

The differences between OE and XE in the role of customer inputs in co-creation could be related to the size of the studio, with XE being a couple of times smaller than OE (where OE has approximately 200 employees, XE has no more than 50).[3] That causes the firm to be in position of benefiting more from co-creation with customers due to more limited resources, as well as facilitates use of co-creation due to smaller, and thus more agile, organizational structure.

Customer Involvement in Game Development

At OE, customer inputs to game development have occurred in the wake of the successful crowdfunding campaign, and were present at all stages of NSD (save for the very earliest stages of conceptualizing the game) from very early prototyping and design, all the way to testing and post-launch fixes (Hight and Novak, 2008).

As the field notes from OE (2014) show, one of the major channels of discussion and information flow between OE and its customers were the regular (occurring at various frequencies, but at least once a month) and extensive email updates sent out to all backers of the *Pillars of Eternity* project. In those updates, the development team described what they were currently working on and what their difficulties or dilemmas were. Those communiques fulfilled a function of not only updating customers with the actions of the firm, but also putting a human face on the company, demonstrating that game development is not performed by 'a corporate machine', but by people with emotions, personalities and preferences (interviews with Press Space PR, 2013). That contributed to the relationship between the company and the customers, and allowed the firm to defend its vision for the game under development.[4] Successful structuring of such communication took skill on the part of the firm, and illustrates both disclosure and user involvement competences. As we read in the field notes from OE (2014):

> In those updates, project team explains the reasons for their decisions, informs the backers about any delays and reasons for them, shares the plans for the project, and informs what is happening inside the firm.

Many staff spent time on forums and engaged with the community. Subsequent transfer of what they learned there into the firm's internal environment was the locus of integration and appropriation competences. This was particularly the case for OE in the very early stages of the production of *Pillars of Eternity*. This is illustrated by the following quote (interviews with OE, 2013):

> [During the KS campaign] I spent roughly four hours every day chatting to players all over the world. Usually late evening or night PST—this way other continents were also online. I would create lists of suggestions from players—and discuss them once or twice a week with [the executive producer and lead designer].

OE's senior staff, for example, the lead designer, spent time on forums. Staff at OE also actively solicited feedback, and the company had seen a lot of 'good feedback' coming from, for example, people with good technical skills in the field of user interface (UI). OE's staff spent time not only on the forums that are proprietary and 'official' (meaning accessed via the company or game website), but also in the third-party forums on the Internet, independent of the studio, as well as on other channels—such as YouTube, Tumblr, spring.me and Twitch. They would visit these other forums because players tend to be more forthcoming with their opinions on the fora independent of OE (interviews with OE employees, 2013). On the other hand, in the contacts with the OE development team itself (or where they suspect the team might be listening in) players were more restrained in expressing their (particularly critical) opinions (analysis of OE web forums, 2014).

OE employees, when following customers' discussions on forums, sought to understand whether a point or a problem raised was indicative of a wider issue affecting many players. OE employees sometimes found interesting ideas in those discussions (interviews with OE, 2013). That points to the minor, although factual, role of customers as ideators (be that accidental or purposeful) in the firm's innovation processes. This was very unlikely to occur though—this study has no tangible account of even one such occurrence, therefore it will not be taken into consideration as a function of co-creation in this case.

The practicalities of project management, as well as certain requirements of firm strategy, were a limiting factor for co-creation in NSD. Still, the general usefulness of working with customers is highlighted in the quote below, pointing out to the sympathetic attitude of employees towards player inputs (interviews with OE, 2013):

> Sometimes players' discussion provides new perspective and the team revisits the idea which had been discarded previously. Sometimes, although very, very rarely, 'nuggets' of interesting ideas from players appear that the team hasn't thought of. The ideas that we get from the players are definitely beneficial, and it is much better to work on the game this way, getting immediate feedback from the customers. Players will be discussing things, and they might mention something of real use.

This demonstrates the role of organizational culture in catalyzing co-creation in firms. Customers also help in refining certain aspects of the game, such as user interface (UI). Again, the studio tends to accept only general ideas and suggestions from the players, not ready-made solutions (O'Hern et al., 2011). The studio has clearly identified the type of input that it can accept from its community (idea-centric inputs) and has no internal capacity for processing solution-centric inputs—relating both to integration competence, as well as to user involvement competence (field notes from GDC, 2014). This is also related to the licensing and IP challenges, as incorporating customers' IP into a commercial product without paying the customers for it could open the firm to misappropriation lawsuits. A firm's understanding of legal landscape is related to its appropriation competence.

Studios also seek to retain all of the control over co-creation. At OE, a selective approach to customer contributors predominates (interviews with OE, 2013):

> On *Pillars of Eternity* development there aren't players who would be directly contributing to the development of the game. Players' inputs pertain more to 'paper design' rather than implementation of the features/mechanics into the game itself. Backers will not be building assets but they will be designing properties of various in-game details.

For OE, "the customers fulfil mostly the function of a barometer of the community's mood and attitude" (field notes from OE, 2014). The co-creative relations between the firm and the community are catalyzed by the prior use of crowdsourcing for raising finance (thus by the funding arrangements).

The exact practices of customer involvement in game development at XE are much more structured and transparent to the customers. Most unique and interesting of these is the use of the Unity Asset Store in the course of development of *Torment: Tides of Numenera* [TOM]. According to the field notes from XE (2014):

> TOM is developed in Unity game engine. That technology is well known and available in the community of its customers, and overall in the community of people who are interested in videogames and game-making.

Therefore, it is easier for the community to contribute to the development of the game, as they do not need to learn the specific and complicated skills that normally accompany a proprietary game engine (interviews with Square Enix Collective, 2014). Moreover, such proprietary game engines are normally developed in-house and are closely guarded secrets by game development studios. This causes XE's increased affinity to customer co-creation—the technological barriers to co-creation have been greatly lowered at the outset of the project. Accompanying the Unity game engine is the Unity Asset Store, where various developers and programmers sell and buy assets produced by their peers. XE has been making a good use of that functionality, which allows for external sourcing of certain elements of the game—pertaining to various functions of NSD (for instance to programming and underlying code, art, animation or sound). This is reflected by the field notes from XE (2013):

> XE overall buys a lot of materials from Unity Asset Store: mostly minor art assets or models for the game. This approach has proven both money and time saving for XE, and is safe from the perspective of intellectual property [the relationship between buyer and seller is regulated by Store's terms of use]. By sourcing player inputs via Asset Store, XE pays its customers for their work, and the ownership is unambiguously and legally transferred.

The above note points towards XE's appropriation competence, which underpins its co-creative practice. Still, apart from sourcing assets from Unity Asset Store, the studio relies on releasing guidelines to the community of customers (for example, backers on the UserVoice forums) pertaining to the production of non-critical art assets (also referred to as 'props') for the game. This demonstrates XE's user involvement competence, as well as disclosure competence, and their role in enabling co-creation (interviews with XE, 2013):

> We provide specifications for submissions [of the assets through Unity Asset Store] to the community. We will buy any assets that we like, and will also be marked as "used in the game". For W2, there are some problems to the arrangement of players developing assets. It has been overall successful, but there have been also challenges. There are some regular users, who are better than others at meeting expectations and specifications.[5]

When it comes to the sourcing information from the forums, XE uses two systems: passive and active (interviews with XE, 2013). Passive is about the labelling regimen described above. It is regarded as a very low-cost way of showing that the studio reads the contributions. Active system is described on the XE website (2014):

> Active system is the process that IE uses to get feedback from players—by targeted discussions on a particular topic, for example, as it was the case for a discussion on combat system in-game. Those discussions are encouraged and 'seeded' with topics by the XE team, and can be initiated at a time convenient for the firm. Those specific discussions can be limited only to backers—as it is often done on the UserVoice forums.

Active system is a great example of user involvement competence at work. XE lets the community know what they are thinking and that they hear their opinions, and observes the discussion evolve from there. This is illustrated by the following quote (interviews with XE, 2013):

> When we are going to design a new system, for example inventory, we will look through UserVoice. There can be some ideas that will spark the developers' imagination; we will also get a sense of what is the community's desire. We will not do that for all aspects of the game, but for some. We will be telling our players about various improvements to the game in the updates, and then we will be looking at their reactions and opinions.

In the above example we observe that firms prefer to use idea-centric, not solution-centric, inputs from the customers (O'Hern and Rindfleisch, 2010). This relates to the integration competence: for the reasons relating to intellectual property, project management and causing disruptions to the current work of the firm, it makes more sense to use more modifiable inputs. Idea-centric inputs are also more flexible in terms of their integration with existing ideas and NSD practices, making them adjustable to the firm's vision, technology or service design. They can also be processed from the earlier stages of NSD process, decreasing risk and investment cost.[6]

Internal Practices of Co-Creation

Customer inputs to game development received in the crowdfunding campaign's wake have triggered organizational changes at OE. Nevertheless, the core processes within the firm have retained their characteristics of a traditional game development (field notes from OE, 2014):

> OE, when prototyping *Pillars of Eternity*, used Scrum[7] in the early phases of production—focusing on interdisciplinarity and responsiveness. In the later phases of development, it used more of Waterfall model—which means that the tasks were planned out on the production schedule, and followed one another.

In Waterfall project management, it is difficult to account for sources of external inputs which, by their nature, are unreliable and difficult to plan in advance (a firm has no means of forcing its customers to deliver anything on time or to specifications), as all tasks follow in succession and each task is dependent on the completion of the previous task. Iteration and slack required by co-creation are anathema to the Waterfall model. On the other hand, the adoption of the Scrum model by Obsidian Development might reflect the need to adjust its project management approach exactly to account for the unpredictability of customers' inputs in co-creation. This model is far more responsive to changing priorities, tolerant of shifting schedules and of ambiguity, and tasks are not so interdependent.

OE had used Waterfall with great success in the past. After the crowd-funding campaign, it had to allow for some degree of co-creation—because of the changed nature of its relationship with customers. It found a solution by controlling who would co-create when in NSD, and in what way. This illustrates the role of organizational culture and history in influencing the practice of co-creation. From the OE field notes (2014):

> In the context of OE, co-creation had to be clearly structured and formalized in order to fit with the Waterfall project management technique, as OE didn't want to depart too far from what it knew worked. That's why at OE we observe co-creation only in some, clearly demarcated, aspects of NSD.

The interviews with the studio employees also highlight that the company had never attempted co-creation with its customers in the past. The requirement to incorporate player inputs (from those players who have backed the project with certain amounts of money) was something new to the firm; all processes needed to be learned. This is reflected in the interviews with OE (2013):

> It is costly to get players' feedback from alpha and beta tests; we need to build infrastructure for getting feedback from our players. Today it takes a lot of time out of the game development just to gather this feedback.

It demonstrates that the studio sees the usefulness of customers' feedback and inputs, but at the same time the construction of necessary infrastructure to assimilate it is something that does not make financial or cultural sense to the firm. Furthermore, instead of investment in the development of that capacity (interviews with OE, 2013):

> We prefer simply to hire a junior in-house person for the position [of the curator of community's inputs] and grow this person into an artist that we can have on staff. . . . Getting [customers'] bug reports is difficult and costly for us, we need to build a special [game version] that needs time, put in an infrastructure for feedback, and then we need people to collate this feedback and convey it to developers . . . It's almost a full time job for someone like lead artist or lead environment artist to manage the community to get art form them, review it, make sure it has a place in the game. You would have to have someone fairly senior, with an eye for what's going on in the game, with good technical skills.

The quote above demonstrates the role of organizational culture in influencing the co-creation-related practice. Not only business rationale, but also organizational history (i.e., the experience of what worked for similar problems in the past) and unarticulated attitude of employees toward the customers determine whether co-creation will be used in this instance, or if a more traditional solution will be embraced. This also points to the additional barrier to co-creation in firms. Firms need a fairly senior employee to curate the inputs from the customers and to manage co-creation (i.e., a person with versatile skills, ample experience, production overview, decision-making capacity, etc.). The time of such a person is expensive for any organization. That automatically creates the expectation on part of the firm to receive high-quality inputs from the community (to recoup the costs). If the customers don't deliver (which often is the case, as their inputs are chaotic if not carefully managed), the firm quickly grows cold to the idea of co-creation and abandons it to better use its resources.

What is also highlighted in the quote above is the broad array of skills required to assimilate customer inputs by a firm (for instance, an artist who is both proficient in production of art, but who also has good technical skills). People like that, with two or more specialities, are still fairly rare in the videogames industry (O'Donnell, 2014). Moreover and as mentioned above, the people processing player inputs as they reach the firm need to be fairly senior, with good overview of the project overall, and good judgment of an idea's feasibility. All of these remarks point us towards the importance of competences for co-creation, and integration competence in particular, as well as heavy use of the people resource in organizations that co-creation demands. From the OE field notes (2014):

> To process and successfully integrate customer inputs with game development, managerial decision-making is necessary. OE has established some routines for considering and integrating player inputs with game development. Players' ideas and contributions are discussed in meetings with other team members—those contributions come from the customers who crowdfunded the game.

One established practice accompanying co-creation at OE, personal telephone conversations with the backers who exceeded the 'feature contribution' threshold in crowdfunding, also serves to enhance the relationship between the customers and firm. Looking again into the field notes from OE (2014):

> OE's employees talk to people on the phone, so they get personal treatment, so they feel that they are getting their money's worth. For ideas coming from the Internet fora, the team normally does not discuss them with individuals, but more with groups, also on that platform. Players can also email the studio, and those emails are filtered by the receptionist. The information contained in them then trickles down to the development team and they respond to customer questions.

At XE, the major barriers to co-creation are secrecy from competitors, management of customer expectations, and finding 'safe places' within the development process where customer inputs can be inserted without risking disruption to established work practices (interviews with XE, 2013):

> The quality of ideas coming from the community varies drastically; the problem is also players' lack of context information about game development. Secrecy is also important when communicating with players, as not to spoil the game for them. Overall it can be dangerous to talk to customers—you can create great expectations, and then lose out by not meeting them. That's why it is critical to take proper care when communicating with the players, so the mode and contents of that exchange are controlled by the studio.

This reflects the competences for co-creation: disclosure and appropriation competences in particular. They are linked to the firm's ability to overcome the barriers to co-creation in ways which fit with its established NSD processes, and which are acceptable from the organizational culture point of view (i.e., employees do not view the negative effects of co-creation as outweighing its benefits).

Structured Forms of Co-Creation

The site at OE where player inputs are processed in a structured way is quality assurance (QA). For bugs (issues with the game flagged for resolving) there are separate databases for each project. From the GDC field notes (2014), it seems that co-creation in the QA is the most common form of that phenomenon in the videogames industry:

> Overall, QA manager and then the QA department provide structure to filtering player inputs. This is an important detail that many of the firms have in common—the QA department plays a visible role in co-creation processes, especially in providing the initial structure for the processing of customer inputs.

This is because QA had been structured in the past to account for and understand a large volume of inputs coming from the outside of the organization. The merit of QA inputs is also easier to judge (i.e., they are technical in nature, with a more binary 'right or wrong' type of evaluation) as opposed to determining the quality of art or game design inputs. An example of such practice is given below (interviews with OE, 2013):

> Processing feedback and bugs is not ad hoc at OE. We have a bug database and it changes from project to project. It is usually dictated by

publisher, that's why it changes [as a particular studio often works with different publishers on each of its productions/games]. A developer has a list of bugs that they need to fix. QA team makes sure that there are no duplicate bugs on the list. . . . If you are getting a lot of feedback from the users, that feedback has to go through some sort of filter before it gets to development team, that's usually a QA person. Other things don't get filtered, and are more valuable to the development team: crash bugs. These go directly to the developers. Crash bugs are an easy thing for us to look at and fix.

This demonstrates that the firm sets up categories for customer inputs, designates people to look through those inputs, assigns priorities to them depending on how useful or relevant they are. This adds structure to the co-creation practice in firms, and transforms QA-related functions of the organization (and thus the late stages of the NSD). In the quote below we see that co-creative inputs to NSD can be assimilated by a firm through its QA activities, thus expanding the function of QA not just to hunting bugs, but also considering potential improvements to the service. From the OE field notes (2014):

OE has internal and publisher testing groups, and sometimes there is a third testing group (a contractor). Testing groups are seen as a resource for suggestions [sic]. Bugs go into a database (A, B, C priority) and there are corresponding various priorities of bugs. There is also the 'S priority', which is for suggestions. The team goes through them regularly—sometimes a database entry gets elevated, and turns into a task and is assigned to someone [to work on].

For XE, the efficient production process means effective internal communication. The focus is on internal communication and exchanges between key people on the team—so called 'leads'. XE has a producer who monitors the forums, and when some contributions strike him as exceptionally interesting, he sends an email to the producer, design lead, as well as creative lead (field notes from XE, 2014). Any decision regarding an externally sourced idea must be carefully considered by the key people on the team—which is one of the reasons for co-creation's disruptiveness. There is a high cost to considering such ideas—as the time of key people is scarce and precious within an organization.

At XE, there are 'absolute owners' of aspects of the game in the course of its development—meaning people who can make executive decisions on their aspects of the service under development (for example, game engine, sound direction, art assets, combat design, user interface, etc.). As one of the senior managers at XE puts it, he "believes in benevolent dictatorships" (interviews with XE, 2013). From the XE community emails analysis (2014):

Particular people are in charge of particular aspects of the game, they have creative constraints, but within those constraints they do whatever they like (provided it is possible from the standpoint of technology, narrative etc.). Community feedback falls into the jurisdiction of those absolute owners of game aspects.

Such a cell-like structure of a company plays a role in facilitated judgment and decision-making on player inputs, thus increasing firm's co-creation competences—including integration and appropriation competences. The studio becomes more responsive to inputs from the community, as they can be reviewed more quickly and more efficiently. The need for complex coordination across teams is reduced—thus causing less disruption to a smaller group of people within a firm.

The most expensive aspect of co-creation is getting customer inputs to the firm employees in a structured and intelligible format—a task which is related to the integration competence. This is accompanied by various challenges and dilemmas for the videogame development team, illustrated in the quote below (interviews with OE, 2013):

> At OE, one of our area designers goes through [customer inputs], and talks with [the producers], and asks whether something [a feature based on these inputs] is possible. This designer asks where we draw a line when it comes to scope of these things and how they fit in our game. Then we need to have a discussion with the customer and work with them [i.e., explain the scope and limitations to the customer]. We know how to get the same effect that players want, but doing it in a less costly way for us—due to our experience in game development that we have accumulated over the years.

The quote above points to the large amount of time and effort consumed by co-creation. It is also revealing about the organizational culture, and the attitudes of the employees toward customer inputs. It also highlights the limited expertise of the co-creating customers, in particular when it comes to the understanding of how videogames are made (from the organizational perspective). There seems to be a general feeling of redundancy of customer inputs, and the fact that the only reason for their use by OE is to maintain the customer relationship (by following on the crowdfunding's promises). The quote also mentions the self-perception of the employees as the curators in the practice of co-creation, who have the ultimate responsibility for the quality of the game produced.[8]

Organizational Culture in the Context of Co-Creation

The element of regular exchanges with the customers has always been present at Obsidian Entertainment. It is visible in OE's affinity towards modding and the support that the studio has shown for this kind of activity in their games (in *Neverwinter Nights* series in particular). Firm managers appreciate the need to devote effort and time to exchanges with players, and to re-direct some resources to co-creation, as well as the need to have two-way conversations with players about what they want. The importance of finding the right forum for exchange is often highlighted in the interviews. "We invest a lot of time on our forums, since 1995 or 1996 when we set up message board for the original Fallout game" (interviews with OE, 2013). This organizational culture influences the propensity of individual developers to talk with the players about ideas for the game. It also affects the employees' attitude towards receiving co-creative inputs to game development. OE's experiences with Fallout and message boards since 1995 also help to explain the competences for co-creation that the studio holds—which have been gained through numerous modding-supporting activities throughout the firm's history.

The attitudes of employees towards customer inputs can vary from being very open and enthusiastic (due to creativity of players in interacting with the game, their maturity and understanding when speaking to the industry professionals, efforts that players put into fan activities and fandom, etc.), to being distrustful and guarded (in the aftermath of repeated abuse of game developers by players on online forums, or in the context of a higher corporate or managerial entity prohibiting any form of communication with the customers save for the official marketing and PR channels). Personalities also play a role here—for some employees of the development team it will be easier to face even unjustified criticism, while others prefer to leave that kind of interaction with customers to the community management staff. As OE's employee puts it (interviews with OE, 2013):

> I am in the minority when it comes to reading and responding; there are other people around who also read through forums. Some people on the team get upset with the things that they read, so it is difficult for them. . . . It is part of my routine to read forum feedback; I find value in reading about what players are doing, not necessarily responding to them.

The quote above again underlines the critical role of organizational culture in influencing the form, extent and practice of co-creation within a firm. Organizational culture matters when it comes to selecting the sources of ideas. It also affects self-perceptions of employees (how they see themselves as professionals, and what their relationship is with the customers) and their opinions about the customer community. At OE, the developers stick to the principle that they "know what kinds of things can and can't work" (interviews with OE, 2013). According to the OE field notes (2014):

> Game developers appreciate that there are useful bits of knowledge to be obtained from the players' community, and the general feel of the interactions between PE team and community is positive. Nevertheless, there is a perception in the team that players' community are mostly "churning the same stuff over and over again" in their discussions.

The relationship between the game developers and the players is also affected by the professionalization of the roles in the videogames industry. This industry has roots in a bedroom or garage activity performed by software developers in their spare time (a fact which is of consequence for the prevalence of co-creation in videogames). Today, videogame development has become highly professionalized, and there is a significant skill gap between amateur co-creating customers and industry veterans who have released numerous titles. Moreover, some videogame developers consider themselves the 'auteurs' of the videogames (i.e., displaying attitude similar to a painter's, a composer's or a writer's towards their works). Their service design decisions result from their experiences and skills. According to the words of a videogame developer at OE (interviews with OE, 2013):

> We want to make a game that we want to make [sic]. We have been doing this for a long time, our team is very experienced. We are making our game for them [the players] but we want to make good game at the end of the day. We know how to make games; we also have the entire view of the project—which players don't have. Players also aren't professional game developers like us. We make changes based on feedback, we want to please customers but at the end of the day we will do what we think is best.

Still, the industry professionals appreciate their audience and know their importance. As illustrated by the following quote from another OE employee (2013): "Games are developed for the players, not just for the development team." Studio staff is overall positively predisposed towards its customers and their creativity, as long as it occurs in separation from the internal game development process. From the interviews with OE (2013): "I love seeing what people do, mods that they make, even if they are just goofy." It is only when the customers start assuming some of the videogame development roles (i.e., begin to co-create) some cultural and identity clashes occur.

This underlines the acceptance of customer inputs as long as they don't interfere with the studio's work, without much of a real transformative impact on the firm's functioning and NSD. OE wants to retain all competences for videogame development in-house, relying only on the resources of the studio, and not on customers or any other external (and difficult to control) resources. OE is not seeking to transition into a 'nexus of external competences' or 'coordinator of external resources' type of company (to some extent, we observe that in the case of inXile Entertainment, with their use of Unity Asset Store and problem-based forum discussions). This stems from the tradition of modding at OE. With modding, customer inputs were entirely separate from the game development effort and didn't affect the work of employees. They were entirely optional to the game and to the studio's operations; the studio didn't have any obligation to consider the mods or modding community (an attitude embraced by many other videogame studios, which offered no support whatsoever to modders). In co-creation, it is the interference of customers in internal practices which becomes the issue—together with associated disruptions and a new type of stakeholder in the game development process. In the notes on OE's public email communication to the backers (2013–2015):

> OE staff thinks of their customers in terms customers, or players of the game. In some cases, for those customers who have individually pledged thousands of USD in crowdfunding, this is overlaid with those customers being also significant financiers ('super fans'), whose sanctioned desires must be met.

In a way, studio employees become obliged to listen and integrate customer inputs with game development. This introduces the tension to the organization, between the employees' affinity for more traditional, closed model of game development (i.e., doing what they know how to do), and the need to open that model up to customers because of the use of crowdfunding (i.e., embracing new game development style). The tension is between doing what the studio is used to doing and does well and transitioning to a new and unknown model which might or might not work—thus adding more risk and uncertainty to an already risky and uncertain industry.[9] The practice of co-creation at OE is the resultant force from that tension. It is a compromise of sorts—where customer inputs are allowed only from some selected customers, in clearly formulated ways, in very specific aspects of NSD. All other customer inputs and manifestations of co-creation are optional (interviews with OE, 2013):

> We [the developers] discuss how we are going to guide them [the co-creating customers]. With a player who has dropped two thousand dollars on our game, we simply can't turn their inputs away. We need to work with them, with their input, especially that their input is creative in nature. It can be stressful to people on the team.

That stress has its effect on the team and is associated with co-creation. Some employees are opposed to it. That negatively affects the mood within the firm as well as erodes esprit-de-corps. That is also exacerbated by the power asymmetry that exists between the studio and the players, and that gives the firm employees the right (necessary for successful game development) to overturn any suggestion or request coming from the customer community (interviews with OE, 2013):

> If a whole lot of people say something, and I still think they are wrong, I will still not do it—because I think they are wrong. But sometimes I will not agree with their solution, but I will agree that there is a problem and will work to solve it.

This demonstrates that in OE's organizational culture customers are seen as not necessarily wrong, but unaware of the professional game development effort. As such their inputs might have merit, but are also regarded as associated with a lot of disruption to the 'business as usual'. That points us back to the root tension between the professional videogame developer and an amateur co-creator. Co-creation emerged and thrives in the videogames industry due to the historic proximity between videogame developers and players (due to the industry's origins in the garages or bedrooms, as a hobby activity of software developers). As the videogames industry becomes increasingly professionalized, the skill gap between videogames makers and customers grows, and customers often lack awareness of the complex industrial processes which underpin new service development in the videogames studios. That gap will likely continue to widen, as we observe, for example, the emergence of 'star' videogame developers. The videogames industry might become similar to other creative industries where such separation between the industry and its audiences is already in place e.g., film, music or television. The practices of XE show close collaboration of the studio with its players, especially when it comes to sourcing of ideas. XE focuses on the 'blue sky', or inspirational function of the ideas from the customer community, and the role that they have on the development team in a 'hidden' way (interviews with XE, 2013):

> In game design, there are many subjective aspects, there are many good answers—but some answers are better than the others for particular games. Sometimes our players point us towards interesting solutions to problems as implemented in other games—players are very well versed in various titles. We need to acknowledge that the community assisted in the effort, because we don't keep the track of which idea came from whom even internally. Often that it is not a specific idea, but more like a thing that makes you think of something else, a catalyst [for new game development ideas].

Such behaviour of firm employees points to the co-location of co-creation with hidden innovation. According to this view, firm employees communicate with customers (who belong to a single community which spans the boundaries of an organization; Cohendet and Simon, 2007) and through those numerous and informal interactions, the employees are exposed to the ideas of the customers. In such way, customers' ideas find their way into the organization: not through an officially recognized channel (i.e., a formal R&D function, or a call for submissions, or asset purchase), but by 'seeping into' the firm. This is also reflected in the practices of OE (interviews with OE, 2013):

> [When receiving inputs from the customers] usually there is nothing to act on right away. Usually it is something that we will forget about, or something that will be in the back of our minds and the origin of the idea will be lost—although it still may influence us.

Some of the customers' ideas find their way into firms under the radar of official recognition—albeit influencing the developers in subtle ways. Still, for many firms the only customer inputs that are acknowledged are the ones stemming from formal co-creation (i.e., customers contributing to the paper design of agreed upon details of the game), or QA (as submitters of bug reports and beta testers). Many of the employees' attitudes and firm practices described in this section pertain to this formal type of co-creation. For its hidden version, it could repeatedly occur even in firms which are reluctant to accept inputs from the customers—such as OE. Again, following on Cohendet and Simon (2007), in the creative industries numerous links exist between various communities and groups that include industry employees and also their customers, in various organizations or outside of them. Such cross-pollination and exposure to the ideas of others is very likely to take place in any creative industry firm.[10]

Case Beta

CCP, an Icelandic game development firm, is the focus of the second case study. Having the reputation of a highly innovative company in the industry (embodied by CCP's use of the latest techniques of software development; field notes from EVE Fanfest, 2014), this firm is a favourite object of study to many academic researchers (c.f. Bergstrom et al., 2013; Gibbs et al., 2013). This is because CCP's most popular game *EVE Online* (2003) is a rare example of successful MMO (massively multiplayer online) game that has survived for over 14 years in the sector of the industry which is notorious for high failure rate. *EVE Online* has not only survived—it has done so with an astonishing degree of success, managing to capitalize on a market niche.

Players of *EVE Online* are a particular sort of customer—they enjoy forms of gameplay that aren't appealing to most of the videogames audience. Furthermore, *EVE Online*, due to its open-ended nature, is classified to the 'sandbox' genre, in which players have a high degree of freedom when interacting with games. There are very few videogames that are designed and structured like this (one example is *Second Life*, which has enjoyed a lot of attention from scholars, c.f. Bonsu and Darmody, 2008; Malaby, 2009; Pearce, 2009; Boellstorff et al., 2012).

The observations from CCP are complemented by the accounts from 5th Planet Games. 5th Planet Games is an American studio, located in California, developing web-browser MMO videogames. In this work, the focus is on *Dawn of the Dragons* title (released in 2013). 5th Planet Games is much smaller than CCP (it has around 60 employees, whereas CCP has over 500). Its main revenue stream is 'microtransactions', i.e., the game itself is free to download and it costs nothing to play, but players are enticed by the game design to repeatedly spend small amounts of money on improving their experience. By contrasting and comparing the practices of those two firms, we can produce interesting insights and observations into the semi-structured dynamic of player involvement in NSD.

Additional insights into co-creation of massively multiplayer online videogames that do not rely on crowdfunding are provided by Zenimax Online Studios and ArenaNet. ZOS is headquartered in Maryland, USA and developed *Elder Scrolls Online* (2014), a fantasy-themed RPG for both personal computers and consoles. It has around 250 employees[11] as well as offices in two other locations in USA and Ireland. ArenaNet are developers of another fantasy-themed RPG, *Guild Wars 2* (2012). The company is based in Washington, USA, and has around 300 employees.[12] *Guild Wars 2* realizes the concept of a 'living world', where the game is being regularly updated (on a weekly or bi-weekly basis) with new content to improve player experience.

EVE Online and Its Niche

EVE Online is a subscription-based MMO game set in a science fiction, space opera setting, released in 2003. For a long time, it had been the only game produced and maintained by CCP. Only recently the company released its second and third titles, *Dust 514* (2013) and *Valkyrie* (2016). *EVE Online*'s subscriptions are the chief means of generating revenue—meaning that the first prerogative for CCP is maintenance of stable and committed customer base that keeps on playing the game. The company is majority-owned by its founders and staff. That captures some differences between this case and the Case Alpha, where OE's game *Pillars of Eternity* was single-player and crowdfunded.

EVE Online, as an online multiplayer game, is characterized by a deep integration of inter-player dynamics into its core gameplay. As a 'sandbox' game, it places a lot of emphasis on players' creativity and its role in affecting the service experience. Furthermore, development of the sandbox type of videogame also fosters open organizational culture, where a firm accepts inputs from the outside more easily (Malaby, 2009). This is because the very design of the service calls for meaningful inputs from the players throughout the game. A sandbox game therefore forms an excellent backdrop for a firm's use of co-creation. Its customers are already familiar with a high degree of agency and autonomy, and its staff with empowered players.

Another major difference setting this case apart from Case Alpha and Case Gamma is the stage in *EVE Online*'s development. The game has been released commercially over 14 years ago.[13] CCP continues to heavily support it by continuously adding major pieces of content, new functionalities as well as options (together with the improvements to underlying game technology, graphics, systems, etc.). This generates significant differences in the way customers are integrated with internal game development—for instance, secrecy concerns to ward off competitors are lower than for an unreleased product, as well as generating improvements to an existing game is easier than development of novel ideas for a game under production (also these tasks require different expertise).

Case Beta illustrates semi-structured co-creation practice. Here, the firms use both structured, highly formalized practices of co-creating with its customers (illustrated by approaches such as contests and toolkits) together with unstructured, largely informal practices (which are akin to Miles and Green's hidden innovation, and occur via numerous informal contacts, exchanges and relationships between employees and customers; 2008). Case Beta demonstrates a situation where a degree of trust exists between the firm and its customers, and where customers are partners in the development of the service (field notes from CCP, 2014). This could be because of the niche nature of the service itself (meaning that it has a relatively small audience), the design of the service (it attracts more mature customers than industry average), and CCP's practice of hiring mostly from among its customers (field notes from CCP, 2014).

The exceptionally homogeneous player community composition of *EVE Online* (Bergstrom, 2013) contributes to the stronger relationship of players with the game developer than in other videogames. From the interviews with CCP (2013–2014):

> Average age of *EVE* player is 32. Other MMOs have audiences which are much younger. *EVE Online* has players from very unlikely demographics; many very highly qualified people are attracted to play *EVE Online*.

The strength of this community is reinforced by *EVE Online*'s unique single-server configuration and player-driven governance of the game (Gibbs et al., 2013). Design decisions made by CCP decrease the size of the likely audience for *EVE Online*, while making its player base more homogenous and attractive for those who fit the narrowed target demographic (Paul, 2011). Other game design elements, such as departures from conventions of how a player is represented in *EVE Online*, further contribute to that[14] (Bergstrom et al., 2013).

In those idiosyncratic gameplay circumstances, in a system which encourages emergent, sandbox interactions and player self-governance, the community of players as a source of knowledge about *EVE Online* is an asset of enormous value to CCP. This view is also corroborated by Burger-Helmchen and Cohendet (2011: 321) in their observation that "[game players] can be considered genuine experts in this field, and as such they are an important source of knowledge, which circulates through . . . channels that lead to the firm". This is a sentiment expressed by CCP employees (interviews with CCP, 2013–2014):

> Players are experts at playing *EVE Online*, with their knowledge about the game surpassing that of ours [developers'] on many occasions . . . Our players are best informed about the ways they like to engage with *EVE Online*.

Moreover, players of *EVE Online* have proven their usefulness as developers of software enhancing the service experience. By development of such toolkits as EVEMon (Battleclinic), EVE Fitting Tool (EFT) or Dotlan Evemaps, the players have not only contributed to the quality of *EVE*'s gameplay, but also established new ways of playing the game, as well as delivered value to the customers and CCP as a company (c.f. Nardi, 2010). In the field notes from CCP (2014):

> CCP considers players a valuable source of information about their needs and gameplay habits, as well as a resource for creativity equipped with the skills necessary for game development (many of the *EVE Online* players are skilled programmers, talented artists, or competent IT project managers).

The community of *EVE Online* players, just like for many other games, is comprised of members with various sets of skills and interests (interviews with ICO Partners, 2014). Managing these diverse player types and thus various sub-segments of *EVE Online* community requires strong competences for co-creation from CCP, which are components of the studio's commercial success with *EVE Online*. These competences grant CCP competitive advantage in MMOG sector, and allow it to succeed in the industry and in a market niche. User involvement and integration competences seem of highest importance, followed by the appropriation and disclosure competences (i.e., being able to create the conditions for and attract customers' solution-centric inputs for the former, and to balance the degree of information openness against potential IP risks).

Similarly, at 5th Planet, catering to customer communities has always played a key role in the studio's strategy. In the interview with a 5th Planet employee (2014):

> I like to think that we have a special relationship with our players. I feel that a lot of people care about the well-being of our games and community.

The ability to build a relationship with customers falls under the user involvement competence. Consequently, the creativity of community members is present in 5th Planet Games as an important resource for the studio. At the same time, we observe how those community inputs at times fit uneasily with the goals of the firm, as well as how they can generate problematic situations (interviews with 5th Planet, 2014):

> A portion of our community enjoys making tools for our games; some of those tools go against our terms of service. In terms of risks we have had some situations when we listened too much to the community, we introduced what they wanted, we had to then take it out of the game, but this has happened rarely.

A firm's ability to resolve those tensions corresponds to its integration competence. Sometimes the TOS (terms of service), as well as EULA (end user license agreement) also contribute to the narrowing or expanding of the possible scope of player inputs to game development. Depending on how relaxed or how restrictive these are, players' creativity will be directed to some, and not other, outlets (or barred altogether). For instance, Blizzard Entertainment's TOS and EULA for their MMOG hit *World of Warcraft* (2005) are famously restrictive, allowing only very specific types of co-creation to occur (Nardi, 2010).

In the interviews with ArenaNet (2014), the role of customer feedback in influencing NSD is underlined: "[Customers'] feedback influences us in a myriad of ways, probably sub-consciously." This quote also accents the proximity of hidden innovation and co-creation, and the informal 'osmosis' of customers' inputs into an organization via mechanisms not accounted for on the formal, strategic level. Setting the appropriate organizational and customer relationship management conditions for such osmosis is also a part of firm's competences for co-creation, and does not happen accidentally.

Customer Involvement at CCP

Integrating customer inputs with the studio's service development practices is critical to CCP's success with *EVE Online*. Various tools for interacting with the community, as well as multiple practices to engage players in co-creating *EVE Online*, are all parts of an open dialogue between the company and its customers. From the CCP field notes (2014):

> There is a constant review happening within CCP, taking player inputs and reflecting on them in the context of CCP's vision.

Formally, co-creation of *EVE Online* occurs via three main channels: physical gatherings, internet-mediated communication (such as discussion forums, emails and mailing lists, etc.) and players' voluntary advisory bodies to CCP (player council, as well as the volunteer program). The other roles of these channels are to 'filter the noise out'—to create outlets for communication that will be transparent to CCP's analysis, and that will yield information relevant to NSD. Another application is to produce information that is possible to assimilate into game production practices of CCP. In the field notes from CCP (2014) we read:

> The practice of assimilating player inputs via these channels [the structure and effectiveness of these channels stem from CCP's user involvement competences] is relatively flexible. CCP displays a degree of organizational flexibility when integrating customer inputs coming into the organization. How the employees deal with them, the composition of teams discussing them, and the profiles of people responsible

for them within the organization—they are all relatively fluid [pointing towards the semi-structure practice of co-creation at CCP].

The note above suggests that CCP's integration competence does not reside only in rigid routines. To large extent it resides in 'on-the-job' practices of employees, their experience and 'professional intuition'.

Fanfests and Other Physical Gatherings

The largest and most important of *EVE Online* player gatherings is Fanfest, held annually in the spring in Reykjavik, Iceland. "Up to two thousand *EVE Online* players and fans come to celebrate their involvement in the game, as well as to meet the developers. Additional fifteen to twenty thousand watch the live broadcast from Fanfest on the internet" (interviews with CCP, 2013–2014). For CCP this presents an opportunity to connect with their players, but more importantly, to gather their feedback about the game in an informal, personal way. Conversely, it is an occasion for the players to give their suggestions to the developers. Such direct communication allows CCP a better insight into players' needs. According to interviews with CCP (2013–2014):

> There have been many instances where EVE was changed as a result of these informal chats [at a Fanfest].

During Fanfests the activities are geared towards enhancing the communication between players and the developers, as well as ensuring that both formal and informal channels for information flow are open. CCP takes this opportunity to announce new expansions, new features, to present upcoming products and a long-term vision for the game. It also uses these events to familiarize the players with some business aspects of CCP. Important community announcements, such as Council of Stellar Management election results, are also made in Fanfests. Finally, Fanfests encompass rich informal interactions between players and CCP employees. Events such as pub crawls, trips around Iceland, concerts as well as spontaneous activities such as hotel and house parties are all venues of informal and in-depth information exchange between the players and developers. As we read in the field notes from CCP (2014):

> It is possible to specify couple of various activity types during Fanfest, such as roundtables, presentations, keynote talks and social events. During roundtables, developers sit down together with players and discuss the game. Such events are recorded; their time and location are advertised in the Fanfest's programme to ensure attendance of interested parties. The discussions pertain to upcoming and existing features of *EVE Online*. There are dedicated roundtables for various aspects of

the game. Presentations are about developers familiarizing the players with CCP's work and where the studio is going with new or existing features, as well as what will happen in the future of the game. There is always a Q&A session at the end of a presentation, and those discussions are another source of feedback and ideas for CCP.

Nevertheless, Fanfests are not the only gatherings of this type. Other events include EVE Vegas (held in Las Vegas, USA), EVE Down Under (held in Sydney, Australia) and many other smaller player gatherings throughout the world. Many of those events are organized and run entirely by the players. Often CCP sends some developers to participate in the gathering, bringing news and promotional materials. CCP delegates developers even to events which are attended by as few as 40–50 people. For other events, CCP developers will often connect with their players via Skype (interviews with CCP, 2013–14).

All of those activities greatly contribute to the customer-firm relationship, as well as to the opportunities for the idea transfer between the customers and the firm's NSD. They illustrate CCP's user involvement competence—pointing towards their ability and resources to engage with the customers in meaningful ways, which flows out of CCP's understanding of customers' needs and motivations for co-creation. Fanfests also embody the semi-structured nature of co-creation at CCP. Over iterations of Fanfests, CCP has learned how to plan and structure the sessions, how to record them, what kinds of events to prepare, etc., to get as much feedback from the customers as possible in a structured or unstructured way. This is because feedback on one aspect of a videogame experience can be more easily conveyed in informal environments, while feedback on another aspect might benefit from analytical and formal discussion. The choice of that structure is dependent on CCP's internal needs (i.e., current game design dilemmas, strategic business decisions based on customers' sentiment, etc.) and it is meant to readily fit into CCP's game development procedures, team structure and project management practices.

Forums, Social Media and Blogs

Online discussion forums serve the function of communicating players' feedback, ideas, concerns and wishes to the game developers. Forums themselves are also indispensable for the game-related exchanges between players to occur, and thus vibrant forums are a condition *sine qua non* for the emergence of players' community. For the purposes of co-creation, a section of the forums that is of most interest is the 'Features and Ideas', where players are invited to share their ideas and participate in the discussion about the existing and upcoming features. Another section of forums which is instrumental to *EVE Online*'s co-creation is the 'Test Server Feedback' section—from which CCP can gather players' opinions, as well as observe how players utilize game features. Game developers and community managers frequent those forums.

The idea of a capital ship, which arose from a discussion in the 'Features and ideas' section, is one example of co-creative activity in CCP's context. From the CCP field notes (2014):

> As players were discussing their ideas for the ship design, the developers were listening in (and getting involved in the discussion as well). Eventually the discussion fizzled out, but sometime later the players' design got incorporated into *EVE Online*—with some alterations as compared to the original discussion, which resulted from CCP making sure that the design fit within the artistic vision and aesthetic theme of the game.

In this case CCP sourced some ideas from the community of players for subsequent internal development and introduction into the game. This kind of practice requires all four competences for co-creation from the studio, as well as the right type of organizational culture. A firm must be able to explain to the players what ideas would be useful (disclosure), have an infrastructure for customer discussion and ideation in place (user involvement), carry the customers' ideas across the firm boundary in a from useful to staff (integration), and finally resolve any legal and intellectual property challenges that might arise (appropriation). The firm's employees must be willing to see their customers as sources of valuable ideas, and to recognize the benefits to the company stemming from collaborating with them (i.e., relationship improvement, customers brand loyalty, increased maximum willingness to pay, spreading of the positive word of mouth). From the analysis of CCP's web forums (2014):

> CCP also organizes contests where customers are invited to submit their entries on a particular problem—for example their designs for ship hulls [ships and their properties, including their appearance, are a critically important aspect of *EVE Online*].

Such practice not only has a chance of generating innovative inputs to the game (developed by the people who are free of organizational 'group think' and have a different perspective), but also creates good will and enhances the customers' feelings of ownership of the game. CCP and its customers also communicate via the comments section below '*EVE* dev blogs'. It illustrates CCP's user involvement competence, as well as their semi-structured practices of co-creation (which depend on the employees' visiting and reading of the forums in an unstructured way). Following on the analysis of CCP's website (2014):

> *EVE Online* developers describe their work on new or existing features in those blogs, where the players' community is invited to leave

comments and suggestions. From there, CCP can get a good idea what the players' preferences and issues are ahead of time, before any tensions with the community caused by changes to the existing gameplay can occur. Other valuable outlets for listening in to players' feedback and ideas include third-party forums (such as Reddit or themittani. com), as well as social media. Players also help in the marketing of *EVE Online* by spreading word of mouth, but also by making videos, writing stories, developing lore, as well as costume and role playing.

One detail that recurs in interviews is the problem of 'management of expectations', revealing inherent challenges of maintaining positive relationship with the players (interviews with CCP, 2013–2014). A studio must be careful not to promise or reveal too much to the community of players. This links back to the disclosure competence. The use of co-creation in game development does not necessarily produce only positive impact on the customer-firm relationship; it is also possible that unsuccessful co-creation will lead to degradation of that relationship (as observed in the case of Auran; Banks, 2013 and 2009; Gebauer et al., 2013).

C: Council of Stellar Management and ISD Volunteer Program

Council of Stellar Management is a democratically elected group of players assigned an advisory function to *EVE Online*'s development (the rules and rationale for this democratic process have been outlined in CSM White Paper written by firm's employees; Oskarsson, 2014). From that document analysis (2014):

> The members of CSM are flown to CCP's headquarters twice during their one-year term, where after signing a non-disclosure agreement they are invited to participate in *EVE Online* development meetings with the studio's staff. CSM members also have access to dedicated section of the forums, where they can discuss *EVE Online* and its community with developers, as well as their communication with CCP is facilitated overall (for instance, CSM members can Skype-call developers or community managers directly).

Also in the field notes from CCP (2014) we read:

> A Council of Stellar Management (CSM) Summit normally lasts three days. There are separate sessions for marketing, PR, community and business leadership of CCP. During those meetings, CSM members are brought up to speed in terms of what CCP is currently working on and provide their inputs and perspective. After the summit, CCP goes through compiled meeting minutes and ensures their compliance with

non-disclosure agreement (the minutes are later released to the public). Once the summit ends, those minutes are distributed to respective development teams, and the issues which have been identified as valid during those meetings are put to development.

Feedback from CSM in such format is tailored to CCP's NSD, and the practice of acting upon CSM feedback is to an extent routinized within the studio's production. It is an example of formal co-creation, embodied by internal practice of assimilating customers' inputs. The exact practice of internal processing of co-creation inputs may vary at CCP from case to case, but an overall map of responsibilities and decision-makers is known to the employees.

Apart from CSM, CCP has established another tool for involving players in *EVE Online*'s development. Interstellar Services Department (ISD) is a volunteer program that invites players to become collaborators of CCP on some aspects of game development (aspects selected by the firm). Similar to CSM, after a successful application process, those volunteer players are asked to sign an NDA (interviews with CCP, 2013–2014):

> Players sign NDAs and are required to do a specific amount of work, but they also get access to developers' tools. They try to reproduce bugs that other players reported, then rewrite the bugs into CCP's standard format and send to the developers (or have a dialogue with developers about them). Bug hunters are given access to various private IRC channels, that's where primary coordination is done. They also have access to defect tracking system—JIRA, as well as to internal mailing lists, as well as exploit reporting system. There is an employee in the QA department who is a bug hunter liaison, looking after the volunteer division.
>
> Players involved in ISD do not become employees of CCP in any way, and are under no obligation to fulfil any duties for the studio; nevertheless, they become involved in the development of *EVE Online*.

From the field notes from EVE Fanfest (2014):

> ISD displays some basic organizational hierarchy; volunteer players are given tasks by the development team, as well as they remain in closer communication with CCP than regular players. Those players are not explicitly rewarded by the studio (they are granted no special privileges and are not paid), except for recognition and higher chances of getting employed by CCP, if they want it.

Player councils and volunteer player programs are examples of structured co-creation, with an established practice of assimilating player inputs, procedures, objectives and hierarchy. Still, within that matrix, CCP grants the players a high degree of self-governance, allowing them to operate outside the organizational boundaries of the firm. That points toward semi-structured nature of CCP's co-creation practice. Player inputs are accepted in various forms and formats, at different times, pertaining to all functions of the firm. Such practice requires excellent integration competence, where co-creation is inscribed into the firm's project management and organizational culture, as well as other day-to-day operations.

Furthermore, player councils and volunteer programs also embody co-creation geared towards NSD inputs from the players (as opposed to co-creation geared towards relationship building, as we saw in the case of Obsidian Entertainment), tapping into their need-related knowledge. Because of CCP's organizational structure and culture (embodied, for example, by the practices described above), it has become much less resource-intensive and disruptive for that studio to process customer inputs for integration into NSD. Interestingly, that doesn't preclude the studio from extracting customer relationship benefits out of co-creation, too. As we read in the notes from EVE Fanfest (2014):

> There are gains for customer-firm relationship resulting from player councils and volunteer programs. All customers are engaged in for example democratically electing player councils, or can witness how the firm listens to them—because both of these practices are highly visible to all of the community, and the firm also celebrates them on every occasion (for instance during Fanfests, or in communication with the players).

Similar to CCP, 5th Planet Games and its game *Dawn of the Dragons* have been available in the market for some time already. In the interviews, company employees mention that as much as 25% of staff is dedicated to community management, pointing towards the importance of customer relationship in 5th Planet's business model. The firm has also established close collaboration with its customers in the format of player councils (interviews with 5th Planet, 2014):

> We gather one council every 9 months for each of our games. At the high level, it is a focus group consisting of people representing different types of players. They speak on behalf of various groups of players. Prior to the council meeting, we prepare an agenda that we want to discuss with the council, we have the time period for the council to bring ideas etc. After the weekend of the council summit, council members are asked to remain available for Skype conversations and feedback. We drop design documents on this Skype group. Player council members have their own dedicated forum tag and they act a bit as community managers: they put out many fires, which works very well both for the player community and for us [the studio].

The quote above demonstrates another approach to a player council theme, but with some differences when compared with CCP's. Player council practice at 5th Planet seems less structured than at CCP—which could be due to the smaller organization size of 5th Planet, and thus greater visibility of all staff's activities and less bureaucratic work environment. The firm has an agenda, provides the customers with various documents, sets deadlines for inputs—but all of these are not framed as 'guaranteed' to be reviewed by the firm. There is no obligation for the firm to listen. The practice of assimilation of inputs can also vary from case to case, leaving the company a lot of freedom in choosing how they use customer inputs, and if at all.

Outside of the player councils, there are numerous similarities between the approach of 5th Planet Games and CCP. 5th Planet Games also does monthly 'state of the game updates', as well as discusses upcoming features on the forums with players. The characteristics of 5th Planet's organizational culture, which are conducive to co-creation practice, are described in the passage below (field notes from GDC 2015):

> For 5th Planet Games, involvement of customers means maintaining a level of organizational transparency to allow people to participate in the development process within the studio (also demonstrating changes to the internal functioning of the organization induced by co-creation). 5th Planet Games seeks to reply to everything that appears on the forums; not replying is viewed by the company as one of the biggest mistakes that developers do. This is because it's not possible to get the good posts if the less useful go unnoticed and without validation form the studio. Making players feel that they are being listened to, that somebody looks at their submissions, is key to creating conducive environment for co-creation.

Going through the totality of community input is the priority for 5th Planet Games, as it is seen as a technique for ensuring co-creation success (i.e., both in terms of finding the best customer inputs, as well as building a strong customer relationship based on trust). It is highlighted in the interviews with 5th Planet (2014):

> Filtering through the customer inputs that are not useful and grabbing golden eggs of player creativity—that is an ongoing struggle for the studio. There is no 'catch all' solution for capitalizing on customers' inputs, and that's the biggest challenge.

The quote above demonstrates the burden placed by co-creation on the organization. Such individual approach to all customer inputs and manual sifting through them is both resource- and time-consuming. Moreover, the issue of vocal minority remains one of the biggest concerns to 5th Planet

Games and risks in the process of analyzing customers' inputs and feedback. Therefore, thinking of the ramifications of what players say is really important during the employees' community training: people who are the loudest may not be representative of the community of all customers (interviews with Valve Corporation, 2014).

5th Planet Games also has volunteer players helping with some aspects of game development (for example, chat channel moderators or testing), but no formalized programme for those volunteers exist (pointing towards a semi-structured practice of co-creation). The company also organizes contests (for example, for game lore creation), where the staff narrows down the submissions to the top 10 and the community votes on the winner. This also illustrates a fairly relaxed, but still to some degree formalized, practice of co-creation.

At ArenaNet, the customer involvement in NSD takes the form of 'CDI project'. It again displays the characteristics of a semi-structured co-creation practice. It is described in the interviews with ArenaNet (2014):

> We put forward a topic and a call for votes. Normally we seek players' input on what are the top three, or perhaps the single most important topic to us. We still don't have a voting mechanism in our forums, but you get a feeling about what's most important to players. Make a separate forum thread specifically dedicated to this topic, with the person in our company who is the biggest stakeholder of that feature involved. We experiment with the structure of that: how long players are allowed to rant for (paragraphs, focus), how do we communicate what we are looking for. It is a process by which we are trying to change our internal company philosophy, as well as to honour and give voice to the players. . . . We have done CDI three times now, three different iterations. Our Director of Development involves the community in each iteration, and also invites them to make improvements to it so it works even better next time.

ArenaNet is characterized by an experimental co-creation approach. The studio tests various co-creation processes and tweaks them every time they are deployed, fine-tuning them. Interestingly, the company also involves customers in designing new iterations and introducing improvements. This is an example of the transformative influence of co-creation on organizations.

Assimilation of Customer Inputs

At CCP, there are many practices of assimilation of player inputs, facilitated by the CCP's use of Scrum project management practice (c.f., Keith, 2010). Some of these practices offer insight into the structured co-creation at CCP—others are flexible and have a certain degree of freedom to them. From the CCP field notes (2014):

Feedback is systematically consolidated and brought on a regular basis to the developers by Customer Support and Community Management teams. Those teams use both quantitative (e.g., software searching for key words in players' forum posts) and qualitative methods (e.g., judging of the players' sentiment by community managers and game masters) to synthesize feedback from the players. One rule of thumb used by CCP for determining the pertinence of an issue is how frequently it appears in the reports on the state of community. If any of those issues becomes a recurrent theme, it is taken on as a development or marketing project (the issues do not only pertain to strictly in-game problems).

Another interesting description is provided below (field notes from CCP, 2014):

During a design department's daily 10–15-minute stand-up meeting, one of the developers can bring up an issue encountered on a forum. Then the group checks whether that is a pertinent issue, or something not to worry about (design department on the aggregate level has a very good holistic overview of the game and they excel at determining the urgency of such issues).

If the issue can be solved by the design team, it is taken to the production level where a senior producer takes it to the product owners and lead game designer, who will then come up with the team who should take it on; the problem or issue becomes inserted into that team's backlog. There are regular meetings of business leadership team for each project—including the representatives from development, marketing, finance and community departments. This team copes with responding to those player issues, which require significant or composite changes to *EVE Online* (if the team is conflicted, executive producer casts the tie-breaking vote).

This demonstrates CCP's integration competence, as well as (to a lesser extent) user involvement and disclosure competences. They also show how deeply co-creation practice has been integrated with the functioning of the organization; it would be actually difficult to draw the boundary of the firm in CCP's case. CCP exemplifies the transformative impact of co-creation on firms: its influence becomes present in meetings, project management, communication routines, employee responsibilities and other sites. Those transformations are also accompanied by a particular organizational culture, as illustrated later in this chapter (field notes from CCP, 2014):

For dealing with technical issues (for example a bug in the game code) formal and informal channels exist. In the formal channel, a bug petition is reported, normally coming from a player or one of the bug hunters (who are volunteer players themselves). Subsequently it is formally tracked via defect tracking system and goes into bucket of a relevant department, and a person responsible for fixing it is assigned to that bug together with its priority.

We also observe how the need of an organization to cope with players' inputs translates into externally facing techniques for managing the influx of those inputs (interviews with CCP, 2013–2014):

> [Processing players' inputs to QA] is very chaotic, and hence some processes were introduced such as volunteer bug hunters—to bring some order to the QA reports. Without that CCP might not be able to cope with all the issues.

We observe formal and informal dimensions of co-creation practice. Formal co-creation practice is officially recognized by the firm. The firm determines its structure, plans for it, and treats it as integral to strategy. Its elements and opportunities are advertised to the community of customers; very often it is accompanied by a process to legally acquire the customers' IP (i.e., appropriation competence). Informal co-creation takes place on-the-job and is embodied in daily routines and activities of studio staff communicating and interacting with the customers. This is not to say that studio management is unaware of this practice taking place—very often it is recognized as beneficial and resulting from firm's resources (e.g., dedicated and creative community of customers). The studio prefers to stick to the 'closed' NSD practices which have been proven to work, as opposed to taking a risk and restructuring its organizational structure to accommodate formal co-creation. From that it would appear that formal co-creation is more difficult to implement in studios overall, unless they are newly established or structured with co-creation in mind. On the other hand, for studios with ample game development experience informal co-creation might work better as the staff of those studios are normally more experienced and have better professional judgment of what works and does not work in NSD (field notes from CCP, 2014):

> In the informal channel, staff members who are involved as players in *EVE Online* will personally push for the bug to be fixed (despite the fact that bug flagging is not part of their job description)—becoming sort of champions for fixing that bug. After such champion successfully advocates for addressing that bug with the relevant members of the development team, the bug is brought into the official track (for bookkeeping reasons), and processed formally from that point onwards.

These practices reveal the attention paid to player inputs by individual game developers, as well as deeply ingrained responsiveness to them in CCP's organizational culture, which are the organizational cultural cornerstones of informal co-creation. Similar practices are also observed at ArenaNet, where some prominent employees argue for listening to the customers and involving them in NSD (interviews with ArenaNet, 2014). They effectively act as champions for co-creation within a firm, spearheading some of the organizational transformations which are a prerequisite for co-creation.

The ability to use both formal and informal practices in co-creation for gathering player inputs is linked to user involvement competence. Still, once those inputs reach the organization, it is the integration competence that determines how successfully a firm copes with co-creation. At CCP we observe formal and informal practices for gathering player inputs (interviews with CCP, 2013–2014):

> One of the biggest advantages of CSM is that it provides CCP with distilled, coherent feedback aggregated from the players.

The mention of 'distilled' and 'coherent' are noteworthy here. They point us to the underlying rationale of ordering the chaos of external inputs, making them friendly for the more hierarchical and regulated environment of a company. The details of those practices are described in the field notes from Fanfest (2014):

> Within CCP, there is a community management team member who is entirely responsible for managing the activities of CSM, as well as monitoring its interactions with CCP. Overheads required to run and manage CSM include communication infrastructure, internal mailing lists and involvement of CSM in sprint reviews; CSM members also are stakeholders on various development teams.

These overheads also provide an intra-studio framework for processing CSM's inputs, which facilitates their integration with game development. This interaction between CCP and CSM occurs normally via forums, email and Skype, with the most intensive periods of interaction being the summits. The mode and format of CCP's collaboration with CSM have been evolving over the years before reaching their current shape (in May 2015 the CSM was in its 10th term).

One barrier to successful processing of player inputs is the legacy of technical decisions (i.e., the legacy of software architecture and implementation decisions undertaken by the studio since the very beginning of new service development), as well as specific fields of expertise of the firm's employees. That limits the possible scope of what can be feasibly processed by the firm employees without devoting huge amounts of time to understanding a piece of player input (interviews with Square Enix Collective, 2014). This problem is also underlined in the interviews with CCP (2013–2014):

> Sometimes players suggest changes to the game in other programming languages, but they also don't know about the surrounding systems

around that issue. Sometimes feedback from players is of high quality, but there is no time or priority to investigate; or it pertains to something that can't be changed because of the nature of other systems in game. And about the latter [player's suggestion invalidated because of legacy systems limitations] you don't want to talk on forums due to confidentiality and community management reasons.

This legacy of old programming languages and systems has accrued with *EVE Online*'s age—when it was first made in early 2000's, there were other technical standards and practices than there are today. Therefore, the technical age of the game is a factor potentially negatively influencing co-creation (while other aspects of a game's age, such as established brand and strong customer communities, have the opposite effect). A firm's ability to overcome this limitation and co-create despite it is a part of appropriation competence.

Another factor limiting a firm's propensity to engage in co-creation is the size of the organization. In larger organizations in particular, only public relations or human resources departments contact players directly, and they control how much an individual employee communicates with the customers (interviews with ZOS, 2013). The above is also true for smaller firms owned by large multinational umbrella organizations, for example, small studios working on particular titles commissioned by game publisher firms such as Activision, EA or Ubisoft. On the other hand, in smaller studios, organizational structures are flatter, there is more communication between all departments, and staff tend to vaguely know what other teams are doing (and thus, if they need to interact with someone on another team, for example, they don't have to follow a formal channel). Interactions among employees of all specialities tend to be less formal. In such an environment, co-creation (which we already linked to informal, 'on-the-job', everyday practices of videogame developers) might likely have a greater chance of occurring. In these videogame studios, the customer service or community management departments are smaller, and line employees from all NSD functions tend to interact with customers more. This leads to exchanges of ideas across the firm-customer boundary, and to increased probability of co-creation in the long run.

The role of volunteer bug hunters is important in the integration of customer inputs with a firm's NSD. As the quality of QA reports submitted by the players to the firm varies greatly, volunteer bug hunters standardize the reports and reproduce them and investigate them so the developers don't need to. As mentioned in the interviews with CCP (2013–2014):

Overall we get far less quality reports that we would like, and player bug-hunters bring those reports to high quality.

When describing the difficulties of integrating customer inputs to game development, CCP employees (2013–2014) mention not being able to give customers the access to CCP's tools. That limits the usefulness of customer inputs to game development team: bug hunters who have this access produce much more insightful and useful reports, while regular players' reports are more speculative unless the issue happens to be very clear. The ability to overcome this limitation is an example of disclosure competence of a firm, as the firm needs to render some of its potentially sensitive processes visible to the public (i.e., in their communications with customers and the software used in-house).

The co-existence of structured and unstructured practices of co-creation at CCP is demonstrated in the interviews (2013–2014):

> Within CCP, there are both established and ad hoc methods for processing players' inputs to game development. Quality Assurance forms a point of entry for a lot of player inputs to game development. At QA we get the feedback and help to obtain the information, but follow-up on this feedback is done by the feature teams. The type of feedback given to us also affects what happens with it [i.e., how it is processed internally]. In some cases, it is handled completely by the Features Team and QA has nothing to do with it. In other cases QA collects the feedback, analyzes it and provides it in a clearer form to relevant teams within CCP. QA team sends the reports to involved parties (Production, Feature Team etc.). For example, processing feedback in the form of mass test surveys is an established process. On the other hand, processing direct feedback from forums (i.e., the posts and discussions) is more ad hoc.

At 5th Planet Games, after developers talk to players and obtain their feedback, they discuss customers' ideas among themselves. Even brief chats on the forums can become very drawn out processes when discussed internally. Employees consult user data (i.e., the big data collected about the players' interactions with the game) in that practice as well. According to the interviews with 5th Planet (2014):

> There are definitely some established processes for players' inputs, but they also sometimes change. On the most general level, customer inputs follow the path of community managers reading the feedback, then bringing it to the lead designer, which feedback is then discussed with the team.

In this example, we witness both the structured and unstructured elements of co-creation practice. On one hand, people responsible for processing customer inputs within an organization are known to their colleagues (as well as, at times, to the NSD process-savvy customers as well). On the other hand, it is up to their own *personal* judgment and preference that determines which customer inputs will be taken forward. Further details of those practices are reflected in the quote below (interviews with 5th Planet, 2014):

For something quick, we will hash it out then and there—in the instances, when the decision on a piece of customer feedback can be made easily. If it is a more complicated decision, the team will discuss it around desk or even in a meeting. The developers also may establish internal chat group for everybody within the firm to leave their feedback when they have a chance, and meeting is organized after that.

The above observations are corroborated by the field notes from GDC (2014):

Three things are always considered when making a decision in such scenario: how much of firm's resources are required to make the change, how many players it is going to affect, and the merit of the change itself. Correspondingly, the people sitting in those meetings depend on the level of change required. Typically, it is just the design lead, production team, assistant designers, project manager, and a community manager. If the group feels that the issue needs escalation (especially on highly technical issues to do with code, programming, software architecture, etc.), then other people also get involved. If need arises, for the changes affecting significant proportion of the videogame service, things can be taken even higher—to the head of design or CEO.

Processing players' feedback and their inputs to NSD is a multi-tiered system at 5th Planet. It points us towards a degree of structure to the co-creation practice in that firm, but at the same time the lack of documentation or formalization of that practice is underlined (interviews with 5th Planet, 2014):

The first point of entry is the player council. Council members are on the forums a lot. Second line is the community managers. They know how to interact with the player community; they know what's going on within the company as well. Third tier is the lead designer of the game. They don't post a lot, except for 'state of the game' posts. It is also the person known as the 'head honcho' for a particular game. Fourth and final tier is the people at the 'chief executive' level within the company. Most things are contained within tier 1 and 2, but sometimes it goes up to 4. It is not a documented process, but that's how things often shake out [sic].

Even less structure is seen at ArenaNet, where there is no formal practice for sorting and distributing action items to individual teams based on the inputs from customers. Still, the inputs from the customers are shared around the team and discussed before being taken forward in NSD. The following account of the informal co-creation practice is given in an interview with ArenaNet employee (2014):

A player will post an exploit, bug, cheat or hack information on the forums, maybe together with a YouTube video. One of us [the game developers] will see that and will send the link to relevant colleagues. After the information is received, the development team still needs to go through proper production channels to get that exploit, bug, cheat or hack fixed.

Such practice of co-creation is linked to integration competence in particular. ArenaNet orders and focuses the customer inputs in the areas where that feedback is most needed, in a form which is most comprehensive to the NSD team. We see that practice underlined in the interviews with ZOS (2013):

We aggregate players' voices. Individual players will often be very strongly convinced; the question is in the numbers.

ArenaNet displays a number of 'best practices' for co-creation, which allow the firm to order, judge and act on the customers' feedback. These practices are accompanied by a disclosure competence, which allows the firm to clearly communicate its co-creative needs to the customers. It is captured in the field notes from GDC (2014):

Best ways of responding to customer inputs are honest answers from developers, transparent production methodologies, rationalization of features, as well as regular communicating with the community of customers.

Another problem that firms face when wishing to integrate players' inputs with their NSD is the legal challenges. A firm's ability to positively resolve them is determined by appropriation competence. According to an interview with ArenaNet (2014):

We have had a lot of [customer inputs] for music; I spoke with someone from legal department about it. This person said that the amount of paperwork and lawyering that would have to occur [to use those customers' inputs] would outweigh any benefits.

This demonstrates that the firm must have the ability to navigate the complex and redefined relationships of ownership of intellectual property when engaging in co-creation. The knowledge, procedures and resources must be in place within a firm in order to achieve that (i.e., to have appropriate contracts ready; money and time set aside for the lawyers; a co-creative platform as the one we observed in the case of inXile Entertainment). The boundaries between producers and consumers of content are shifting, and the traditional division between the makers of a videogame and its consumers is blurring as well. A co-creating firm must have the ability to cope with this new landscape and develop appropriate legal knowledge, approaches and tools.

C: Organizational Culture and Co-Creation

Such rich interaction between the users of *EVE Online*, as well as its developers, is possible because of the single community that transcends the boundary of the firm. The presence of such unifying body, which includes both customers and firm employees, creates the foundations for organizational culture of increased respect for customer inputs. According to the interviews with CCP (2013–2014):

> The game is the topic of many conversations during the Fanfest, and other fan gatherings as well. We [the developers] try to be like 'dry sponges' soaking up all the feedback and information throughout the event. Developers record their conversations with fans [in order to capture all of their feedback and ideas], or write themselves emails with notes.

CCP has established an organizational culture where the customers are seen as valuable collaborators and partners. The firm devotes a lot of effort and resources to maintaining a positive relationship with its customers. For instance, CCP engages with the customer community to ensure that players' interest in contributing to *EVE Online* remains high and that they know their contributions are appreciated. In the interviews with CCP (2013–2014) we read:

> Community's sentiment is usually at its highest around the Fanfest, or right after it, and we try to keep this feeling going throughout the year [by releasing videos from CCP's offices, providing the community with updates, by writing developer blogs].

At the same time, CCP understands that feedback from the customer community can be purposefully inflammatory, or represent the opinions of a very small portion of the customer base (which is still very visible, hence the name 'vocal minority'). Therefore, the skills of aggregating feedback trends and not taking negative opinions personally among the employees are important (interviews with ZOS, 2013). This links to the user involvement and disclosure competences in particular, as well as is embodied by a co-creation friendly organizational culture.

CCP's employees are characterized by a cooperative and enthusiastic attitude towards their players' inputs—a trait which is fostered throughout the firm. This is illustrated in the field notes (2014):

In the case of ship rebalancing [an activity important for maintaining *EVE Online*'s playability], the developers provided statistics and raw mathematical data about ships requiring balancing to the community by posting them on forums. Players started working with the numbers and discussing possible changes, resulting in very long forum threads. The development team was involved in those discussions as well and went through multiple iterations with the players, listening to their feedback. Finally, the CCP balancing team and the community came to a compromise between innovating and staying true to the classic *EVE Online*'s feel and gameplay.

This is an example of how CCP delegates some tasks which players are adept at solving (due to deeper individual familiarity with *EVE Online*, their numbers, and their ever-emergent gameplay habits), or have better knowledge of, to the community of its customers. These tasks are also fairly mundane and peripheral to the core NSD activity. This saves the firm's resources, which frees the employees to focus on other tasks. This is reinforced by the following quote from the field notes (2014):

> Players only occasionally provide CCP with innovative ideas—it is rare for CCP to take up some completely new ideas from players' activity on forums and assimilate them into NSD.

On the other hand, in some functions of the firm, such as Quality Assurance discussed above, players' inputs can be hugely useful. In co-creation, a part of the firm's integration competence is understanding which aspects of game development it is best to apply players' inputs to. Sometimes these are fairly peripheral activities to the main NSD effort (especially in the later stages of NSD, as outlined by Hoyer et al., 2010). On other occasions, players might be co-creating high-level systems design or gameplay flow for a game's aspect in early stages of NSD. That nature of players' involvement at CCP is captured in the quote below (interviews with CCP, 2013–2014):

> Players' ideas and propositions have a very high take-up rate when it comes to balancing and tweak work [which is part of Quality Assurance activities] on *EVE Online*—amounting to roughly 70–80% of all work done.

This shows that CCP mostly follows its own vision for the game, which nevertheless is moderated by the high input from players and close monitoring of their needs. That vision is at times vehemently negotiated—as it was, for example, shown by the *Incarna* affair in 2011. Still, what seems to be of the highest priority to CCP is maintaining the good relationship with its customers, as well as ensuring that the service is tailored to their needs. This is ensured by engaging with customers in many different ways, for inputs of varying nature, across the functions of the development effort. The overall importance of involving customers in NSD is underlined in the following quote (interviews with CCP, 2013–2014):

> Players are usually very knowledgeable about the game, while developers find it at times difficult to stay on top of the shifting game dynamics. If we never listened to our customers, EVE Online would not be running.

This reflects the organizational culture which recognizes customers as valuable sources of ideas, a resource for completing more mundane NSD tasks, as well as their role overall in the firm's success. Still, probably the best reflection of CCP employees' attitudes towards the community of *EVE Online* players is captured in the following quote (interviews with CCP, 2013–2014):

> We are not the gods of EVE, we are her janitors. We help players to make EVE great. Studio has an approach characterized by humility towards their players' wishes and feedback. It is also important for the game developers to grow a thick skin, as players give all kinds of very harsh feedback. Players are central to CCP's functioning.

From that quote it appears that working with customers takes a particular type of professional attitude. The employees of CCP should be characterized by 'thick skin' and 'humility'. Those traits are promoted within the organization, and they correspond to the user involvement competence. At the same time, the NSD process at CCP can be characterized as 'customer-centric', where good service experience for customers is a priority. CCP skilfully accesses the customers' need information in-situ—meaning within the community of customers, where it is sticky (von Hippel, 2005). It then uses it, to some extent, to inform the game development efforts in-house.

Another interesting aspect of CCP's organizational culture and attitude towards co-creation in general is seeing the customer community as a new employee recruitment pool. According to the interview data (interviews with CCP, 2013–2014):

> CCP prefers to hire a new employee from amongst the players, who understand the principles and dynamics of *EVE Online*, as opposed to hiring a developer with experience in the industry, but who has not played the game.

This means that the familiarity with the culture of *EVE Online*, including the close collaboration between the customers and the studio staff, is highly prized by the firm. The firm wants to hire staff that will match and further strengthen the firm's co-creation competences. This reflects the nature of CCP as a studio tapping into the co-creation processes as a resource in NSD (to increase the resource pool of the studio) and in firm strategy (for instance to guide aspects such as enhancing existing services or ideation of new ones).

There is also a strong culture of collaboration with the customers at 5th Planet Games. According to the interviews, that collaboration is an integral part to the functioning of the 5th Planet business model. According to the words of a senior manager (interviews with 5th Planet, 2014):

> nothing at 5th Planet would work without collaboration with customers. We want the players to post things; we want them to know what we look for in their ideas, we will reply even to ridiculous ideas.

Also, in the field notes from GDC (2014) we observe:

> Lead designers are on the forums all the time. 5th Planet Games has players who have suggested whole parts of the game.

Often company employees develop personal relationships with the players on the forums, pointing to the close nature of collaboration between them and the frequency of exchanges of idea, feedback and knowledge. The general feeling and attitude of studio employees toward player inputs is captured by the following quote (interviews with 5th Planet, 2014):

> We all like to read through the feedback. We can put a product out and get immediate feedback. It is inspiring because you put your heart on everything that you put into the game. That passion of players and seeing it—that's part of why I do that job, I think everybody feels that way, that's why we love it. I have great passion for what our community produces, we are blown away by their knowledge of the game, creativity; we have players who have huge spreadsheets with data. Interesting to see that, players making those data a little bit of their own and running with it.

The above quote links back to the nature of the videogames industry overall—the mission of which is delivering positive (entertaining) experiences to the customers through its services. Listening to the customers and expanding that positive experience through co-creation appears to be the natural extension of the videogame firms' core activity, and to some degree explains the propensity of the videogames industry overall for co-creation.

An account of how co-creation relates to organizational culture was mentioned in the ArenaNet interview (2014). It underlines the new possibilities for communication arising in the wake of co-creation, thus demonstrating the organizational transformations that accompany customers' involvement in NSD:

[Co-creation] influences our company culture in two ways: it leaves us paralyzed because we see all of this community feedback contradicting itself; there is no consistent voice in our community. But it also helps us to articulate the feelings that we have about issues as individual developers to the rest of the team.

Employees know that the exchanges with customers are not always easy or pleasant. Management of players' expectations surfaces again and again as a problematic issue. That's where a dedicated community management department steps in to help 'regular' developers in communicating with the community—very often they act as intermediaries or 'filters' of information flows (from the studio to the players, but also the other way, too). Community managers are skilled in communication and public relations, and are careful to 'manage community expectations' (so that these expectations match the services and functionalities offered by the videogame). This reflects an organizational need to develop appropriate functions, such as community management or customer services, to embody some of the corresponding competences for co-creation (such as user involvement or disclosure). This is particularly well observed at ArenaNet, where the employees describe how some exchanges with the customer community are toxic because of some customers' aggressive criticism. Consequently, many employees develop 'guarded hearts' and become less inclined to even communicate with the customers (interviews with ArenaNet, 2014). Also, according to the interviews with ZOS (2013), the negativity on forums is one of the reasons why companies don't want 'line employees' to go on them, instead of leaving this task to specialized community managers (who know how not to 'fuel the hate' on Internet forums).

C: Role of Co-Creation in Firm Strategy

Over the lifetime of *EVE Online*, the degree of players' influence on the game has been changing (interviews with CCP, 2013–2014):

In the early days [of *EVE Online*] player inputs were quite innovative. Today, long-term vision has become important. Currently the players' don't really influence high-level game development activities. Productively engaging players today is more about giving them tools.

In the early days of *EVE Online*, the inputs from the players had the tendency to be more innovative and open up new trajectories for *EVE Online* gameplay. That was because the game itself was still new, and was developing in directions not always anticipated by the studio. Also, there was less competition in the market in the MMOG sector, and the market niches (such as the one occupied by *EVE Online* today) hadn't formed yet. Currently, mostly because of the existence of long-term plans for *EVE Online*'s development, as well as other titles which are designed to be integrated with *EVE Online*, players' inputs cannot influence high-level vision for the game—which is tightly linked to the studio's strategy. Instead, CCP focuses on giving players tools which allow for the emergent gameplay[15] to occur within *EVE Online*'s existing systems. This is accompanied by increasing the formalization of co-creation practices within the firm, and the recognition of its importance as a resource by the studio management and in firm strategy. Co-creation's usefulness to firms varies across the different stages of NSD—more formal and structured ways of co-creation are likely to be more applicable in the late stages of NSD, while informal and unstructured approaches might be more useful in the early stages of NSD. Similarly, players' inputs can be mapped onto O'Hern and Rindfleisch's (2010) contribution-versus-selection activity matrix, with the tasks moving across it as the NSD effort progresses. In the early NSD stages, customers will tend to be involved in selection activity as well as contribution activity. As the NSD progresses, their role in selection activity will diminish and the role in contribution activity will increase. This ensures that the studio retains its power in determining the form of the service offered while still being able to tap into the resource of customers' creativity. This general transition could also be compared to the gradual evolution of co-creation into crowdsourcing, where the tasks to be completed by the players are increasingly formalized and predetermined by the firm as the NSD progresses and a service is released. This could also be mirrored in the transition from unstructured and informal elements of co-creation to structured and formal ones. Still, this is not to say that all co-creation ultimately becomes crowdsourcing—firms can retain co-creative (in particular its unstructured and informal parts) elements even in the very late stages of NSD, as in *EVE Online*'s example. They can also determine the degree of structure and formality in their co-creative practices, as embodied by their co-creation competences.

One example of a structured element of co-creation in the very late stages of NSD is a player council (as observed in the *EVE Online* and 5th Planet cases). In *EVE Online*, the Council of Stellar Management (CSM) is a player council, and as such has come to play an important role in the firm strategy, especially after the failure of *Incarna* (an expansion to *EVE Online*) in 2011. During that time, CSM played a pivotal role in communicating and mediating between the community of very disgruntled players and the firm. This was because CSM is seen as neither part of the firm, nor part of the customer community—instead, it combines the characteristics of both. CSM is designed to fulfil the following functions (interviews with CCP, 2013–14; Oskarsson, 2014):

a. Represent players' interests and their voice, influencing the development of *EVE Online* so that players do not feel that their interests are being threatened, as well as ensuring that their feedback is given a fair consideration (for example, when CCP wants to introduce changes to ToS or EULA);

b.   Function as a review board for CCP when planning to make changes to the game, such as introducing new features, and to highlight any potential problems with these changes (for example, the balancing of *Marauder* ship, when CSM was providing direction and insight to the many iterations of developers' work);

c.   Mediate between CCP and the community in crisis or otherwise acute situations (for example, during the *Incarna* expansion's aftermath, when CSM was a conduit to speak with the estranged community in a controlled and civil manner; CSM was instrumental in calming things down and acting as a buffer for emotion-laden communications);

d.   Convey the community's sentiment and mood to CCP (for example, speaking to CSM after the release of a new expansion and inquiring how the new features and content have been received by the community).

Moreover, the inclusion of players' designs into the game serves as an element of deepening their relationship with the game (which becomes more of their creation with each such successful submission). Therefore, co-creation not only serves to improve the game by including customers' ideas into NSD, but also works as a PR and marketing tool, drawing the customers closer to the product as well as increasing the likelihood of positive network effects (manifested, for example, as favourable word of mouth and increased maximum willingness to pay; Gebauer et al., 2013; Banks and Potts, 2010). This demonstrates that co-creation can be used not only for NSD purposes, but also as a relationship-building tool, where the customers' inputs themselves are not paramount.

CSM is the most structured element of CCP's co-creation practice. Described in a dedicated white paper (Oskarsson, 2014), its goals, practices and outcomes are clearly outlined. The white paper clearly defines the procedure of electing new members, their functions, mode of communication with the firm, etc. What the document does not mention are the procedures for internal processing of CSM's suggestions and recommendations. When it comes to the internal processing of the inputs delivered by CSM, the company has a lot of freedom and choice. Only by observing CCP we perceived some consistent patterns in how the inputs from CSM are assimilated (for instance people responsible, how CSM inputs fit with project management, etc.), but these can vary from case to case. CCP also does not have the obligation to follow what CSM says, highlighting the imbalance of power between the studio and customers in co-creation (in favour of the former). The selection activity described by O'Hern and Rindfleisch (2010) for customer inputs is retained by the firm.

The role of the collaboration of CCP with its customers is demonstrated in the quote below. It expands on the observations made by Hoyer et al. (2010) and gives a sense of the strategic positioning of the resource 'crowd' in high-level organizational thinking (interviews with CCP, 2013–2014):

Community interaction can provide you with a proof of concept, make
the game more fun, instil more passion in your community, ensure business' success, and it is not an altruistic endeavour.

This quote reflects the utilitarian approach to co-creation. Customers are
a versatile and flexible resource in game development, marketing and pro-
longing the shelf life of a service. Videogames are commercial services,
which at the end of the day must generate profits for the stakeholders, and
co-creation cannot escape that paradigm (even if it's presented as a democratic process, the purpose of which is to serve the customers). A similar
account is mentioned in the field notes from CCP (2014):

People feel more vested in *EVE Online* because it gives them the opportunity to be more vested, more involved; they see the results of their
actions reflected in totality of it. Such dynamic generates terrific PR
opportunities.

Co-creation is, in a way, a non-zero-sum game. It is beneficial to both the
firm and the customers—the firm gets to offer a better service with increased
shelf life and dedicated customer base, while the customers can enjoy a service which better matches their needs and preferences (some of the customers, by co-creating, benefit by belonging to a community, developing their
skills, etc. as outlined by von Hippel, 2005).

Firm strategy trickles down to the service design decisions and implemen-
tations that employees make. The role of the players within the game, the
degree of their freedom in managing gameplay, and the game's technological
availability for reconfiguration (by modding for instance) are all determined
by those decisions—so is the relationship and working closeness of employees to the customers.

Interestingly, once embraced, co-creation seems to transform all functions
of the firm, and becomes an indispensable element of its functioning and its
service offering. In other words, a firm would find it difficult to cease co-
creating with its customers without endangering the market performance of
the service itself (see Banks, 2013 for a case study of co-creation failure).
NSD, marketing and co-creation become involved in a symbiotic relationship. According to the interviews with CCP (2013–2014):

EVE Online is a game designed to be open-ended, which is the cornerstone of allowing a wide array of player inputs into it. In such a game, it
is vital to follow the flow of players' gameplay patters. As much contact
as possible with the community of players is absolutely essential. *EVE
Online* can't really survive without it.

Here we observe how the close interaction with customers has become the
pivotal element of the firm's business model. Co-creation has become an

integral part of the firm's functioning. It has been recognized by the firm strategy, and the resource 'crowd' in its context is regarded as strategic. Such prevalent attitude in both the organization's functioning and culture is a significant facilitator of co-creation practice, as it reinforces the symbiotic relationship between a studio's NSD and marketing functions, and co-creation.

Case Gamma

Cloud Imperium Games (CIG) became well known even before the release of their first game. Founded in 2012 and having offices all over the world (from California, via Texas, to United Kingdom and Germany), it is helmed by a widely renowned videogames designer Chris Roberts. In the course of the crowdfunding campaign for the *Star Citizen*, their yet unreleased game, the studio has gathered over 156 million USD in funds from its community (as of July 2017; the crowdfunding campaign is still ongoing). Contrary to what we observe in Case Alpha (Obisidian Entertainment), where the crowdfunding campaign had a clear beginning and end, and after which the studio functioned without much input from its customers, CIG decided to do otherwise. The crowdfunding campaign has been going on since the announcement of the project in 2012 and is still active today.[16] According to the studio description on the company's official website:[17]

> CIG aims to pave new ground in game development by sharing the process with the players. Where game development was once hidden, Cloud Imperium has opted to share the process with those backing Star Citizen. Supporters come to know the team and follow them every step of the way as the game created. The community is closely engaged and their feedback is considered in all aspects of game development, avoiding standard publicity to put Roberts' epic vision directly in players' hands.

In CIG case, the customers pay the studio to be a part of the NSD process as external observers, advisors and voters. There is a large variety of ways in which the studio extracts revenue from its customers—for example, through the sales of in-game accessories (note that the game still has not been released), or through a monthly subscription fee to have privileged access to the game development information. Co-creation which occurs in such a context is unlike its counterparts in Cases Alpha and Beta, in terms of its structure, formality and purpose.

The observations from CIG are accompanied by the insights gathered at Born Ready Games, a British game development studio which developed the *Strike Suit Zero* (2013). The studio also relied on crowdfunding to finance its NSD, raising approximately 175,000 USD on Kickstarter.com.[18] Interestingly, this crowdfunding effort was conducted towards the end of the NSD, which is a unique occurrence—as crowdfunding is normally used to raise initial funding for a service. Nevertheless, this approach makes Born Ready Games similar to CIG, where the firm tapped into its existing community of customers for funds to improve the game already in development.

Case Gamma also represents an example of unstructured co-creation practice on the level of the everyday practices of CIG. Many of the co-creative mechanisms and interactions occur informally between the players and studio staff. Still, on the level of organizational strategy and business model, the practice of co-creation is well-recognized and vital to the player relationship-building activities of CIG. In this case study, we observe how co-creation can occur via the individual relationships between employees and members of the customer community, without many formal practices associated with it, while at the same time being recognized formally by the studio management as a process vital to its business model (unlike the Case Beta and CCP, where co-creation was vital to the NSD effort).

Co-creation at CIG is very different from that described in Cases Alpha and Beta. *Star Citizen* has already gained popularity and media attention while still being in development. When eventually released, it will consist of numerous modules of gameplay, each of them different and belonging to a different genre—making it a very ambitious videogame project (normally studios develop games belonging to a single, narrowly defined genre, and attempts at mixing genres have a high risk of failure). *Star Citizen* will be a MMO title, but at the same time it will be a space simulator, as well as contain a single-player storyline. CIG has adopted a model of continuous crowdfunding of its game, where the players, in lieu of being able to play the actual game, are invited to participate in the game development process. From the field notes from CIG (2015):

> This participation is not simply about accepting as many customers' inputs into NSD as possible. Because of its unique funding arrangement, CIG engages in such extensive co-creation in order to maintain continued influx of monies into its project. The richer, closer and more engaged the relationship of CIG with its customers, the more money those customers are spending on game production updates, purchasing of service add-ons, or spread the word of it to their fellow players.

CIG's approach could be described as having players subscribe to game development and observe it, as well as have the power to influence some aspects of it. The company has been gathering funds in that manner since the very beginning of the project (initially the Kickstarter platform was used, but immediately after it the crowdfunding campaign was moved to *Star Citizen*'s own website[19]). To illustrate that point is the analysis of CIG's website (2015):

> The initial funding goal for the game was 500.000 USD. Within one month (and at the end of that Kickstarter campaign) the game has

gathered over 2.1 million USD, and went on to continue gathering funds via its own website. These funds come from the sales of in-game assets, subscriptions to special updates, customization items, discounts, priority tickets to various community events, as well as access to early testing opportunities and viewing of in-progress works of the studio.

The case of CIG is largely defined by the unique function of customers in its co-creation efforts. They are fans as well as a source of funding, and the company has found a way to directly transform the strength of that relationship into money. It is possible to be a fan of the game and follow it without paying any money; but it is the paying customers who enjoy deeper (or facilitated) access to the firm as well as are recognized as part of the *Star Citizen* development effort. Hence, apart from unstructured co-creation practice, we observe the transformative influence of co-creation on the functioning of the firm—including profound changes to its revenue streams, business model and strategy.

To CIG, the main benefit of community involvement in game development is the boosting and maintenance of the relationship with its customers. We can classify the nature of co-creation occurring at CIG as 'co-creation for relationship', as it is the continued interest and support from the customers that keeps the NSD effort going at CIG. According to the field notes from CIG (2015):

> CIG seeks to make the experience of *Star Citizen* different than just "consuming something"—instead, the company speaks of '*Star Citizen* Universe' which is to elicit the feelings of belonging from the customers, and which encompasses not only the game, but also the community of fans and the firm. The experience of *Star Citizen* is about participation in the making of a 'landmark' project, an ambitious game that follows in the footsteps of *Wing Commander* games (which themselves are widely regarded as excellent, and have also been helmed by Chris Roberts).

Heavy focus on the customer relationship in all firm activities and placing it at the centre of CIG's business model has more benefits than tapping into innovative revenue streams. It allows for harnessing word of mouth and social network in marketing, advertising and generation of positive publicity for the game. For instance, the marketing materials developed by the fans (such as video reviews) are considered more authentic by fellow community members, and their recommendations are more trusted than the studio's or established press opinions. This is even admitted by the studio employees, who recognize the value of user-generated content on social media such as YouTube, Twitter, Twitch, various forums and others (interviews with CIG; 2014–2015):

Videos from fans have different flavour; they feel more authentic than our marketing materials.

CIG's management frames their goal for community involvement more as an empowerment of the customers, rather than just harvesting their labour or creativity (something that we also see at Square Enix Collective; interviews, 2014). That high-level objective sets the tone for all co-creative exchanges between customers and the firm, thus underlining the importance of firm strategy (and articulation of its goals and use of resources) for shaping the practice of co-creation. Such attitude also reflects a certain degree of trust that the firm has in its customers, and is linked to the informal and unstructured forms of co-creation (where the customers are treated more as equals and partners rather than a resource). On the other hand, CIG taps en masse into the unique benefits of having customers engaged as marketers and advocates for the service. The company has realized that the best way to achieve that is to enable individual relationships between key community members and the firm's employees to develop. These reinforce the narrative of partnership between players and the studio in *Star Citizen* development, and frame the ongoing crowdsourcing campaign as a joint effort in realizing an ambitious project.

Consequently, CIG doesn't appear interested in the customers' inputs as new ideas or improvements to the NSD itself. We read in the field notes from CIG (2015):

> CIG doesn't provide its customers with many incentives to get involved in co-creation for NSD. A studio such as CIG has an ample capacity for production of assets (be they art, programming, sound or any others) in-house. Frequent and ubiquitous inputs from customers could easily disrupt already difficult (because geographically dispersed, and because it is the firm's very first development) NSD processes.

The studio's employees are creative professionals and the general sentiment at the firm is that (interviews with CIG, 2014–2015):

> we already have more material than we can work with; we don't need more material. Best material gets filtered by the community and highlighted, because it is so active.

The latter half of the above quote demonstrates that some content produced by the community is of interest to CIG, although the expectations for the quality of that content are very high. In the context of the young age of the firm and its relative inexperience (employees haven't been working together for long; teams and line managers aren't yet well established; the organizational culture doesn't have a long tradition; the business model of the firm is highly innovative and different from even the most experienced employees' professional track record), the increased protection of the firm's formal structure and processes is warranted. If customers were allowed to interfere with those processes with their inputs coming via highly formalized channels, the disruptions to NSD stemming from the vastly increased workload and staff responsibilities shifted towards curation of external inputs would be too hard to manage and the whole game development effort would be at risk.

Hence co-creation at CIG is seen primarily as a marketing device, but its capacity for occasional generation of high-quality inputs to game development is recognized. In the course of Case Gamma, we observe one highly structured co-creation practice—one which, despite its usefulness at producing high-quality NSD inputs, is still heavily geared towards marketing and customer relationship benefits. Moreover, the huge amount of feedback on forums helps the studio with prioritization of game development tasks (as the game is still in development and is being released in modules or interoperable pieces). The examples of that are customization of controls and leaderboards.

One manifestation of user involvement competence at CIG is the profiling of the community of its customers. The studio understands the differences in various players' involvement as co-creators, akin to what Burger-Helmchen and Cohendet (2011) described (interviews with CIG, 2014–2015):

> We have some players who pledged very early and those players will have different weight to their opinion than people who just joined.

Those oldest supporters of the project are an important asset to the company's strategy; they are considered 'core' audience for the game, who create positive word of mouth and set the tone and culture for the community of customers. It is also predominantly those customers who have the individual relationships with employees of the firm (for example, their usernames are recognized by the studio employees in various forms of communication). This is in line with Burger-Helmchen and Cohendet's (2011) observations, as well as those of von Hippel (2005), who identify lead users and customers who are overall involved in the design and development of the service itself. Recognizing those users and enabling them to co-create with the firm empowers them and motivates them to continue generating valuable inputs, suggestions and ideas.

CIG, thanks to its emphasis on the individual relationships between employees and customers, has a good ability to identify those pivotal key members of the customer community and respond to their needs. The role of that aspect of user involvement competence is underlined in the field notes from CIG (2015):

> The community's overall sentiment is an important indicator for the studio. Knowing that the players agree or are happy reaffirms the

direction of the studio's work and employees feel that they are 'on the right track'. Dissenting voices are also of importance to the developers and are not ignored—trying to figure out why players don't like the game or some of its aspects can be equally important.

This allows the firm to understand what is happening within their community. CIG constantly takes the pulse of it—whether customers are happy with new additions to the game, what they might need, how likely they are to recommend the game to others, etc. This is of vital importance to the CIG's revenue model as well—with unhappy or dissatisfied customers, who are estranged from the development team and process, the influx of monies from the ongoing crowdfunding campaign might be reduced. The firm is highly dependent on the positive word of mouth and social media marketing. That's why it prioritizes customer relations and community management activities, with numerous channels, initiatives and tools (they will be discussed in more detail below). These efforts of CIG are answered by the players, who are involved and emotionally invested in the yet-unreleased game, which is highlighted in the following quote (interviews with CIG, 2014–2015):

> [What is also great about the community is] the fact that the community has the patience, and they are really into giving their feedback—which is opposite from a normal focus group. They want to give the feedback, they are invested in the quality of feedback that they are giving.

The firm recognizes the unique nature of inputs that the customers can provide to its NSD. Players contribute to certain functions of the firm, such as quality assurance (as we also saw in the case of CCP) differently than for instance externally contracted firms or professional groups. In quality assurance, internal testing conducted by a firm can be formulaic and regimented, while player testing is free and unrestricted; thus players are more likely to come up with new things or non-standard approaches. Players are better at testing the boundaries of the software (so called 'stress testing') and interacting with it in ways not always foreseen by the developers. This can also have a positive effect on the morale of staff, who can see the effects of their labour in actual use by intended audiences. It also has the added benefit of breaking up the routines dominant in the workplace. This is reflected by the following quote (interviews with CIG, 2014–2015):

> YouTube is almost like a database of bugs. Good for us to be able to see players having fun. QA can sometimes be boring, the same. Seeing people doing crazy stuff makes our staff a bit happier.

The above are the examples of CIG's user involvement competence, as well as its roots in the organizational culture and firm strategy (related to the recognition of the role of customers in the non-NSD functions of the firm—funding, marketing and quality assurance in particular). CIG's ability to identify and establish relationships with key community members is the best illustration of user involvement competence. In the following sections we observe how this is linked to organizational culture, as well as the funding arrangements.

This occurs in the context of unstructured co-creation practice, where customer inputs are rather reluctantly assimilated formally by the firm (in particular via visible and official channels). At the same time, through the dynamics akin to hidden innovation, we notice that the individual staff are open to receiving some ideas (in particular feedback and improvements on the employees' ideas) and collaborating with the members of customer community. At the same time, studio management allows this due to the benefits to the customer relationship, which then is translated into the influx of monies and positive word-of-mouth marketing (Gebauer et al., 2013). This is illustrated in the field notes from the visits to CIG offices (2015):

> At CIG offices employees communicate directly to a few members of the customer community. They recognize them by their forum handle or some other nickname. They communicate via forums but not only— sometimes also via email or Skype, as their relationship grows more personal. This is further strengthened by the fact that CIG approves of fans' visits to the offices. During those visits, after a general tour, the fans will sit down with individual employees at their work stations. CIG employees are enthusiastic about their exchanges with members of the community, they treat them almost as an extension to the intra-studio game development team. They genuinely respect the inputs from the customers, as they see them as mature, of high quality, and quite professional in nature.

This dichotomy between the lack of formal channels for customer inputs and the enthusiasm towards it displayed by the line employees constitutes the cornerstone of the unstructured practice of co-creation at CIG. The high informality of processing customer inputs emphasizes the relationship-building role of co-creation at CIG. It also demonstrates the function of lead users emerging from among the customers (i.e., established community members who have been consistently providing the studio with constructive inputs, have been with the *Star Citizen* development effort from the start, and who established social links to individual employees) as the actual contributors to the NSD and the design of the game, in the fashion described by von Hippel (2005).

Contrary to the lead user inputs described above, the contributions from the majority of customers tend to be small contributions and improvements along the existing trajectories of firm's game development efforts. This is reflected in practice by the fact that CIG customers are mostly involved in contributing to QA, and it corroborates the observations of

Burger-Helmchen and Cohendet (2011) in academic theory. It is also illustrated by the CIG field notes (2015):

> The employees at CIG do not recall a single 'big', innovative input from the community, but they do admit to having assimilated many small ideas and suggestions. In their own words, these were "good ideas that we decided to use".

Overall, the changes suggested by the customers are implemented only if the lead systems design (i.e., a senior function within the game development) agrees with those changes. This process is similar to the route taken by new ideas generated by employees themselves: the lead systems designer needs to approve all changes to the NSD, including those introduced by the staff. At CIG, many customer inputs enter the organization at the level of individual employees via the relationships described above, and then follow that single route for all changes and ideas, whether originating internally or externally. The question remains how many of those customers' inputs are later bundled and not differentiated from the ideas generated by the employees themselves, and approved as internal by lead systems design (also, whether the categories of 'internal' and 'external' exist at all for various ideas and suggestions). A brief overview of that practice follows (interviews with CIG, 2014–2015):

> We do respond to players' suggestions for changes to the game or new features; those do get filtered up [within the studio]. Those suggestions do not precipitate huge changes to the game, but we definitely look at them. A lot of feedback is about players' commenting on how things should work in-game, that we get a lot of. Still, at CIG the design department is more involved in the blue sky thinking stuff. It is the QA staff who gathers all the information from feedback and condenses it into a format which is then conveyed to the design team and to Chris Roberts [CEO]. I can't remember one massive thing [a piece of feedback from customers that would influence NSD] though.

Overall, CIG has the practice of releasing a lot of information to the community of customers so they can comment and build on those materials. From their comments, CIG can also learn whether the players will like a particular feature, or whether it needs some changes before implementation. This practice can serve to further strengthen co-creation through the mechanism of hidden innovation (interviews with CIG, 2014–2015):

> Players are often riffing off the ideas that we give them, or come up with their own ideas.

There is no doubt that there is close collaboration between employees and customers in the game development, which could be working in the two-way fashion (as implied in the quote above). A degree of 'cross-pollination' of ideas takes place in the conditions of close relationship and informal (and content-rich) communications between the studio staff and customers. Still, the majority of customers do not appear to provide feedback that would be valuable from the NSD perspective. A note from the field notes (2015) says:

> The inputs of customers to NSD at CIG are limited and pertain mostly to the functions of providing feedback and validating the decisions made by the firm.

Again, this corresponds to Burger-Helmchen and Cohendet's (2011) bottom layer of the pyramid classifying co-creating customers, and underlines the fact that co-creative activity at CIG is mostly for relationship-building purposes. Moreover, the category of 'feedback provision' is very broad, where the exact nature of the feedback given (and how much novelty is contained within it) is difficult to capture. Such elusive nature of the contents of co-creation in terms of their innovative potential confirms the observations of Miles and Green (2008) about hidden innovation.

It would appear that in Case Gamma, the minority of players are seen as having some valuable knowledge, although they are not trusted as innovators (interviews with ICO Partners, 2014). The majority of players can be useful as stress testers or providers of inputs to QA, but most importantly they are considered a resource for marketing and (in the case of CIG, but also OE in Case Alpha) funding. Players are not professional game developers; they don't understand the business rationale of making videogames, as well as they can easily stray from the core vision for the service. They cannot articulate their own needs (von Hippel, 2005) and often will favour incremental improvements over radical innovation (Aoyama and Izushi, 2008). A similar trend is observed at Born Ready Games, where the dominant opinion is that customers are very enthusiastic to aid the studio in its NSD efforts, but at the same time they are 'child-like', i.e., their inputs do not always fit with the vision for the service, or are unrealistic to implement (interviews with Born Ready Games, 2014).

Benefits of Co-Creation

The importance of co-creation with customers for its relationship-building purposes is prioritized at CIG, as it has direct consequences for the firm's revenue streams and marketing effort. According to the interviews with CIG (2014–2015):

> Players' feedback has defined some of the directions we have taken with the game in macro and micro scale.

From that we see that customer inputs do influence CIG to some extent even on the high level of service design. The firm responds to the preferences and wishes of the players—although, as we demonstrate below, it does not follow them blindly. The studio stays true to its own videogame development experiences and skills, and all changes requested (or, at times, demanded!) by players are carefully negotiated and considered. The primary form of CIG's interaction with the community of customers is via forums (interviews with CIG, 2014–2015):

> We have very active forums; people post their hearts out there. We want people to have the conversations there, and to have our players posting their work. We watch that and we swoop in when there is something special there, we start working with that person. . . .

That again demonstrates that CIG engages in true co-creation only with select players: the lead users (von Hippel, 2005) or customers occupying the top of Burger-Helmchen and Cohendet's (2011) pyramid. Further details are provided in another interview with a CIG employee which point to the individual relations between the firm employees and customers that cross the firm boundary and that, by the mechanism of hidden innovation, contribute to informal co-creation (2014–2015):

> A lot of people in the studio are giving one to one feedback to people on forums: coders do that, designers do that, and writers do that too.

Apart from that informal co-creation, the studio also has mechanisms for building the relationships with its customers. Here the official website of the game plays an important role. Its design is very player-centric—it has sections dedicated to the crowdfunding players available only once a player backs the crowdfunding effort or subscribes to the game development updates. The website also reports a lot of information to the community on the latest developments in the NSD effort, which resembles the communications that videogame developers would normally have with producers or publishers.[20] According to the analysis of the Roberts Space Industries[21] website (2015):

> There is a significant amount of communication on the website between the studio and the players. The website has a section dedicated to forums, which are the main communication channel between the firm and the fans. There is also plenty of information about the crowdfunding effort—how much money has been raised so far, per month, per day, per hour, etc., with many graphs, special achievements and options to display the information in different ways. There are also sections where the customers can contribute money to *Star Citizen* in different ways (and with many financial tiers), as well as buy various in-game enhancements and items.

The website is an excellent demonstration of the co-location of a co-creation interface together with a crowdfunding conduit. It gives the primacy to the player, and puts the community of customers at the centre of attention—recent activities, development, player contributions (such as printing of the game's starships designs using 3D printers). It emphasizes the perception of the democratic nature of *Star Citizen* development—downplaying the role of the studio and glorifying the player community, underlining the collaborative aspects and spirit of *Star Citizen*. Related practices in other channels are described in the field notes from CIG (2015):

> CIG has a major YouTube channel—'Around the Verse', which is meant to be more of a fan interaction-based show. Comments are left under each video episode on YouTube, which [comments section] functions almost like another forum. The company also uses more bespoke channels, for when the players are encouraged to discuss various topics—for example, in response to 'ask a developer' blog posts. The company regularly releases fanzines which collate information, as well as makes sure that official and dedicated wikis are updated. CIG also uses other channels for listening to the customers—for example, voice chat in the released portions of the game, when the QA department will be playing with or against the community.

Additional details are provided when reading further into the field notes from CIG (2015):

> It is not just the community management or customer support employees who read the forums and observe social media. Everybody within the organization is encouraged to do so. Chris Roberts is "obsessive" [according to the words of one employee] with reading forums and listening to players' opinions. The figure of Chris Roberts remains very present and involved in the continued communications with the community. Among the fans he is considered a visionary and his name carries a huge weight in shaping the fandom around Star Citizen. His attitude towards players and listening to their input is widely known both within and outside of CIG. He often personally responds to forum threads, as well as regularly creates videos called 'Ten for the Chairman' in which he answers community's questions and provides updates about the latest game developments and what's happening at the studio.

All of the above points to the wide array of diverse and established methods of communicating with customers used by CIG. Their role is to inform about the game, market it, ensure the continued influx of monies into the development effort, provide channels for interaction with the community of customers, offer help and customer support, as well as to promote co-creation. Not all interaction taking place via these channels is co-creation; in fact, co-creation constitutes a minority of all activity. Nevertheless, it is in those conditions of well-structured, diverse, enticing and vibrant conditions of interaction between the players and studio staff that co-creation can originate and develop. This points to the high user involvement and disclosure competences on the part of CIG, where the firm has the ability to tailor its interactions with customers depending on its needs and moment in NSD. The approach towards co-creation is informal and unstructured, strongly correlated with employees' interactions with involved and engaged customers on an everyday, 'on-the-job' basis.

CIG organizes contests for the players to submit entries based on their ideas for *Star Citizen*. Next Great Starship (NGS) was a contest conducted in 2014 which provided both the firm and the customer community with many benefits. For instance, it primarily resulted in CIG boosting its relationship with customers, demonstrating the central role of players in *Star Citizen* development, receiving some high-quality ship designs to be included in the game, as well as gaining exposure with new customer groups and market segments. For the customers, the most interesting result was the top contestants getting employed by the studio (as well as prestige and community standing to the contestants whose designs were accepted into the game, considerable monetary prizes, learning experience, etc.). For the studio, the usefulness of such format of customer inputs to game development is highlighted in the following quote (interviews with CIG, 2014–2015):

> NGS is a great way of having players produce assets, but they have their own pipelines, so good to keep things formalized and separated.

It points out to the fact that for a studio it is often difficult to integrate player inputs with internal game development, as the routines, technology and standards of work are different for the company and for an individual external contributor. A contest allows for bypassing this problem. The contest format also has the advantage of creating formal and clear rules for what happens with customer inputs—for example, allowing for alleviating intellectual property concerns (Edwards et al., 2015), setting clear quality expectations and criteria, or preventing accusations of being unfair or biased in the selection of the winner (Gebauer et al., 2013).

NGS is an example of structured and formal co-creation practice taking place at CIG. This demonstrates that CIG has the ability to use both structured, as well as unstructured forms of co-creation. The firm has the competences, as well as strategic vision to deploy co-creation as a process driven by the firm and contributing to the studio's bottom line of customer relationship gains, primarily. A contest such as NGS is a highly visible method for attracting customers' attention and producing positive word-of-mouth effects across their communities—and as such it has powerful marketing benefits. This is illustrated in the analysis of the contest website (2014):

> Many of the highly engaged customers aspire to be employed by CIG or to work in the games industry. NGS shows them that such fantasies

can be true; it borrows its format from similar very successful TV shows (The X Factor, Britain's Got Talent). The provision of inputs to NSD is a valuable function of this contest, but still it is probably the marketing outcomes (positive word of mouth, increased willingness to contribute money to the development effort) which are its key benefits. NGS produces high-quality inputs (from the entries and works of the contestants), identifies candidates for employment (the winners, apart from money, are offered jobs by CIG), as well as creates a lot of very positive word of mouth. CIG also improves its public image: it is shown as being fair, transparent, modern and loving its customers and their community.

The ability to stage such a contest, which was done by CIG with very high production value, is a reflection of strong user involvement and appropriation competences for co-creation.[22]

The studio also organizes physical gatherings with players—at large game industry events (such as Gamescom in Germany), but also it has its own dedicated annual event called CitizenCon. From the CIG field notes (2015):

> During CitizenCon the company presents the players with large updates on the development of the game, reveals new content, and communicates with them on a personal basis. It improves its overall relationship with customers.

Apart from that, CIG accepts the studio visits form regular fans (and not only from player council members at a designated time, as in Case Beta). The account of this comes from the field notes from CIG (2015):

> People fly in from all over the world and have a tour around the studio, and game developers chat to them and show them what they are currently working on. Those visits need to be prearranged, but they are a direct interaction between the community and the firm—a phenomenon unique in the game industry at large, as developers tend to be reclusive and focused on game development effort. The developers at CIG enjoy these tours: once a month on average they have a group of backers, show them what they are doing, spend half a day with them, show stuff that's not out yet . . . Those fans can talk one to one with developers, and individual developers will often take individual fans to their workstations to discuss things.

Soliciting such visits reflects the resources that CIG devotes to building and maintaining a good relationship with its customers. The studio visitors talk to the game developers, for whom this is a distraction from their core duties (of coding, art creation, game design, sound engineering, etc.). Still, through these conversations, the visits might have a role in creativity exchanges and co-creation of the game. This is illustrated in the interviews with CIG employees (2014–2015):

> We don't know until the players come, whether those visits will be beneficial in terms of creativity or ideas. We certainly want to give things back to our players, to show them gratitude for their support and money. It also gives us good feedback whilst they are here, and showing what they really want.

The quote above again emphasizes the role of visits in relationship building, but it also points to the feedback that game developers receive from the customers. In the course of informal discussions at the workstations, or during conversations at fan gatherings, ideas could be exchanged between the customers and the employees. More commonly, the developers receive direct feedback from the players on the game features—which, as we saw in the Case Gamma (CCP), tends to be more honest than when provided via forums or other formal channels. This again underlines the importance of informal communication with customers as an important form of co-creation in firms, and the co-location of hidden innovation with unstructured co-creation practice.

Organizational Practices: Integration Competence

CIG is characterized by a dispersed organizational structure. Its intra-organizational communications, work delivery and task management rely heavily on the use of the Internet. It can be easier to integrate customers with internal processes. With such a dispersed organizational structure, CIG could be particularly prone to disruptions arising from co-creation—i.e., attempting to assimilate inputs from outside of its structure. What is more, CIG is a young company which is still developing its practices, consolidating its organizational culture, and changing internal routines and project management approaches. It also has a compartmentalized structure—with some of CIG's subsidiaries (such as Foundry 42) being separate, self-contained studios themselves, with their own routines and culture. CIG's business model, relying on continued funding and focus on relationship building with the customers, as well as modular releasing of game elements, is unseen before in the industry. In such context, assimilating en masse external inputs from customers could add to the already high uncertainty, thus resulting in heavy disruptions to the firm's work. That's why integration competence at CIG is manifested by its emphasis on the 'on-the-job' co-creation, occurring between individual employees and customers in a highly informal manner. This is illustrated by the following paragraph from the field notes from CIG (2015):

> There isn't an established practice for processing player inputs. At CIG, it is done in a more organic way—because of individual communications between the developers [i.e., studio employees] and members of

the customer community, many ideas and player inputs are looked at and considered by the developers, who then discuss them informally and on an 'on-the-job' basis with their colleagues.

This kind of practice fits the definition of hidden innovation well (Miles and Green, 2008). Nevertheless, we identified some practices for assimilating customer inputs at CIG. These practices reflect the firm's integration and appropriation competences. In the field notes from CIG (2015):

> What happens most often is as follows: a list of interesting player suggestions is made by the Quality Assurance or Customer Services staff, passed on to the relevant group within the company. At the end of the day game design employees look at this list and flag the interesting ideas, then it goes to Chris Roberts [the CEO] who makes decisions.

Apart from that general, company-wide practice, we also observe more specialized practices of co-creation (of integrating players' inputs into NSD). We read in the field notes (2015):

> The job of QA, apart from the usual responsibilities of testing the game and fixing the bugs, is to filter all the comments from the community, and production of a list. That list contains the summary of the feedback and commenting activity going on at the forums. It is sent out by email to all of CIG production team, as well as to the entire leads team (leads team is composed of the decision-makers in every major aspect of game production, such as programing, art, design, animation, and sound). It is part of a QA specialists' job to read the feedback and to prepare that list. It tends to be collected two days after a patch is released.

Accurate conveyance of customers' sentiment is of importance in the context of such practices and is something that co-creation practices within CIG rely on (interviews with CIG, 2014–2015):

> When we [the QA staff] send the email with 'community feedback digest' to production and leads, all of QA is cc'ed [sic] on it. We [the QA staff] as a department are passing on both positive and negative feedback from customers. Feedback is passed on and received, but not always acted upon by the production. Leads will highlight some things that they think are most important. Production sometimes will get back to us and ask to investigate something in more detail, to see how much validity there is in a piece of feedback. This is accompanied by a lot of talking to different people around the company. The way we deal with such feedback grows and changes. The main pattern I see is that the things that get looked at the most are the things that have most forum threads about them.

The practice described above is to large extent informal and does not have a fixed routine. This underlines the unstructured practice of co-creation at CIG, which is enabled by the firm's integration and appropriation competences for co-creation. The quote above also demonstrates how disruptive external inputs from the customers can be to an organization. The amount of discussions and people involved following on receiving feedback from the players could easily have negative implications for the usual work practices of individual employees, causing the firm to decrease its resource use efficiency. The feedback itself might not be worth such an expenditure (as it can be biased, incorrect, uninformed about business or technical realities, etc.)—hence underpinning the precarious nature of co-creation.

CIG uses agile game development methodology (a methodology in which requirements and solutions evolve through collaboration between self-organizing, cross-functional teams, emphasizing face-to-face communication, frequent delivery of new deployable business value and collaboration between the development team and business experts; Agile Alliance, 2015). CIG also uses project management software assisting in tracking various tasks within the organization—Jira. The studio also uses various milestones. Those NSD approaches facilitate the use of co-creation in the organization by making the organization more capable of processing external inputs which do not fit easily into any particular department's responsibilities. Similarly, agile game development methodologies are used at Born Ready Games. From the interviews with Born Ready Games (2014):

> Inputs from customers go into backlog and become a task to be completed by the firm. Customer inputs are vetted for their suitability and quality as they are received by the firm, although this practice (despite being unstructured and subjective) is seen as adequate, as employees screening the customers' ideas are professionals.

Born Ready Games practices emphasize the individual employees' ability to screen, process and approve (or reject) the inputs from customers. This underlines their role in co-creation, where the studio staff duties are expanded to include those of curators of external inputs (a dynamic that we also see at CIG and in other cases presented in this book). In agile videogame development methodologies, such skills are instrumental to quick decision-making, 'on-the-job' judgments (e.g., whether a customer input has merit or not), and overall to the firms' integration competences.

Organizational Culture

Organizational culture appears to have a pronounced effect on co-creation practice in firms. It determines the way in which studio managers see their customers, and how their usefulness as a resource is framed in the long-term strategy. Decisions such as use of crowdfunding, or asking the players for help with QA testing or generation of non-critical software assets, are connected to organizational culture. An overview of CIG's organizational culture is conveyed in the field notes (2015):

> The company treats its close links to the community as one of its priorities, and the culture at CIG appears largely customer-centric.

This strategy is linked to the practices and 'on-the-job' attitudes of the developers towards the customers, and influences the informal interactions between these two groups. CIG uses multiple methods to forge closer links between itself and the community of customers. Again, from the CIG field notes (2015):

> Some players who are active on forums and who contribute regularly have their names recognized by the developers. Developers recognize those players for good or bad. All developers are encouraged to go on the CIG chat and speak to the backers [i.e., players who have contributed funds during the crowdfunding campaign]. Some CIG employees are online all the time on game chats, talking to players and just 'being themselves'. They not only talk about the game, and work with the customers.

Open links between the development team and the customers are uncommon in the videogames industry at large, and are a unique feature of CIG's organizational culture (interviews with CIG, 2014–2015):

> Some people are better at [communicating with players], and some people are worse at it. We push the culture of going out and answering questions, letting people know in the community. In the games industry, it is common not being allowed to share things with the customers, but here we encourage developers to share.

As a result, the players are advocates for the game, generating positive word-of-mouth effects (and helping the game marketing in the long run). The studio also taps into their ability to come up with feedback, as well as at times insightful and creative inputs (interviews with CIG, 2014–2015):

> One good thing about the way we build games with community is that everyone sees the community as a part of the team, extended part of the team. People are open about getting feedback. When it comes to the community inputs their ideas are very appreciated.

CIG attempts to include players' feedback in various elements of the game, but they also point out to the players that the game is still work in progress (field notes from CIG, 2015). That integration of customer inputs constructs

Star Citizen as an artefact attributed both to the company, as well as to the players (such players' 'ownership' of the game functions only in the socio-cultural dimension; in the market dimension the ownership is purely that of the company, as per the usual crowdfunding rules). That also serves to forge working relationship between the community and the firm, creating a rich environment for game marketing through social network channels and co-creation in NSD. Furthermore, some aspects of engaging customers have a positive impact on the employees' morale: players' messages approving of new features in their comments on forums, high-quality fan art, or positive interactions with players (either online, or during studio visits or fan gatherings).

CIG's customer-focused organizational culture has been introduced by Chris Roberts, the founder and CEO (who himself is an experienced video-game developer). From the CIG field notes (2015):

> Chris Roberts sets the tone for, and leads by example the interactions with the customers. His strategic vision for the firm influences CIG's organizational attitude towards the players, and places them at the centre of CIG's marketing and funding efforts. He is deeply engaged with the community members.

This attitude permeates the company and is adopted throughout the organizational ranks (interviews with CIG, 2014–2015):

> You watch people around the company talking with the players, and then you start realizing the benefit of it. And you just adopt it and want to see how it's like and how it works. I had never done it before at other studios [in previous employment]. Here aren't solid 'ten commandments' on the wall; we are all just watching Chris Roberts and seeing that he has all those fans around, and respecting that. It has never been said that we are supposed to listen [to the customers]. Maybe it trickles down from the top in the company emails, that at CIG we are listening to everyone's voice.

This organizational culture and attitude is also viewed by the employees as an advantage, making their current workplace different and more interesting from their previous experiences. Developers appreciate not only the relaxed culture of communicating with the players, for whom the game is essentially being made, but also having access to customers' feedback in their everyday duties. This is reflected in the following quote (interviews with CIG, 2014–2015):

> I think that approach [to customers] is definitely open. People [at CIG] come with this fresh, hopeful stance, and no one has been critical of it. Everyone is excited about being so close to the players. The culture

[at CIG] is open, but no one is too worried about it. I think such an approach is worth its risks; that's what makes our studio different.

Similar characteristics are observed at Born Ready Games, where the CEO is also a proponent of integrating feedback from customers into NSD. The focus is placed on improving the organizational ability to listen to the customers. This is manifested by the hiring of external firms specializing in analyzing customer behaviour (interviews with Born Ready Games, 2014). Such close integration of customers with organizational strategy and NSD practices is a sentiment shared by many firms in the videogames industry overall (interviews with UKIE, 2014). That in turn causes the general shift in the practices of that industry, which is becoming more customer-centric. The culture of its organizations and attitudes of game development professionals are increasingly open to communication and inputs from the players, as the firms recognize and learn to harness the resource of customer community.

Still, that transition does not come without any problems. There are some concerns at CIG when collaborating closely with the customers. One such example is the exploitation of the customers by firms. We see an example of this in the CIG field notes (2015):

The worry is of ethical nature (but also one that translates itself into issues of legal ownership, need for remuneration or acknowledgment of intellectual property), and pertains to the point at which accepting high-quality customer inputs, even if freely given, becomes problematic.

Issues like that are symptomatic for the participatory culture at large, and it is not only CIG that faces them. Co-creation as a NSD practice requires resolving accompanying legal and ethical problems (pertaining to the intellectual property, copyright, nature of exploitation, free labour, audiences consisting of minors, etc.) before it can be adopted with ease by majority of firms. At CIG, one answer to that concern was having players offering their inputs by participating in a contest—such as Next Great Starship. That way, the rules governing players' collaboration with the company, as well as the issues of ownership of intellectual property, were clearly defined in a standard format (as contests have rules that all entrants must agree to before making any submissions). The idea of the contest arose because (interviews with CIG, 2014–2015):

[CIG] needed a legal framework in case we use the work [of players in the game], so it became a process.

Such strategic structuring of the co-creation practice contributes to the legal security of the firm, as well as can be further developed to serve as a public relations and marketing device. Still, many other issues of intellectual property and labour exploitation in particular remain unresolved in the space of co-creation, and as such must be addressed by both academic research and the industry.

Another group of problems associated with co-creation is linked to the at times charged nature of firm-customer communications. Interactions with players can get emotional, and customers do get critical of the developers' work—and make it known in at times abrasive ways. In the traditional videogame development arrangement, that rarely was a problem—as the developers did not have to interact with their audiences at all (the audiences simply received the game once it was ready, and either liked it or didn't). It is co-creation and crowdfunding which cause the videogame studios to become more permeable and transparent to the players, who now become involved at much earlier stages of NSD (which is a significant change from being passive audiences). From the CIG field notes (2015):

> In some interactions with the CIG staff, the customers directly remind them in anger that if it wasn't for their money, all developers at CIG would be out of work. The customers haven't forgotten, and will not forget, that they are funding the game. In a way, it is their money which is allowing the firm to operate, basing on the trust that the customers have for the firm (that it will deliver a quality service). CIG has to walk on a high rope, balancing its vision and professional expertise against fulfilling customers' wishes and just keeping them happy. To an extent, CIG is a hostage of its own popularity with the customers, who do have the ways of pressuring the company, sometimes against its will.

That's why dealing with such negative comments is an important ability for an organization—they have a negative impact on the positive word of mouth that the customers are expected to be spreading, as well as may discourage the studio staff by estranging them from their audiences. To prevent this, CIG has a dedicated customer support as well as community management teams whose job is to avoid or diffuse such negative scenarios. Such organizational functions, when well developed and staffed, are manifestations of co-creative organizational culture. They also reflect the integration and user involvement competences of a firm.

Such open organizational culture at times causes studio staff to disclose too much information or say something out of place. The reaction of the firm's management to an employee's mistake in communicating with the customers is not about accusing and blaming. Instead, such communication or customer relationship failures are seen as learning opportunities (interviews with CIG, 2014–2015):

> [Negative behaviour of customers happens] but it has not been extreme—our customer services and community team are good at diffusing those [toxic] situations. Having colleagues in these two departments ready to help is a bit of a safety net; I feel more comfortable knowing they are

there to have my back. When there is a problem, it's not about blaming someone or punishing the person responsible—instead, it is more about 'lesson learned'.

At times prolonged exchanges with customers, as well as their observation of some of the internal practices of the firm, becomes problematic and difficult for the employees. This is reflected below (interviews with CIG, 2014–2015):

> Developers like some of the ideas from the players, but mostly they see them a bit as a nuisance. Players don't quite understand the physics engine, for example. Developers are then irritated by prolonged exchanges.

Also, this is corroborated by the CIG field notes (2015):

> When employees don't want the customers to get involved, they avoid contact. On the other hand, when an individual employee is interested in customers' feedback or inputs, he or she can always seek them out among the customer community.

All in all, at CIG we observe an organizational culture which is customer-centric: open to the inputs from customers, investing in the relationship with customers, as well as developing its services by closely following customer needs.

Firm Strategy

In a company such as CIG, game developers always work guided by the vision for a game, described in various design documents (interviews with ICO Partners, 2014). Still, within any development team there are conflicting interests, as captured in the field notes from GDC'Eu (2014):

> [Within a videogame studio] there are designers wanting to make the best game, production team which wants predictable schedule, and business team which wants to keep the studio alive. Then there are artists, who want their art to be spectacular, and don't worry too much about technical implementation of their ideas. There are the programmers and coders, who want all game systems to work reliably and efficiently. Examples can be listed on . . . Even the high-level principles of iteration, redesign and interaction, which are required for making a successful game, run contrast to other interests about predictability, reduction of risk, and cost efficiency.

Predictability of game development timetables and team deliverables is something that the videogames industry at large strives for. Firms in the industry also seek consolidation of cash flows, reliability of business models, as well as reduction of risk stemming from demand uncertainty (Franklin et al., 2013). That's why, despite the fact that customers have been recognized overall as a valuable resource in videogame development, learning how to harness that resource needs to fit well with all of the above priorities. For instance, the disruptive nature of co-creation on internal routines, or the risks it poses to the customer-firm relationship (as we saw, for example, in Case Beta) are problematic and act as deterrents to the use of co-creation. The benefits of co-creation have been recognized by the firms, but so have its risks and disadvantages. CIG as a firm deploys a unique business model, where the customers are central to marketing and funding of the game (and thus, in many respects, to its commercial success). It makes sense, because of the market niche of the *Star Citizen* (space simulator game, planned to be released on the PC platform, with massively multiplayer game design) and the unique vision for the game (e.g., Chris Roberts, the CEO, returns to the videogames industry from filmmaking industry and uses crowdfunding to realize his vision). The same customer-centric strategy might not work for other firms. This unique position of CIG and its success in co-creation are reflected in the words of a studio employee (interviews with CIG, 2014–2015):

> CIG has been very fortunate that its players have been so supportive. One of the main reasons for players to give us money is to enable us to focus on making the best possible game without worrying too much about the business side of things.

What demonstrates the central role of customer relationship in CIG strategy is the fact that CIG doesn't have a marketing budget (interviews with CIG, 2014–2015). For the studio, the players are a resource when marketing a game; that mechanism is working mainly via positive word of mouth and increasing maximum willingness to pay. Involvement of players contributes greatly to their satisfaction with the game, which means more positive word of mouth marketing, continued influx of new customers (and retention of existing ones), and steady revenue stream (through the customers' subscription to *Star Citizen* development and crowdfunding). In the interviews with CIG (2014–2015) it was pointed out that CIG is "making players happy by making them feel that they are being listened to". This reflects the role of co-creation at CIG as subordinate to tapping into players' community as a resource, particularly for marketing purposes.

CIG's funding arrangements (i.e., the crowdfunding) play a pivotal role. The studio must interact and collaborate with its customers, especially because the crowdfunding effort is ongoing (which is different than the approaches described in Case Alpha and Obsidian Entertainment). Such choice allows the company to embrace an innovative business model and better tap into resource 'crowd', but at the same time makes it more dependent on the relationship with the customer community. It is the 'making players happy' approach that must be balanced against sticking to the company's vision for the service, and exercising the firm's professional expertise in the context of the demanding and empowered customers.

The role of the customer community is seen by the studio as useful for refinement of the game's vision. That vision is first and foremost held internally—its main curator is the CEO of the company, who provides leadership and guidance on how to realize it. The above approach is contrasted in the accounts of CIG employees to 'making games by committee'. That means a situation where that central vision is absent and the game is made based on the popular vote, or on metrics of customer behaviour (so called 'data-driven design'; interviews with CIG, 2014–2015):

> You can't make games by committee. What the community does is helping us to refine our vision. They are telling us what they like and don't like. But as far as core vision is involved, the community can't change it, because Chris [Roberts] makes the decisions here. We do integrate ideas from our players, but they do not affect the core vision for the game.

One of the biggest risks stemming from co-creation that arises is issues surrounding misrepresentation of the original content created by the firm. This has the potential of affecting public image of the company, as well as deeming the game inappropriate for some age groups (interviews with CIG, 2014–2015):

> There are also downsides [to customers' inputs to videogame development]: dishonest representations of our material; people try to pass our material as their own. Another thing is people taking our stuff and modifying it, reconfiguring it. It could be construed negatively if customers did something negative with it; also, our competitors could take those things and steal our ideas.

This is linked to the issues of secrecy and revealing the information about the internal activities of a studio to the customers during the process of co-creation (which is an aspect of disclosure competence). It is easy to imagine CIG's competitors listening on the exchanges between the studio and its players and benefitting from either information about the studio, or data about its community of customers. Other risks to involvement of players are discussed in the interviews with CIG (2014–2015):

> The risks are where you draw the line between what you tell and don't tell your community. During a long development process, that also means keeping players involved, as the community can easily get bored. But then communicating with the players frequently also elongates the development process, as it means more iterations of doing and redoing following on the community's feedback, inputs, opinions, and sentiments.

The ability to manage and mitigate those risks feed back into the firm's appropriation and disclosure competences.

Chapter Summary

This chapter discussed three cases central to this study. It provided an account of practices and characteristics occurring in various departments and functions of those firms. Those cases were largely similar to one another, but some significant differences between them also occur (which is in line with replication logic; Robson, 2011). Table 3.1 presents the summary of the three cases presented in this chapter.

Table 3.1 Comparison of the Main Characteristics of the Cases Discussed in This Chapter

Case	Case Alpha	Case Beta	Case Gamma
Focus on co-creation outcome	Focus is strongly on fulfilling the obligations towards the customers incurred during the crowdfunding campaign. Apart from that firm is conservative in its NSD methodologies.	Customers' inputs are vital for NSD; they largely constitute the game's unique feature. The firm has embraced customers as a core element of their business model, as well as part of their organizational structure.	Use of customers as a marketing and funding resource. Heavy focus on customer-firm relationship, and all co-creation is subordinate to it.
Formal vs. informal co-creation	Firms in this case like to stick to the proven methods of game development. Co-creation is regulated and accounted for.	Firms here like to experiment with innovative NSD methods; customer inputs are welcome in various forms and formats.	A lot of one-to-one exchanges between customers and firm employees point towards informality of co-creation. Customers' role as game co-creators is highlighted in marketing materials and communications.
Co-creation practice	Highly structured co-creation practice, where how customers inputs are provided and what happens to them internally is clearly defined.	Semi-structured co-creation practice, where we observe a large number of various methods and channels for co-creation, which still are flexible and changing.	Unstructured practice of co-creation, relying on the skills and judgment of individual employees of the firm. Relatively few and informal practices of co-creation are present.

(*Continued*)

Table 3.1 Continued

Case	Case Alpha	Case Beta	Case Gamma
Structuring of co-creation experience	Only for selected customers who have contributed premium sums of money in crowdfunding effort.	Sandbox design and focus on customer innovation define the game. They are the centrepiece of attention. All customers are encouraged to co-create.	Rewarding customers' loyalty and financial contributions with access to insider's perspective of NSD effort. Co-creation experience is rich, as customers involved receive in-game and in-kind rewards (e.g., studio visits).
NSD stage	Prior-release stage.	Long-relased into the marketplace.	Prior-release stage.
Use of crowd-funding	Used crowdfunding at the early stage of NSD.	No crowdfunding use at all.	Essentially structured around continued crowdfunding revenue model.
Organi-zational attitude towards customers and studio traditions	Has been making videogames for a long time, sticking to traditional model of game development.	Only recently begun to work on its second game, and from the beginning of its operations it was focused on player-driven videogames.	A new studio that is established with the help of the customers, dispersed geographically and working on its first title, characterized by highly innovative (and still unproven) business model.
Videogame genre	Single-player, story-driven experiences tapping into a niche market of RPG players.	Massively multiplayer videogames tapping into a niche market of sandbox space simulators.	Massively multiplayer videogames tapping into the mass market.[23]

Selected material reprinted from *Internet Spaceships Are Serious Business: An EVE Online Reader*, edited by Marcus Carter, Kelly Bergstrom, Darryl Woodford. Copyright © 2016 by University of Minnesota Press. Reprinted by permission of University of Minnesota Press. Material excerpted from 167–186.

Notes

1. RPGs are videogames where a player creates and takes control of an avatar in a world (usually fantasy or science fiction themed). The avatar experiences adventures and interacts with other characters (be they controlled by the computer or other players). Players have complete control and agency over the actions and development of that character, choosing skills, personality traits, appearances and many other elements.
2. Asset is an element of the game which is not critical for the core functionality or experience of gameplay, and instead contributes variety and aesthetic value to the overall experience. Examples of assets at OE are trees, rock formations, weapon descriptions, non-player character profiles and stories, etc.

3. LinkedIn, accessed on 17.08.2015
4. In the context of co-creation, NSD increasingly involves negotiation of how the game will be shaped and what its key characteristics will be.
5. The latter part of this vignette points to lead users as identified by von Hippel (2005) in a slightly different understanding. Here they are not ahead of the market (technology adoption curve), but better understanding the aesthetics and 'spirit' of the service under development.
6. For example, if a studio receives a solution-centric input at a late stage of NSD process, it must likely expend a large amount of resources to make that idea compliant with existing systems, solutions and visions of a service in advanced stages of development. On the other hand, if a studio receives an idea-centric input at an early stage of a service development, it can integrate it with a service which is still largely in flux and bears no irreversible commitments to particular technologies or designs.
7. Project management technique, popularly used in the videogames industry. For more, see Keith (2010).
8. This is a correct and warranted impression. Even if a game is co-created, once it has been marketed, it will be the studio and its employees who will be credited with its success or burdened with its failure—see for example the case of Auran Games described by Banks (2013).
9. The videogames industry overall devotes a lot of effort towards reducing the uncertainty and risk (Franklin et al., 2013). For instance, their extensive use of title franchises (i.e., repeated development of sequels to successful games instead of developing new game ideas or designs) illustrates this. See *FarCry*, *Call of Duty*, *Civilization* or *Uncharted* series.
10. For more detailed discussion of hidden innovation in creative industries, see Miles and Green (2008).
11. www.gamesindustry.biz/articles/2012-07-17-the-elder-scrolls-online-reinventing-a-franchise-in-an-online-world [accessed on 14.09.2015]
12. https://forum-en.guildwars2.com/forum/archive/bltc/What-to-buy-with-800-gems#post1218058 [accessed on 14.09.2015]
13. For Cases Alpha and Gamma (Obsidian Entertainment and Cloud Imperium Games), the games are still in development and have not been commercially released.
14. In *EVE Online*, players are not represented by an anthropoid avatar as it is the case in most of the games, but by a destructible spacecraft. Media studies point to the importance of a player's identification with the avatar for the enjoyment of a game (Boellstorff, 2008; Pearce, 2009; Yee, 2014)—and it is much harder for humans to see themselves as a spaceship.
15. Emergent gameplay is a form of interaction with the game where the players find ways of playing which hadn't been strictly planned for by the developers. Emergent gameplay is linked to 'sandbox game design' where developers, rather than forming predefined gameplay patterns, build a software environment where players can find their own interaction styles, creatively use the game's affordances, and engage in gameplay that suits their tastes (and the theme of the sandbox). For example, *EVE Online* is a sandbox game about the politics, economy and conflict of spaceships in space.
16. The Cloud Imperium Game's crowdfunding campaign is unlike any other crowdfunding effort and deserves a separate publication just discussing its design and implementation. It goes as far as to make it an integral element of revenue stream of the firm. We will try to showcase as much of that crowdfunding effort as possible here, but the readers are encouraged to investigate that phenomenon in further detail themselves.
17. Sourced from: https://cloudimperiumgames.com/about [accessed on 14.09.2015]
18. Sourced from: www.kickstarter.com/projects/43153532/strike-suit-zero/description [accessed on 14.09.2015]

19. This is linked to the Kickstarter's terms of service (www.kickstarter.com). Crowdfunding campaigns often last around 30 days on Kickstarter, after which they decisively end with either success (project funding goal has been reached) or failure (the funding goal has not been met, backers keep their money, and the firm behind the crowdfunded project gets nothing).
20. Which is not surprising. With the studio's use of crowdfunding, the customers take on some of the traditional roles of a videogames publisher and producer (i.e., the organizations which normally would fund a studio to develop a game) in exchange for an equity or intellectual property share. Many studios find it appropriate to inform the crowdfunding customers how their money is being spent (even though the crowdfunding customers have no leverage over the firm if they don't like it—they essentially donate money by crowdfunding) and when they can expect the finished product.
21. https://robertsspaceindustries.com [accessed on 1.08.2017]
22. A reader interested in watching some of the NGS episodes should follow this link: www.youtube.com/watch?v=CIb4rTrP_9w&index=20&list=PLVct2QDh DrB03tueI9SKQMO9XA86wiXR1 [accessed on 4.08.2017].
23. Various genres tap either market niches (different ones) or mass market, and thus the composition and characteristics of the customer community will differ accordingly. Differences in skills, motivations, spending power and many other dimensions occur here.

References

Aoyama, Y., and Izushi, H., (2008). User-led innovation and the video game industry. IRP Conference, London, May 22–23, 2008.

Banks, J., (2009). Co-creative expertise: Auran games and fury—a case study. *Media International Australia: Incorporating Culture and Policy*, 130(February), pages 77–89.

Banks, J., (2013). *Co-Creating Videogames*. London: Bloomsbury Academic.

Banks, J., and Potts, J., (2010). Co-creating games: A co-evolutionary analysis. *New Media and Society*, 12(2), pages 252–270.

Bergstrom, K., (2013). EVE Online newbie guides: Helpful information or gatekeeping mechanisms at work? In Selected Papers of Internet Research, Denver, USA.

Bergstrom, K., Carter, M., Woodford, D., and Paul, C., (2013). Constructing the ideal EVE Online player. In Proceedings of DiGRA 2013: DeFragging Game Studies, Atlanta, USA.

Boellstorff, T., (2008). *Coming of Age in Second Life. An Anthropologist Explores the Virtually Human*. Princeton and Oxford: Princeton University Press.

Boellstorff, T., Nardi, B., Pearce, C., and Taylor, T.L., (2012). *Ethnography and Virtual Worlds*. Oxford: Princeton University Press.

Bonsu, S.K., and Darmody, A., (2008). Co-creating second life market—consumer cooperation in contemporary economy. *Journal of Macromarketing*, 28(4), pages 355–368.

Burger-Helmchen, T., and Cohendet, P., (2011). User communities and social software in the video game industry. *Long Range Planning*, 44, pages 317–343.

Castronova, E., (2005). *Synthetic Worlds: The Business and Culture of Online Games*. Chicago and London: The University of Chicago Press.

Cohendet, P., and Simon, L., (2007). Playing across the playground: Paradoxes of knowledge creation in the videogame firm. *Journal of Organizational Behavior*, 28, pages 587–605.

Edwards, M., Logue, D., and Schweitzer, J., (2015). Towards an understanding of open innovation in services: Beyond the firm and towards relational co-creation. In: Agarwal, R., Selen, W., Roos, G., and Green, R., (eds). *The Handbook of Service Innovation*. London: Springer London, pages 75–90.

Franklin, M., Searle, N., Stoyanova, D., and Townley, B., (2013). Innovation in the application of digital tools for managing uncertainty: The case of UK independent film. *Creativity and Innovation Management*, 22(3), pages 320–333.

Gebauer, J., Füller, J., and Pezzei, R., (2013). The dark and the bright side of co-creation: Triggers of member behaviour in online innovation communities. *Journal of Business Research*, 66, pages 1516–1527.

Gibbs, M.R., Carter, M., and Mori, J., (2013). Vile rat: Spontaneous shrines in EVE online. Paper presented at the EVE Online Workshop, Chania, Greece, May 14–17, 2013.

Hight, J., and Novak, J., (2008). *Game Development Essentials: Game Project Management*. Clifton Park, NY: Delmar.

Hoyer, W.D., Chandy, R., Dorotic, M., Krafft, M., and Singh, S.S., (2010). Consumer co-creation in new product development. *Journal of Service Research*, 13(3), pages 283–296.

Keith, C., (2010). *Agile Game Development With Scrum*. Upper Saddle River, NJ: Addison-Wesley.

King, B., and Borland, J., (2014). *Dungeons and Dreamers*. Carnegie Mellon University: ETC Press.

Lettl, C., (2007). User involvement competence for radical innovation. *Journal of Engineering and Technology Management*, 24, pages 53–75.

Malaby, T.M., (2009). *Making Virtual Worlds: Linden Lab and Second Life*. Ithaca and London: Cornell University Press.

Marchand, A., and Hennig-Thurau, T., (2013). Value creation in the video game industry: Industry economics, consumer benefits, and research opportunities. *Journal of Interactive Marketing*, 27(3), pages 141–157.

Miles, I., and Green, L., (2008). *Hidden Innovation in Creative Industries*. London: NESTA.

Nardi, B.M., (2010). *My Life as a Night Elf Priest*. Ann Arbor: The University of Michigan Press and The University of Michigan Library.

O'Donnell, C., (2014). *Developer's Dilemma*. London, England: MIT Press.

O'Hern, M.S., and Rindfleisch, A., (2010). Customer co-creation: A typology and research Agenda. In: Malhotra, N.K., (ed). *Review of Marketing Research*, 6, pages 84–106, Bigley: Emerald Books.

O'Hern, M.S., Rindfleisch, A., Antia, K.D., and Schweidel, D.A., (2011). The impact of user-generated content on product innovation. SSRN. http://ssrn.com/abstract=1843250 or http://dx.doi.org/10.2139/ssrn.1843250

Oskarsson, P.J., (2014). The council of stellar management: Implementation of deliberative, democratically elected, council in EVE. White Paper. http://web.ccpgamescdn.com/communityassets/pdf/csm/CSMSummary.pdf (accessed on 6.04.2014).

Paul, C., (2011). Don't play me: EVE online, new players and rhetoric. In: *Proceedings of the 6th International Conference on Foundations of Digital Games*. ACM Press, pages 262–264.

Pearce, C., (2009). *Communities of Play: Emergent Cultures in Multiplayer Games and Virtual Worlds*. Cambridge, MA and London, England: MIT Press.

Robson, C., (2011). Real World Research (Third ed.). New YorK: John Wiley & Sons.

Rowlands, T., (2012). *Video Game Worlds*. Walnut Creek, CA: Left Coast Press, Inc.

Saur-Amaral, I., (2012). Wisdom-of-the-crowds to enhance innovation: A conceptual framework. ISPIM Conference Proceedings 1–7. Barcelona, Spain, 17–20. 06.2012.

Taylor, T.L., (2006). *Play Between Worlds: Exploring Online Game Culture*. Cambridge, MA: MIT Press.

Tschang, F.T., (2005). Videogames as interactive experiential products and their manner of development. *International Journal of Innovation Management*, 9(1), pages 103–131.

Tschang, F.T., (2007). Balancing the Tensions between rationalization and creativity in the video games industry. *Organization Science*, 18(6), pages 989–1005.

Van der Graaf, S., (2012). Get organized at work! A look inside the game design process of valve and linden lab. *Bulletin of Science, Technology & Society*, pages 1–9, 0270467612469079.

Von Hippel, E., (2005). *Democratizing Innovation*. Cambridge, MA: MIT Press.

Yee, N., (2014). *The Proteus Paradox*. London: Yale University Press.

Zackariasson, P., and Wilson, T.L., (2012). *The Video Games Industry: Formation, Present State, and Future*. London and New York: Routledge.

4 Managerial Insights for Creative Services

Many of the observations that we described above pertain not only to the videogames industry but to all creative industries at large. In order to map the impact that co-creation has on NSD and innovation in creative industries firms, we take into account three characteristics of co-creation. These are competences for co-creation, organizational culture and funding arrangements. We also observe various outcomes of co-creation and their impacts on innovation and organizational change. Table 4.1 below compares these characteristics as they occur in the Cases Alpha, Beta and Gamma.

The role of a firm's strategic orientation plays a moderating function for the competences for co-creation. We observe how strategy that relies on tapping the co-creation mostly for its marketing and PR benefits favours disclosure competence as well as innovation sites of 'marketing and customer relationship management' and 'users' interactions' as captured by Miles and Green (2008). Firm strategy that focuses on innovation and exploration of new models of production and customer relationship favours integration competence. In this strategy, customers are seen as a resource in various functions of the firm, resulting in strong innovations in 'internal communications and organizational culture' and 'back-office production processes'. Strategy that relies on maximization of existing resources and making them fit in with established production practices does not favour co-creation strongly—but where it does, appropriation competence comes into play, and few innovation outcomes pertain to the 'value chain location and positioning' site.[1]

Organizational culture plays a role similar to strategic orientation—it moderates the action of competences for co-creation on innovation practices as well as outcomes. Framing customers as members of an 'extended studio family' by studio executives, as well as encouraging all employees to communicate with customers contributes to the building of a strong customer-firm relationship as well as tapping into its marketing potential. Radical innovations occurring in the 'marketing and customer relationship management' site result from this, as well as new possibilities of 'transactions, financing and revenue model' are enabled. Strong partnership between customers and studio employees, consisting of mutual respect, social bonds,

Table 4.1 Key Characteristics of the Three Cases

Concept	Competences for Co-Creation	Organizational Culture	Funding Arrangements	Outcomes of Co-Creation
Alpha	Moderate user involvement and appropriation competence; low integration and disclosure competence.	Strategic focus relies on the maximization of existing resources—chief of which is the community. Traditional game development practices. Single-player genre. Clear division between fans and the studio employees. When co-creating, customers' main strength is in their numbers, as well as in their videogame literacy.	Strong presence and significance of crowdfunding. Project crowdfunded from the early stages of NSD. Select customers (based on their financial contribution) provide inputs to game development in a defined and formalized practice. Game in development, i.e., currently under NSD—ideation and production, as well as testing.	Some innovation observed in the 'transactions, financing and revenue model'. Changes to 'marketing and customer relationship management', as well as 'value chain location and positioning' (especially for inXile) are also present.
Beta	High user involvement, disclosure and integration competence; moderate appropriation competence.	Strategic orientation is focused around innovation and entrepreneurship, and competing in the market based on offering unique service. Innovative and experimental game development processes. Multiplayer, online, sandbox-type experience. Strong partner-like relationship between customer community and studio developers. Customers are skilled technically, but also strong in numbers. Customers seen as innovators in the context of the sandbox and beyond.	Revenue from existing subscriptions from players. Catering to market niche—players with specific taste in gameplay. Game post-launch, although under repeated cycles of improvement works, i.e., expansions and add-ons that are in production.	Organizational changes visible in many sites: 'user interface and user capabilities', 'users' interactions', 'internal communications and organizational culture', 'back-office production processes', as well as 'content of service or genre'. Other sites are also affected by the presence of co-creation, although to a lesser degree.

Gamma				
High user involvement and disclosure competence; moderate integration and appropriation competence.	Cultural match between the community and the organization. Many diverse channels for communication with players. Use of contests.	Strategic orientation is focused on marketing—and expanding the reach of the game to new audiences and constructing the relationship with customers. Multiplayer game with different elements potentially appealing to diverse types of customer. Relationship with customers is a priority for the firm. Marketing-like communication with customers encouraged for all employees. Strong community-focused leadership demonstrated by the CEO. Numerous channels for communication with players, although not very diverse. Open calls for participation and inputs manifested as contests.	Innovative revenue model, relying on continuous crowdfunding and players' participation in internal NSD processes of the firm. Early stages of NSD; the service is still far from being released.	Most organizational changes are visible in 'users' interactions', 'marketing and customer relationship management', 'value chain location and positioning' and 'transactions, financing and revenue model', but innovations resulting from the use of co-creation are also present in other sites.

cultural and worldview similarities, as well as a similar background demographic, fosters innovations in the 'back-office production process' as well as in 'content of service and genre'. On the other hand, organizational culture which relies on the distinctive separation of the customer community and the firm promotes innovations in 'value chain location in positioning' where new means of productively engaging customers are sought, without diminishing strategic control of the firm over its services and their content.

Competences for Co-Creation

Here we discuss the first of the co-creation characteristics, which is 'co-creation competences'. Building on the work of Piller and Ihl (2009) and Lettl (2007), we identified four competences of a firm for co-creation: integration competence, disclosure competence, appropriation competence, as well as user involvement competence. The configuration of those competences, as well as their strength in a firm, determine the propensity and style of co-creation, together with the firm's use of crowdfunding and its organizational culture. Nevertheless, the role of those competences in affecting the propensity and style of co-creation in the setting of a firm varies, meaning that each individual competence's role in affecting the propensity and style of co-creation is limited, and some competences will have more influence than others. We first turn towards exploring those differences.

Disclosure Competence

Service developers overall tend to be very careful when revealing potentially sensitive information. Co-creation therefore can occur only in those aspects of the firm or its service which have been deemed 'safe'. If co-creation is allowed in the 'unsafe' aspects, then customers are required to sign a non-disclosure agreement, as it is the case at CCP (c.f. Case Beta). At the same time, information shared with the customers, which also is the material for and a starting point of co-creation, must be relevant to NSD. A firm's behaviour here can range from releasing marketing-only materials, through opening up some of the underlying code to the customers (example of Valve Corporation), all the way to granting customers access to back-office processes and tools of the firm.

Releasing of appropriate types and amounts of information about a service under development to the community of customers is a prerequisite for successful co-creation. Examples of that competence include, for example, volunteer programs in Case Beta. There, individual customers are invited to participate in the NSD effort almost as if they were the employees of the firm. In order to do that, they must be granted access to sensitive information— and thus are required to sign NDA. Similar applies to player councils in Cases Beta and Gamma.

In Case Gamma there is more reliance on trust and personal relationship between an employee and a customer. Information is revealed only when a particular employee trusts the co-creating customer—this way, customer can provide meaningful and useful inputs to NSD. Similarly, no NDAs are signed in Case Alpha—co-creating customers are provided only the general information about the setting of the service, its artistic feel and mood. Those types of information are not very sensitive, and there is a low risk associated with revealing them to the customers.

Integration Competence

Integration competence is about assimilating external inputs into internal routines and practices of a firm (Piller and Ihl, 2009). As long as the practices for obtaining customer inputs are relatively informal (as it is discussed for the user involvement competence; Lettl, 2007), its internal assimilation is largely done ad hoc in all three cases studied. The exceptions to that rule are the QA (quality assurance) practices, as well as the inputs finding its way into the firm via contests and competitions (those normally stipulate how the entries will be judged, when, by whom, using what criteria, what the rewards will be and so on). These tend to have very formal practices, both outward-facing (in terms of how the community of customers is getting engaged) and internal (how 'bugs' or reports about issues are processed by the QA team and the rest of the firm). We see the examples of that in all three cases.

Structured forms of co-creation, such as contests, purchasing of assets from online stores, or volunteer programs, allow for resolving some of the problems presented in the point above. By introducing clear conditions of exchange of the ideas that are known to co-creating customers a priori (as well as outlining potential rewards) and the rules governing their selection, the companies are on much more legally secure ground. As an outcome, they can assimilate customers' inputs directly that result from such a structured practice without worries of opening themselves up to legal action or causing unrest among the community (Gebauer et al., 2013).

In such dynamic, companies also clearly define what kind of inputs customers will provide them with. The firms are interested only in the inputs that will fit those defined guidelines. We observe the evidence of that in particular in Cases Alpha and Gamma, where specifications of inputs accepted have been released to co-creating customers. That facilitates not only the selection of the highest-quality inputs, but also ensures their compatibility with internal practices of the firm—such as (in the case of videogame industry) programming languages, polygon counts or file types.

Moreover, for QA, the observed formality of the practice is also a by-product of the nature of QA itself—problems in the software code must be internally ordered, responsibilities to fix them must be ascribed, as well as their origin must be recorded. Player councils observed in Case Beta are also typically accompanied by internal practices that allow for efficient and extensive recording of the customers' feedback and then passing it on to the development team. We therefore observe a degree of formality in processing those inputs. Those practices have been developed over years of experience, and the presence of customer co-creation has been evolving together with the firm, growing into its structures gradually. It fits well our broader category of overall semi-structured practice of co-creation dominant in Case Beta.

Nevertheless, the vast majority of inputs from the customers does not fall into any of these three categories. Instead, they are suggestions, requests, materials loosely based on the firm's offerings, poll results, personal conversations, workshops and others. It is impractical to establish a practice for integrating those, as that is done mostly by the individual employees on an 'on the job' basis. Together they constitute 'informal' co-creation, which relies on the rich communications and organic relationships between customers and firm's employees, as well as exchange and flows of ideas between them. This is also where the integration competence resides—in the firm's ability to assimilate those inputs and integrate them with its day-to-day functioning and routines without causing much of a disruption.

The potential impact of integration competence on the propensity and style of co-creation is high. Many creative industries firms do not accept inputs from their customers due to their disruptive nature—the traditional model of service development does not account for the presence of customers at any stage of it. Therefore, some degree of organizational flexibility and project management (Agile and Scrum techniques) is required to make use of feedback from the customers. It also must be accompanied by relatively experienced staff (as we see for instance in Case Beta) who know how to juggle internal work together with the inputs from customers, as well as how to manage the relationship with such involved customers. In Case Alpha we read how the experiences of modding enabled the firms to engage in co-creation, as those two practices bear some semblance to one another.

One interesting result is that integration competence is the one that firms struggle the most with. It remains a problem for all companies—even the ones for which that competence is high. Integration competence does not necessarily have to be about formal ways of processing customer inputs by a firm—after all, a large proportion of co-creation is informal in nature. Therefore, this competence includes a firm's ability to be flexible about its NSD practices and processes, responding to external inputs in a timely and targeted fashion.

Appropriation Competence

Appropriation competence hinges on the firm's ability to protect the knowledge generated with the customers, as well as bar the free-riders from benefitting from the open innovation practice (Piller and Ihl, 2009). The current understandings of intellectual property do not sit well with participatory cultures, open innovation or the dynamics of 'playbour', and with how firms deal with the inputs from their customers. Therefore, how a firm manages to bypass those limitations to enable co-creation, both of its own NSD methodologies as well as resulting from imperfect legal systems, constitutes this competence.

If customer inputs are used in their original form, then for legal reasons those inputs must be originating via an established and clear channel which allows for transparent rules. An example of that is the Next Great Starship contest described in Case Gamma, or purchasing of assets from the Unity Store in Case Alpha. That way, it is legally clear what the conditions of co-creation are, what are the rewards, and who the author is. It is possible to have legally binding terms and conditions determining the process. The customers are legally consenting to any such rules, including the transfer of intellectual property ownership. Other forms of co-creation lack this formalized aspect and are treated more as feedback or loosely defined source of ideas. In the course of this latter category, customer inputs are reconfigured before becoming integrated with the service development, for the reasons of safe appropriation of customer-generated knowledge and intellectual property considerations.

Appropriation competence also implies the firm's ability to attract talented co-creators to its cause, i.e., to co-create their service, and not that of the competitors. As the time of co-creating customers is limited, their co-creative attention is a subject of competition among firms. They tend to co-create that service which fulfils their motivations for co-creation the best. Those motivations have been already discussed as either intrinsic or extrinsic (Füller, 2010; Roberts et al., 2014), and correspond to opportunities of employment, learning or belonging to a community of like-minded individuals. Hence the appropriation competence captures what the firm is able to do in return for the customers' involvement as co-creators of their service to meet their motivations and reasons.

The above is well visible in all three cases, although there is a degree of variation between them. Those differences stem from the fact that firms described tap into different types of co-creating customers, or different cognitive communities (Burger-Helmchen and Cohendet, 2011). For instance, Case Gamma in the NGS contest relies on extrinsic motivations of customers to co-create by offering financial rewards and offers of employment. Case Beta on the other hands focuses on the intrinsic motivations—as the reward for co-creation customers get the feelings of belonging, customization of their experiences, as well as forging new social ties.

User Involvement Competence

This competence is closely linked to the characteristics of the community of customers (Lettl, 2007). It describes a firm's ability to systematically involve customers in the innovation practice, and it has two dimensions: one, in which firms need to have a good understanding of their customer community and their creative or innovative potential; and two, in which the firm identifies the best interaction patterns with customers to bring their inputs into the organization. Therefore, this competence describes a firm's ability to construct a co-creative interface with the community of its customers, and is the most outward-looking of all four competences characterizing a firm's propensity and style of co-creation.

When it comes to the first dimension of that competence, a firm has close ties and numerous links to the community of its customers. Those links rely not only on long-term coexistence between the firm and its customers, but also on the fact that those services occupy market niches. This is strengthened by personal links between the community of customers and the employees, as well as recruitment of staff from among the community of customers. Firms also collect data on their customers (when it comes to in-game behaviour for instance), which is then statistically analyzed. The cases studied vary in the amount of data that they collect—demonstrating differences in user involvement competence across firms.

For instance, in Cases Beta and Gamma a lot of information, Big Data, statistics, behavioural patterns and similar types of information are collected. That data can then be analyzed using scientific method by the firm to understand the behaviour and needs of the customers. On the other hand, in Case Alpha, no such very formalized practice is visible—instead, that firm prefers to rely on its own perceptions and experiences, as well as interactions with the customers on forums and via other channels. Overall, community management and customer service functions contribute visibly to that competence in organizations.

The second dimension of user involvement competence describes the firm's ability to select the best format of interaction with its customers, so that their inputs can flow into the organization's NSD and innovation processes as efficiently as possible. We observe variation across the cases in the use of such devices as player councils, volunteer programs, crowdvoting, contests, purchasing of assets, studio visits and physical gatherings. Those are also formal means of tapping the customers' creative potential. On the other hand, there are also forms of interaction that are displayed by all cases—staff activity on forums, regular updates provided by the firm to its community and related solicitation of feedback, as well as calls for community inputs to NSD (which also take form as an element of crowdfunding campaign).

The benefits that incentivize customers to generate inputs to NSD differ between formal and informal modes of co-creation. In informal co-creation, customers are motivated to participate by product use and improvements, network effects, reputation, enjoyment of the activity, and fulfilment of norms (Piller and Ihl, 2009). In the formal mode of co-creation, firms add benefits corresponding to extrinsic motivations—such as chances of employment, in-game rewards and official recognition—on top of the afore-mentioned benefits. Again, this is very well visible, for example, in the case of contests described in Cases Beta and Gamma.

As co-creation in the creative industries stems from participatory culture (Jenkins, 2006) and is underpinned by both socio-cultural and market dimensions (Banks and Potts, 2010), the customers demonstrate high propensity to become engaged in co-creation. Firms are in the position of deciding whether or not to use their customers as a resource—and if so, in what form (whether for NSD or for relationship building). Firms vary in their ability to incentivize their customers—due to, for example, their service development methodologies, the level of understanding of their community's composition and motivations, or organizational structure. Also, a firm that uses mixed methods of co-creation (i.e., both formal and informal) will be able to tap into a wider array of incentives, and thus engage more customers in co-creation—the best example of that is visible in Case Beta, where CCP deploys an array of co-creation practices. This competence therefore reflects a firm's responsiveness to its customers, and therefore plays a significant role in shaping the propensity and style of co-creation.

Comparing ALL Competences

The two competences that have most potential weight in influencing co-creation within a firm are integration competence (Piller and Ihl, 2009), as well as user involvement competence (Lettl, 2007). The former focuses on the organizational aspects of the firm, its practices, and whether routines exist for assimilating customers' inputs. The latter looks to the outside of the firm, and towards the communities of customers. It determines the format of interactions between the firm and its customers when it comes to exchanges of ideas and creativity. It resides in the firm's ability to understand its customers and their potential, as well as to select the right tools for allowing their participation in NSD.

For disclosure competence, its impact on shaping co-creation in organizations is less significant. Firms are already guarded when it comes to revealing the information about their internal practices and works; some types of information are very rarely revealed to significant extent. Moreover, the aesthetic and experiential nature of services under study further cautions firms when disclosing details of yet unreleased services. Firms are very well aware that once a piece of information is out, it becomes available on the Internet and in other media quickly. Still, information must be disclosed to the customers if co-creation is to take place. Choosing how much can be revealed of what type of information, to whom, at what time, and in what circumstances of the marketplace is a skill reflected by this competence.

Appropriation competence does not have a dominant influence on firm's propensity and style of co-creation. As customers who contribute their work to creative services are also their fans, their inputs are highly tailored to the aesthetics of that particular service. Creative industries' services are characterized by their unique art, design, experience, mechanics, as well as technical solutions, which determine their aesthetics and style. Therefore, the inputs contributed for a particular service are difficult to be also applied to any other. Still, this competence is not without consequence on a firm's co-creation propensity and style. As discussed above, firms compete for their customers' attention as co-creators. Attracting that attention from skilled co-creating customers is captured by the appropriation competence.

We observe that a firm's propensity for co-creation depends on its co-creation competences—and user involvement and integration competences in particular. The style of co-creation is also determined by those competences, which do not only exist on a binary scale of zero or one (where a firm either has a particular competence or doesn't have it). Instead, they exist in a number of varieties, as for one firm integration competence stems from highly formal practices for processing customer inputs (e.g., Case Alpha), while for the other it will rely on the flexibility of project management and collaborative teamwork practices (e.g., Case Beta). Therefore, we look towards the four co-creation competences to best describe a firm's propensity for, as well as style of co-creation. Examples of such practices that illustrate competences for co-creation, and thus allow us to describe a firm's propensity for and style of co-creation, are given in the Table 4.2 below.

Furthermore, a firm's propensity for co-creation depends on the cumulative strength of its competences. The more and stronger its competences for co-creation, the more propensity for co-creation a firm displays. On the other hand, the style of co-creation is a resultant force of co-creation activities enabled by competences. Finally, institutional arrangements of a firm (i.e., organizational culture and funding arrangements) also influence its propensity and style. We discuss them in further detail in sections below.

Table 4.2 Table Comparing Examples of Competences as Described in Empirical Data (Chapter 5) Together with Their Effects on a Firm's Propensity For and Style of Co-Creation

Competence	Example in Data	Effect on Co-Creation Propensity* (P) and Style (S)
User involvement	Alpha: Posting regular project updates and emails. Beta: Fan gatherings and democratically elected player councils. Gamma: Studio visits and paid levels of customers' involvement (access to NSD).	P: weak S: low integration of customers P: strong S: customers have a personal stake in co-creation P: moderate S: close integration with crowdfunding and revenue model

Competence	Example in Data	Effect on Co-Creation Propensity* (P) and Style (S)
Integration	Alpha: Customers provide very specific inputs on predetermined topics.	P: weak S: similar to crowdsourcing and submission of work
	Beta: Champions for customers' inputs coupled with cross-disciplinary teams in Scrum project management.	P: strong S: customers become almost a team member and stakeholder in internal practices
	Gamma: Discrete decisions of individual employees basing on their knowledge of the co-creating customer.	P: moderate S: informal co-creation strongly correlated to hidden innovation, occurring 'under the radar'
Disclosure	Alpha: Customers don't need confidential info to co-create.	P: strong S: it is safe to use co-creation
	Beta: Signing NDAs with customers.	P: moderate S: intensive, work-like co-creation
	Gamma: Personal trust between customers and employees.	P: strong S: the paramount role of relationship in co-creation, informality
Appropriation	Alpha: Using assets from Unity Store.	P: strong S: transparent co-creation, no legal concerns
	Beta: Belonging to a unique and respected community.	P: moderate S: tightening the links with community
	Gamma: Winners of the contests gain employment and financial award.	P: strong S: only the best inputs are accepted, increasing visibility

(*) Effect on a firm's co-creation propensity is framed as positive for all competences, as a competence always has positive value.

Configurations of Competences

Firms are characterized by unique mixes of the four competences for co-creation. The propensity and style of co-creation, and their differences across firms, are explained by various sets of competences of firms. The mix of competences for co-creation also reflects firm's dynamic capabilities (Teece, 2007; Rosenbloom and Christensen, 1994; Teece and Pisano, 1994). They capture the firm's ability to shift away from the traditional models of NSD and adopt the organizational changes required for successful innovating in the changed market and socio-cultural environment. In the sections below we discuss the particular array of competences for co-creation in each of the main firms studied. It serves as the demonstration of the correlation between different co-creation practices and particular sets of competences that a firm has.

Case Alpha—Obsidian Entertainment

In this firm, user involvement competence is the most significant. The firm knows its customer community well, and the community of customers plays an important role in the firm's commercial success. The firm selected the best format of interaction with the community of customers, allowing the company to continue using its established work practices (traditional service development), together with satisfying the demands resulting from customers' involvement in the wake of crowdfunding campaign. That's why we only observe extensive use of forums, as well as controlled inputs of customers to pre-determined aspects of the game. The practice of co-creation in that firm is highly structured. There are specific practices, responsibilities and goals of the co-creation in Case Alpha, and almost all of the information flows between customers and the firm are regulated and accounted for.

Such an approach to co-creation is also identified as relationship-focused. A degree of collaboration with customers in NSD does take place, although to a very limited extent. The firm does not need (or want) its customers for making any significant NSD progress, as competences for that are present in-house, as well as co-creation is recognized as being potentially disruptive to work practices. Instead, the firm allows for co-creation in order to deepen its relationship with customers, providing them with expanded experience of the service, capitalizing on positive word of mouth, as well as fulfilling its obligations resulting from crowdfunding campaign.

Overall integration competence is low, as the customers' inputs do not fit easily into the firm's routines and practices. They are treated as a challenge for the organization first and foremost, and the customers' role is seen as mostly that of testers, and their main strength resides in numbers. Finally, appropriation competence relies on the a priori stipulated terms of customers' ability to have their ideas included into the service—following on the promises made during the crowdfunding campaign.

It would seem that this firm's reluctance to depart from the traditional NSD models (that also have proven successful for that firm in the past; Cohen and Levinthal, 1990) reflects its low dynamic capabilities. OE sticks to the practices that have been proven to work, modifying them minimally to enable the use of crowdsourcing in its NSD. Co-creation is permitted to exist within OE only as long as it is controlled, and its influence on the organization and NSD is mapped.

Case Beta—CCP Games

Co-creation practice in the context of CCP is semi-structured. It means that it encompasses both formal and informal elements. Specific practices exist within the firm for assimilating customer inputs, together with assigned responsibilities, tailored project management techniques, as well as communication routines. At the same time, there is a heavy focus on the relationship with the customers, and the means of receiving the inputs from customers are flexible and deeply integrated with the organization. The community of customers is empowered both in formal and informal ways, and it can influence the service development team in a myriad of ways.

Customer involvement in the case of CCP occurs at all stages of NSD, which also contributes to explaining the wealth of various methods for co-creation. User involvement competence in CCP Games is very high (there are employees within CCP whose only job is to analyze customer behaviour, process their inputs internally, as well as liaise with the player councils). The company deploys many methods of analyzing and understanding the community of its customers, as well as engages a wide array of methods to allow customers' creativity to find its way into the firm. Similarly, integration competence is correspondingly high—there are specific routines and posts within the firm that facilitate the assimilation of customer inputs.

In the case of CCP, appropriation competence is strongly linked to organizational culture and the fact that CCP sees its service success as largely dependent on customers' creativity. Customer co-creation is limited only by terms of use and end-user licence agreement. CCP controls customers' engagement with the firm by asking co-creating customers to sign non-disclosure agreements and abide by other practices of confidentiality. Nevertheless, CCP is effective at appropriating customers' creativity (in terms of assets, emergent gameplay and social dynamics), and that practice has become an integral part of the firm's business model.

Disclosure competence is high in the context of CCP—customers who engage in formal co-creation are often informed about the requirements of their task. Employees participate in the discussions with customers, as well as inform them about their work. There are numerous personal links between the individuals on both sides of the organizational boundary. The fact that CCP's service occupies a market niche and caters to idiosyncratic consumer tastes makes it less imitable by the competitors, as well as facilitates social network effects (i.e., social bonds), which reduce the risk of purposefully malicious (confidentiality-breaching) customer behaviour.

Dynamic capabilities at CCP correspond to its ability to remain successful in capitalizing on a market niche for a prolonged period of time. The firm's practices change and shift in response to customer participation in NSD. Firm achieves the 'sandbox' design of its service in part by its flexible NSD methodologies, as well as accommodating organizational culture. The firm has clearly demonstrated that it has the capabilities to adapt and adjust to changing conditions of the market, having thrived in its niche for over 10 years. It has a reputation for being innovative and embracing novel NSD methodologies.

Case Gamma—Cloud Imperium Games

CIG's co-creation practices are unstructured. The focus of co-creation at CIG is the relationship with the customers and generation of increased maximum willingness to pay, positive word of mouth, as well as overall enlisting of the customers' help as marketers and advocates for the service. Co-creation occurs mainly via the rich personal interactions between individual employees and customers, and is characterized by relatively few formal practices accompanying it.

As CIG's service is still in development, the observations of Case Gamma also apply to that stage of NSD. User involvement competence in that setting is very high—the amount of attention and resources that the firm expends to maintain its close relationship with customers is, to the best of the author's knowledge, unprecedented. This is linked to the firm's success in raising the funds in the crowdfunding campaign, as well as widespread attention that its development effort has been receiving. As mentioned before, user involvement competence resides in the ability of individual employees to understand and communicate with customers, and is largely coupled with customer-centric organizational culture.

When it comes to the integration competence, the majority of customer inputs are processed informally and on an ad hoc basis. The firm remains positively disposed to customer inputs. Communicating and working with customer inputs is an organizational priority, so despite the lack of strong formal practices, the integration competence still remains high. The locus of that competence remains informal, and it is also subordinate to the company's focus on customer relationship.

Appropriation competence is on comparable levels to what we observe in other cases, as the customer inputs are highly specific to the service and are not easily transferable to other firms' offerings. CIG's appropriation competence is noticeable when observing the NGS contest, which was designed to attract the most interesting contributions from the most skilled members of the community. Contest format, together with the promise of employment for the winners, attracted many entries from various customers, including also the ones from outside of CIG's usual community.

It is difficult to speak of dynamic capabilities in the context of Case Gamma. The main firm under study is a relatively new organization that has been developed with crowdsourcing and co-creation in mind. Its structure, mission and goals correspond closely to the current dynamics of its environment. It is characterized by an innovative business model, as well as by a highly dispersed organizational structure. Further studies in a few years' time are required to better illustrate CIG's dynamic capabilities and to track this firm's ability to adjust to changing conditions in its environment.

Competences: A Summary

The competences for co-creation that are present in various firms are summarized in Table 4.3 below. Each of the three companies discussed in this section has a unique profile in that classification, showing how different mixes of competences correspond to various practices of co-creation.

Each of the four competences for co-creation has different strength in promoting co-creation (thus increasing firm's propensity for co-creation). All competences for co-creation, by their definition, have a positive influence on a firm's co-creation propensity. The sum of their strengths (here described on a scale from low, through moderate, to strong) is the main factor in determining a firm's propensity for co-creation.

When it comes to the style of co-creation, it is a more descriptive affair. First of all, each company has different array of co-creation competences, manifesting with different strengths at various stages of the NSD. This unique blend of competences influences the style of co-creation—whether formal or informal, for NSD inputs or customer relationship—as well as its practice (structured, semi-structured or unstructured). Second of all, competences for co-creation are manifested differently in each company, and thus must be qualitatively described (instead of being just treated quantitatively on a scale correlated to their strength). The style of co-creation will therefore be a resultant force of those qualitative and quantitative descriptions of what those competences entail and how they affect a particular firm.

Furthermore, the institutional arrangements—organizational culture and funding arrangements—also influence a firm's propensity and style of co-creation. The best examples of that are the role of organizational culture in Case Gamma, as well as the influence of crowdfunding in Case Alpha. We discuss those two factors in detail below.

Similarly to firms, customer communities are also a locus of co-creation competences. It is possible that the communities of CCP and CIG have higher potential for co-creation (defined by their level of skill, demographic and motivation) than the community of Obsidian Entertainment. That factor, which is largely outside of the firm's control (although the characteristics

Table 4.3 A Comparison of Co-Creation Competences, Dynamic Capabilities and Co-Creation Practice in Three Firms[2]

Competence	Obsidian	CCP	Cloud Imperium
User involvement	Moderate	High	High
Integration	Low	High	Moderate
Disclosure	Low	High	High
Appropriation	Moderate	Moderate	Moderate
Dynamic capabilities	Conservative— maintaining old NSD practices	Progressive— adjusting to the shifting environment	?—we lack data as the firm's environment hasn't changed yet
Propensity for co-creation	Low/moderate	High	Moderate/high
Style of co-creation	In response to the crowdfunding effort, guarded and careful.	Bold and innovative, deeply integrated with many aspects of the business model.	Integrated with crowdfunding, relying on informal interactions, coupled to marketing.
Co-creation practice	Structured	Semi-structured	Unstructured

of a service do influence what kind of customer is attracted to it), has a significant role in the firm's propensity and style of co-creation.

Together, competences for co-creation as well as institutional arrangements determine how customer inputs influence the practice of co-creation. We observe three types of co-creation practice: structured, semi-structured and unstructured. They capture the overall dynamic of how customer inputs influence a firm's NSD, regardless of the purposeful or accidental co-creation nature of co-creation, its formal or informal dimensions, or the firm's goals for co-creation (whether for NSD inputs or customer relationship gains).

Customer Inputs Influence Organizations

Various firms, characterized by different mixes of competences for co-creation, embrace their customers as a resource in NSD or for relationship-building purposes (including marketing benefits). Those competences though do not fully describe the role of customers in the innovation practice of the firm (von Hippel, 2005), or the role of co-creation in enhancing the customer-firm relationship (Gebauer et al., 2013). The innovation practice in digital videogames firms occurring in the presence of co-creation can often be ad hoc and performed on an 'on the job' basis (as many creative industries' firms lack a formalized R&D department or budget; Miles and Green, 2008). It is possible that such informal forms of co-creation are more common than formal and structured ones, including a formal call for submissions and an internal practice for assimilating them into NSD.

Hence the outcomes of co-creation on innovation practice can be very subtle and occur 'under the radar' of official identification and classification, or can assume a form of 'adhocracy' (when their processing is unstructured and shifts from case to case; Naranjo-Valencia et al., 2011). In such a dispersed form, they cannot be easily targeted by analytical tools or metrics, such as sector-wide innovation surveys (e.g., in the UK they are conducted by Nesta, a global foundation researching innovation and social challenges – nesta.org.uk). Instead, their form will be most of all affected by the two institutional arrangements that underpin and provide context to all of its activities. These are funding arrangements, as well as organizational culture.

Those institutional arrangements heavily influence a firm's propensity for, as well as style of co-creation. They also modify the nature of the relationship between the firm and its customers. We describe the expectations, attitudes, as well as obligations that determine it.

Significance of Organizational Culture

Co-creation occurs through the everyday practices of studio employees; and compared to the wealth of these interactions, the formalized practices relatively rarely replace that informal co-creation—but that also varies across the firms. This underlines the agency of organizational culture in shaping co-creation. Since co-creative exchanges are dispersed among line employees, it is their individual attitudes that affect their interactions with players. Also on the strategic decision-making level, an organizational culture which frames its customers as valid contributors and partners to NSD aids in absorption of their contributions or tapping them as a marketing resource.

Organizational culture is formed by three characteristics of a firm: its history, strategy and attitudes of its employees. All of them are significant in shaping the practice of co-creation in a firm. Organizational history generates inertia in culture; a firm will tend to stick to the practices (i.e., project management, communication routines, team structure) which worked for it in the past. As things currently are, co-creation is an innovation in NSD practices as well as in organizational structures, and thus represents such unproven and untested methodology—hence the reluctance to embrace it of those firms which have a long track record of prior success (c.f. Case Alpha and Obsidian Entertainment). On the other hand, new firms (CIG), or firms that have built their business model around co-creation, do not face resistance from that inertia.

Firm strategy and stage in NSD will be another factor influencing organizational culture—in particular, how the company formulates its relationship with the community of customers, and how central they are to the service's success in the marketplace. At different stages of NSD organizational culture will be also influenced differently—early stages are normally done without any inputs from the customers, as involving them at this stage would be infeasible (i.e., what the service is, for whom, how it will work—all of that is uncertain or unknown at that stage). That was visible in all three cases—their 'core offering' has been developed without any inputs from the customers. In later stages of NSD it becomes easier and less risky overall to involve customers, as the risk of disruption from co-creation is gradually reduced. It is very well illustrated by Case Beta, which is currently at a very late stage of NSD (what is currently developed is only add-ons and modifications to the basic service) and engages heavily in co-creation. Additional discussion of the role of the NSD stage on co-creation practice follows towards the end of this chapter.

The last element of organizational culture is the attitude of employees. It is a subtle yet powerful effect which determines how individual employees view and think of customers as co-creators (thus, to some extent, peers). In the case studies, we see how firm developers view themselves as professionals (c.f. interviews with OE, 2013; field notes from OE, 2014) who know best what is required for a successful service development. Customers are seen as impostors at times, whose place is not within the firm's internal affairs. On the other hand, both Cases Beta and Gamma illustrate a different approach—where the customers are regarded as having some skills that can be used in the course of NSD. In Case Beta this is connected to the role of customers' creativity in developing the service, while in Case Gamma to their unique ability to generate powerful marketing benefits for the studio, as well as (in individual cases) having genuine service development skills.

Organizational culture partially determines the competences for co-creation that a firm has, as well as modifies their action in the context of a particular firm. Organizational culture underpins many of them as well—we see a lot of differences between firms. For instance, in the organizational culture of OE (Case Alpha) customrs are seen as mostly faithful and cherished fans—but not more. On the other hand, at CCP they are perceived as collective collaborators on many occasions, oftentimes providers of the spark that makes the service unique and special. At CIG (Case Gamma) we see yet another understanding of the customer community dominating organizational culture—as a resource for marketing and funding, and as interesting and skilled individuals.

Therefore, organizational culture determines the attitude of employees towards the customers and their inputs. If a firm has a culture of collaborating with customers and views its customers as valuable (this pertains in particular to whether customer community is seen as a productive body) co-creation will be facilitated, and the customer inputs may take more formal shapes and paths (as we see in Case Beta). If, on the other hand, the customer community is not viewed as a skilled collaborator, then the organizational culture may still promote productive relationships with individual customers. Then the customer inputs will tend towards informal and more linked to hidden innovation, as we see in Case Gamma for instance. Some additional details are illustrated in Table 4.4 below.

Table 4.4 Illustration of the Relationship in Organizational Culture: The Attitude of Employees Towards Co-Creating Customers as Individuals or Collectively (i.e., Customer Community)

Organizational Culture	Individual Customers	Customer Community
For the customers as co-creators	As seen in Case Gamma. Reliance on hidden innovation, co-creation taking place via individual relations between employees and customers. Informal methods.	As seen in Case Beta. Many different practices, democratic and transparent in nature, both externally and internally deployed by the firm. Formal methods.
Against the customers as co-creators	As seen in Case Alpha. Customers are seen as a source of disruption to NSD and lacking professional skills. Closed-off NSD, closely controlled inputs from select customers. Formal methods.	As seen in Case Gamma. Customers as a community don't provide useful inputs, except for QA. Importance of identifying valuable individuals as contributors and deploying appropriate methods. Informal methods.

Organizational culture influences articulation of a firm's competences for co-creation. User involvement and disclosure competences in particular are affected by it—for instance, whether employees take their time to understand their customers' needs, whether a firm designates resources to analyze customers' behaviour, or how much trust there is for the customers overall. As such, organizational culture is very closely linked to a firm's competences for co-creation as well as the practice of co-creating with customers. It is also transformed by the continued and successful presence of co-creation in a firm.

Significance of Funding Arrangements

Crowdfunding is among the most powerful influencers of co-creation's form and prevalence in organizations. At its core, crowdfunding creates a new dynamic in the relationship between a firm and its customers—one where customers also become funders. In exchange for their funding they obtain no equity or profits but the ability to participate in the development of a service that wouldn't otherwise be developed. That participation is a significant aspect of a crowdfunding project: the firms are aware that the crowdfunding customers are their most loyal and devoted fans. Crowdfunding therefore creates a pressure and obligation for the firm to involve their customers in the NSD, as well as to listen to them—at least to some degree.

For firms which decide to use crowdfunding, their propensity for co-creation increases significantly. Those firms must display at least some user involvement and disclosure competences—as they must be able to successfully identify their customer communities, communicate with them effectively, as well as disclose enough confidential information to engage them in the project. Community management and service functions play an important role here. This is well visible in Case Alpha—OE engaged in crowdfunding having sufficient user involvement and disclosure competences gained during its support for modding in the past. This enabled the firm to successfully tap into the customer community as a source of funding.

Moreover, as firms which engage in crowdfunding promise their customers some degree of influence over NSD, they also need to have some integration competence. They need to be able to assimilate and process the inputs of those customers, and integrate them with internal NSD. As a consequence, there is a clear link between funding arrangements, competences for co-creation, as well as firm's propensity for co-creation.

Furthermore, the style of co-creation is also affected by funding arrangements. We observe that in the differences between Cases Alpha and Gamma (which were or are being crowdfunded) and Case Beta (where no crowdfunding was used). In the former two cases, there is a greater need for user involvement and disclosure competences. A large proportion of co-creation is geared towards customer relationship gains, and keeping customers happy by fulfilling promises made during crowdfunding campaign plays a big role.

Interestingly, funding arrangements also interact with organizational culture, where they are mutually influencing (reinforcing or inhibiting) each other. For instance, at CIG (Case Gamma), organizational culture makes a good match with crowdfunding—they are both open to the customers and welcome their inputs, be they financial or creative (provided that they come from individuals, not communities as discussed above). This is contrasted by Case Alpha, where organizational culture sits uneasily with crowdfunding, accepting it more out of necessity, simply because there was no other option for gathering funds for the development of *Pillars of Eternity*.

Funding arrangements are also not without consequence. The presence of crowdfunding spearheads the need for formal co-creation to take place within firms—so that the customers see it fulfilling its obligations and listening to them in the development of a new service. As such it affects the way in which customer inputs affect co-creation practice—especially in the formal space. That drive towards formalization is also accompanied by the increased focus on the customer relationship outcomes of co-creation.

In summary, a firm's culture and funding arrangements play a role in determining the scale and scope of co-creation, as well as its impact on innovation practices at various stages of NSD. This explains the dynamic governing the effect of propensity and style of co-creation on innovation practice in firms. These institutional arrangements fall respectively under the sites of 'transactions, financing and revenue model' and 'internal communications and organizational culture'.

Two Outcomes of Co-Creation

Does co-creation truly allow for bypassing the need for transferring of customers' need-related knowledge across the customer-firm boundary? Considering the organizational changes and tensions introduced by the use of co-creation, this practice could not be classified as 'cheap' or 'risk-free' for a firm. Firms undergo numerous transformations, their work routines are forced to change, and the professional roles and identities of employees also shift. Those tensions are very well illustrated in Case Alpha, where the company, previously successful in the more traditional methodologies of game development, resists the transformations to its practices and routines arising from co-creation. This stems from the organizational history.

Still, the intensity of co-creation in the context of a particular firm can be regulated—as we observe throughout all three cases. Firms control their co-creative practices, but customers are also very quick to form expectations for particular levels of cooperation between studio and their community. As we observed in the cases, firms such as Obsidian Entertainment or ArenaNet do use co-creation in their NSD, although to a relatively minor extent. Customers' inputs are present only in very specific aspects of NSD and at stages chosen by the firm. This is linked to the ingrained belief in an organization that customers' inputs are not really necessary for their innovative value—NSD- or innovation-related activities can be better off carried out internally. Nevertheless, what the customers can be useful for is the funding of new projects, marketing and provision of certain services (ones that take advantage of the large numbers of customers, i.e., quality assurance and testing).

On the other hand, with the culture of openness at Cloud Imperium Games or CCP, those inputs are far more spread across various service development disciplines, from art, via programming, to design, sound and even to some administrative activities. The costs of co-creation, the trans-formations to organizational culture or service development practices will therefore be much higher for those two latter firms as compared to OE. Co-creation therefore becomes one of the core tenets of firm's strategy—one which devotes a sizable portion of its resources to the management of pro-ductive relationship with customers. It becomes closely integrated with vari-ous processes and practices of a firm, its routines and style of management. CCP is the best example of that, with the plethora of various practices, both formal and informal, of tapping the creativity and labour of the customers.

This confirms the observation that co-creation occurs in two varieties in firms: first of all, for its benefits to NSD. This dimension relates to a firm's innovation management and transferring of need-related knowledge from customers to the firm. It is best visible in Case Beta. The second form of co-creation is about gains in the customer-firm relationship. It is mostly about generating positive word of mouth, expanding existing or creating new markets, and increasing maximum willingness to pay among the firm's customers. It is best visible in Case Gamma, but also in Case Alpha.

Stage in NSD

Co-creation's influence over innovation practices evolves in the course of project cycle. The needs for inputs are different (early in the project the ideas can be speculative and novel, while later in the project they need to stick to existing trajectories and be more incremental). The degree of control of the firm is increasing (customers find it easier to provide inputs early on, when they can be more conceptual, as opposed to later stages in NSD, when there are strict guidelines and requirements). At the same time, customer inputs in the early stages of NSD are potentially more disruptive to studio's practices (as they are more likely to influence the high-level decisions for the service), and thus occur rarely. In this work, we have not seen a single occurrence of such practice.

Approaches such as player councils, open tests and volunteer programs work well in the late stages of production, as well as after the service com-mercial release. Some highly formalized co-creation techniques, such as con-tests, use of asset stores, as well as targeted submissions are also deployed at later stages of NSD (as the company provides detailed instructions and requirements, as well as establishes some degree of dedicated routines and practices internally). Use of forums, crowdvoting and open discussions are particularly effective in early to middle stages of NSD.

OE's co-creation occurred during the development phase, after the main concept for the service was established and before it was released to the marketplace. Both the nature of customer inputs and the guidelines were clearly established by the studio, allowing for customer inputs only in pre-determined forms and selected aspects of the game (targeted submissions). The usefulness of the inputs provided through the other major channel used by OE, online forums, was becoming increasingly limited as the project progressed (because forums are best at providing ideas, while the best inputs at later stages of development are refinements). Towards the end of the development cycle, the main strength of customers was that determined by their numbers, as the customers were mainly used for QA and testing.

CCP's case illustrates a different scenario. Long after its initial release to the market, *EVE Online* is being constantly improved and worked on. Channels of various types are used concurrently at CCP, as new features of the service are at different stages of development. Customers co-create both long-existing elements of the game, as well as its aspects currently in development.

CIG's case represents a hybrid state of both elements of unreleased service still under development, as well as improvements to an existing one. This is because CIG's service is released to customers in modules. Those modules are still seen as 'works in progress' to some degree, and thus their features and characteristics are malleable. That creates rich context for the ongoing discussions about these features between the customers and development team. We see no customer inputs at the very earliest stages of NSD; ideation of new service features and making major design decisions are seen as the domain of the firm.

Co-Creation's Effects on the Firm

We propose the framework of eight sites of innovation within a firm which are affected by co-creation. This allows us to understand and map the impact of co-creation practice on organizations. We also trace the competences for co-creation that a particular company displays, together with its institutional arrangements, and compare them to the significance of changes in eight sites within a firm. This way we can understand what kind of effects a particular co-creation practice has on an organization.

In the co-creation dynamic, a firm develops its services with significant input from the customers—resulting in services that will fit customers' needs better. One of the most prominent issues pertaining to innovation is the questioned ability of customers to innovate radically (e.g., Aoyama and Izushi, 2008), which means breaking free of existing market trajectories and incremental improvements to existing services. This is a limitation that we also observe in the case of the data presented in this study. Customers are involved as co-creators on various existing projects of the studio—ones that the studio has established and which direction it controls. Feedback on existing or planned features, contests for inputs on a defined topic, votes on choices provided by the studio, volunteer programs to help with maintenance of existing services and solutions—virtually all observed manifestations of co-creation pertain to incremental innovations.

In the case studies, we don't see an account of a radical innovation stemming from the co-creation, perhaps with the exception of the *Incarna* expansion to CCP's *EVE Online*. Still, it illustrates the community's vehement reaction to a firm-introduced innovation and subsequent backtracking of that change by the firm. So even in the example of very strong and visible influence of customers on NSD, that influence pertains to the preservation of the existing line of the service, and is against change. Such a state of affairs is accompanied by the service developers' general reluctance towards customers' ideas as infeasible, unproven, impossible to implement, or difficult to commercialize. In other words, service developers aren't inclined to innovate radically themselves (also due to the general nature of innovation in the creative industries, and sticking to incremental innovations which are familiar to the consumer; Franklin et al., 2013), not mentioning letting their customers do that for them.

More interesting effects of co-creation are observed not in the domain of the service—but on the side of the firm and its organizational practices. Here, the presence of customers in the immediate environment of the firm, as well as increasingly in its internal practices and culture, forces a series of changes to how studios function, how they establish their professional identity, and how they source labour. Those changes, albeit in most cases gradual, cumulatively are radical departures from how videogame development studios normally operate (or how they used to)—as illustrated in Case Alpha. They are reflected by innovation in the eight sites (see Chapter 1), where we see how co-creation affects organizations. Co-creation introduces incremental improvements to firm's services, while having radical intra-organizational effects.

Firms embracing co-creation are required to adapt their organizational practices, culture and competences, as well as integrate co-creation with their firm strategy—including the funding or revenue model. The implications of co-creation are felt in a number of organizational functions. We take a look at the main sites within a firm in which the co-creation outcomes are observed, as well as which serve as institutional conditions for it. Those sites have been first identified by Miles and Green (2008), and have been subsequently narrowed down for the purposes of this research. Furthermore, following on the work of Voss and Zomerdijk (2007) and Zomerdijk and de Vries (2007), those sites focus mostly on the 'back stage' and 'front stage' areas of an experiential service. Additional co-creation-influenced outcomes of innovation occur also in the 'customers' area, with focus on both customer experience and the role of fellow customers.

Therefore, we split the eight sites of innovation into three categories, corresponding to Voss and Zomerdijk's (2007) experiential service design areas. The perspective of looking at videogames as experiential services allows for the accounting for the role of subjective impression and individual perception of value in consumption of creative services, demonstrating the links and interlocking between socio-cultural and market spheres (Banks and Potts, 2010) also on the very basic level of an individual customer.

'Back Stage' Design Area of Experiential Service

According to Voss and Zomerdijk (2007): "the main innovation related to back stage areas of service delivery involves connecting back office employees to the front stage experience" (p. 15). We observe it within the videogame firms embracing co-creation as well. As co-creation is adopted by the firm, more and more employees whose jobs in no way relate to interacting with customers begin to include elements of communication with them. The impact on the organization, its culture, practices and well as style of management (as well as employee identities) are the most pronounced areas of innovation resulting from co-creation. Organizations are required to undergo a significant change in the wake of co-creation.

Back-Office Production Processes

New forms of work organization emerge from co-creation's presence within an organization. New organizational functions for processing customer inputs and types of employees appear. At CIG, email digests of community inputs, sending them out to selected teams, as well as resulting internal discussion, are another example. The 'S priority' class of entries to the bug database at OE, which denote suggestions from the customers, illustrates how customer inputs are accommodated in the aspects of the service development that so far have been solely the domain of the firm. The process of service development is rendered visible as part of the customer experience.

The outcomes of co-creation on innovation are also enabled, or at least greatly facilitated, by flexible production methodologies in those firms (such as Agile or Scrum). Innovations to back-office production processes are introduced steadily as customers' role grows and the firm learns to harness those inputs. Sometimes new organizations are established with some degree of co-creation inscribed into their structure from the very beginning. Certain pre-existing or independent practices within firms will be a barrier or stimulator of organizational innovation in the wake of co-creation—for instance, geographical dispersion and reliance on Internet communication facilitate the integration of co-creation methodologies in game development. Conversely, at a firm which is located in a single physical site, more communication is done in person and verbally, and that means that player inputs (mostly provided via Internet) are further away from existing organizational routines, and thus assimilating them requires more effort.

In the presence of co-creation in a firm, the roles of employees are also subject to change. Developers are no longer the sole authors of the service. The work practices are also changing, and the curation of customer-generated content is becoming an increasing portion of work. Those changes are seen to a different extent at various firms—CCP is very much about facilitation of customers' creativity, and the developers' job is to build a system for that creativity. On the other hand, inXile Entertainment uses customers to generate art assets from scratch, which is a practice that so far has been solely the domain of the firm. That practice though is tightly controlled by the releasing of strict guidelines for those community inputs, as well as retaining of selection control by the studio (it is the best illustration of the framework of O'Hern and Rindfleisch, 2010). Nevertheless, we see here the change occurring—firm employees prepare the guidelines and orchestrate creative inputs originating outside of the firm.

We observe how the work of the QA department has been afforded new possibilities and new modes of functioning. The role of that department within the organization has also been shifting. The QA department, to that point a low-visible function of the creative firm, now becomes one of the key departments having intensive interactions with the customers. QA employees are also adopting some social and community duties, as QA becomes the main entry point into a profession. We are observing both types of co-creation outcomes—benefits to NSD, as well as to the relationship with the customers. Those changes do not always sit easily with service developers, especially in departments such as art, where the role of personal vision and skills in production of outputs is considerable (O'Donnell, 2014).

Professional identities of staff are also at stake. They consider themselves experts in what they do. Customers on the other hand are seen as uninformed and not fully understanding the practicalities of service development. Still, the researcher has not seen any data corresponding to staff fears of becoming displaced by the free labour of fans and customers (apart from in literature, c.f. Wexler, 2011). Those tensions between the changing role of employees in the context of customer involvement, as well as their fears of being displaced by free labour, may influence the role of co-creation in innovation practices.

Internal Communications and Organizational Culture

Just as organizational culture influences the role of co-creation in innovation practices, the changes to it can be the basis for innovation resulting from co-creation. Compared to the traditional way of service development, the presence of co-creation has triggered major differences in how studio employees approach and think of their customers. Departing from the model of separation of internal firm culture from that of the community of 'fans', creative industries have started involving customers in their organization's life and culture. Numerous personal relationships appear between the employees and customers, especially observed during physical gatherings of the customer community. Employees describe the difference between their current customer-involving work practices and their previous job (i.e., a job without much interaction with customers). The force that is driving those transformations most of all is the presence and widespread use of crowdfunding, which promotes tightening of the relationships between customers, who are now funders and loyal fans, and the employees, who now have also a social and moral obligation to return the trust of their fans.

Similarly, internal communications are another clear innovation outcome appearing in the wake of co-creation. Creative industries overall are departing from the outdated Waterfall-based production models (where tasks and assets are produced in a sequence) and instead embrace the use of Agile and Scrum methodologies (which allow more flexibility and simultaneity, as well as rely on iterative production cycles and extensive coordination across multidisciplinary teams). Such environment is also more conducive to accepting customer inputs (as they are largely unpredictable in production schedules, so only production schedules allowing for a degree of slack and unpredictability can fit them in).

Daily stand-up meetings, making decisions as a team, coordination of requirements and deliverables across the teams—those are all influencing NSD and innovation practice at firms, allowing for organization-wide communication with customers, and thus increasing their effect on innovation. We observe how certain communication routines and channels have been established and evolved around the need to convey customers' feedback. Dedicated internal mailing lists, email forum digests, as well as allowing some insight into firm's project management and database tools—these forms of communication appear or are adopted more widely as an organization's response to co-creation. Interestingly, some communications that have been strictly internal, such as service design documents and transcripts from internal meetings, are beginning to be made available to the community in order to further co-creation. Use of those documents for that purpose is an innovation which transforms how a vision for a service is articulated.

Co-creation's impact on NSD and innovation practices hinges on the attitudes of individual employees within that firm. Historically, creative industries firms tend to be weary of the customers' involvement in service development due to the disruptions to organizational practices. Also, confidentiality issues play a role here. More importantly, exchanges between the staff and customers can sometimes take a bad turn and become toxic, becoming a source of stress.

At all firms studied, the relationship between customers and the employees is good or very good. That results from the sample bias—only firms that use co-creation have been sampled, and customer relationship benefits are one of the two main outcomes of co-creation. Nevertheless, individual employees will vary in their perception of customers, and some of them have negative opinions about their involvement or have had bad experiences with them. If customers are seen as partners for the employees, the doors are open for co-creation—the type that resides on the level of individual, 'under the radar' interactions between firm employees and customers and is performed on an 'on the job' basis. On the other hand, formal manifestations of co-creation are not as heavily affected by the attitudes of individual employees. Instead, they largely rely on top-down managerial decisions and cannot be contested by the lower echelons of an organization.

Different personal attitudes towards customers affect where in an organization there will be more co-creation taking place (or, in other words, in which sites within a creative firm, as outlined by Miles and Green, 2008). Visible exemplars of community interaction affect the tone of exchanges and attitude of lower-tier employees, becoming in time associated with that particular organization's culture.

The general attitude among employees is that customers do not have skills that would in any way exceed those resident within the firm. Customers, in such light, do not have the ability to provide the firm with innovative inputs. What customers are seen as good at is their knowledge of the genre, as well as their excellent overview of the service (as individual developers are very focused on their field, they compromise their understanding of it as a whole). Customers are also seen as useful in numbers to test as part of QA. The problem of customers having difficulty articulating their needs is highlighted. That aspect of organizational culture determines the limited scope of co-creation, close controls on co-creating customers, as well as relatively sparse use of customers for guidance.

Customers innovate new service use patterns and expand the service software. Customers are seen as very competent in reaffirming the direction in which the firm should go, as well as a valuable marketing and public relations tool. The fact that there are close personal links between the employees and the members of the customer community, as well as common interests and shared social background, further contributes to the perceptions of partnership and collaboration.

Customers' skills and knowledge are at times difficult to integrate with the firm's practices, or come in excess to the internal competences of the firm. Intellectual property issues, as well as the issue of coping with too many inputs are the main limiting factors to accepting customers' creativity. Customers are seen as being able to come up with valuable ideas, but their community is also seen as the best judge of the quality of those ideas (mostly because it eliminates all but the best ideas before firm staff become involved, thus saving the employees time and effort). Still, it is the customers' affinity for spreading the word about a service, and thus contributing to its marketing, that is also highly valued by firms.

Transactions, Financing and Revenue Model

One of the biggest innovations that is linked to co-creation, and which also is the easiest to observe, is crowdfunding. This model of financing transforms how organizations function. The ability to have the customers fund NSD, on the capital investment basis, in exchange for nothing more but recognition and belonging to a community (as well as other optional rewards, but those rewards have mostly sentimental value associated with the feelings of fandom and community membership) has allowed many firms to function. Through the crowdfunding mechanism, customers' role in voting with their money has increased in significance. It is therefore an articulation of customer needs in its bare form—after all, customers are backing ideas, not finished services.

Similarly, another big change was the rise of 'microtransactions' and the subscription model of revenue. Although not directly linked with co-creation, in the videogames industry they drive the formulation of games as services, as opposed to products. Before these two revenue models, videogames were simply purchased on a one-off transaction basis, making them more similar to products. In the new model, videogames can even be first played for free, and only once a customer has been involved for some time in the service do they begin to pay the firm. That forces the firms to keep their customers happy and closely listen to their wishes and demands. That has created the now-growing need for positions such as community managers and customer service. For some firms, it means granting customers an active stake in NSD and getting them involved in the firm's internal practices.

A firm's strategic goals and their influence on the innovation practice are to large extent determined by the use of crowdfunding. That approach forces the firm to maintain close links with its customers, permitting them insight and influence over the game development—as the phenomenon of crowdfunding is driven by customers' desire to be involved. In exchange for money, customers do not receive any shares in the firm or rights to intellectual property—a firm incentivizes their participation by various rewards, some of which are formalized opportunities to co-create.

The successful maintenance of the revenue from subscriptions hinges on the stable and satisfied community of customers. In the case of CCP, the service that is being offered (*EVE Online*) attracts customers of a particular taste, constituting a niche in the market. Those customers seek to innovate, tinker and push the boundaries of the service—and the firm seeks to satisfy them. In order for the service to truly respond to those desires, a high degree of control must be ceded to the customers—therefore creating the situation in which there are strong and close links between the firm and customers.

'Front Stage' Design Area of Experiential Service

There are numerous innovations arising in response to active customers. The firms realize how much can be gained by forging close links with the community of customers—for some firms it is about public relations and marketing, while for others about complementing some functions of the firm (such as QA) and sourcing NSD inputs from the customers.

Marketing and Customer Relationship Management

As customers are becoming participants in service development, the maintenance of relationship with them becomes paramount to organizations. Customers are vocal and highly networked, and word of mouth and maximum willingness to pay form powerful forces. It can be argued that any co-creation effort undertaken by the firm has a role in marketing of the service.

Innovations in this area pertain mostly to structuring of the communications between the firm employees and the customers—the official channel for communication is now only one of the many channels, the majority of which rely on informality. User involvement competence feeds into this—studios deploy various means and channels for communication with their customers in order to fully tap into their creative potential, or to ensure the maximum gains to the customer-firm relationship. The investment in those functions of the firm has increased greatly, which is reflected by the number of community managers and customer service representatives. Management and understanding of a community's mood and sentiment has become widely practiced by the collection of various metrics and data about the community (as well as talking to some key community members), together with controlling their expectations.

Value Chain Location and Positioning

Co-creation opens up new possibilities for value chain and positioning. Some firms choose to tap into their customers' creativity and make it into an important part of their value proposition. Similarly, some firms choose to source many of their assets from the community. They also establish marketplaces where customers can sell their designs, but the firm will also generate revenues out of it (e.g., Steam Community Market—the majority of profits goes to the creators, but the firm will extract a share from the sales as well—up to 25% in some cases). Firms can reduce their costs of NSD by sourcing some of the labour from the community (such co-creation also has marketing and customer-firm relationship benefits for instance, as well as helps to identify and vet the best candidates for employment).

Therefore, more aspects of a service can be produced outside of the firm by the customers (while other aspects can be sourced from software purchased from other firms, e.g., middleware). In that scenario, a creative firm becomes a coordinator of external competencies. It is a significant departure from the traditional model of creative service development, which relies on the solely in-house effort. The role of co-creation in value chain location and positioning differs from firm to firm, and can occur both during the NSD, as well as after the launch. In both instances customers can be a source of free labour to the firm, helping the firm with ideation, creation of assets, testing, marketing and public relations (Pearce, 2009; Malaby, 2009; Boellstorff, 2008; Castronova, 2005).

Following on Cheng and Huizingh (2014) and Grant (2010), the strategy at OE is identified as maximization of resources. The firm embraces the attitude of making the most out of its existing NSD practices, as well as of the resource 'crowd' (which is seen mostly as a source of funds, not of knowledge or creativity). This is also the most conservative strategy—the firm is relatively reluctant to open itself up to the inputs from customers.

This is contrasted by the practices of CCP, whose strategy relies of innovation and entrepreneurship. Their service is a system for enabling customers' innovativeness. Such approach is also embraced by the firm in its experimentation with service development and delivery methodologies, new forms of involving community of customers, as well as fostering open organizational culture. Entrepreneurship of the firm, and that of the customers, is promoted (Chandra and Leenders, 2012).

CIG's strategic orientation is focused on marketing and building their service's presence in the market. They put a heavy emphasis on the communication with the customers, as well as the exchanges of creativity and ideas with them. Community, which is CIG's chief resource, plays an important role of both funders, as well as marketers in the firm's strategy. Complex integration of customers in the NSD has become commoditized at CIG, and the customers' participation in internal processes of the firm is among its chief value- and revenue-generating mechanisms.

'Customers' Design Area of Experiential Service

In the following section, customer experience of a service, as well as related innovations that stem from co-creation, are discussed. This section reflects the changing roles of customers not only in the NSD, but also their role as customers, members of the community and important influencers of fellow customers' experience. Co-creation has profound effects on those dimensions, but it also influences how the firms design the role of customers into their services.

Users' Interactions

Customers discuss services on online forums, contribute ideas, and provide comments and feedback. With the firm listening in on those discussions, some interactions between customers become productive. Employees 'seed' the forums with topics for discussion, open contests for customers, or encourage customers to form teams and participate in various activities. The community becomes a more tightly knit institution as the firm deploys various community-building programs and tools. Certain aspects of the service discussion can 'spill out' and take place in other places on the Internet, via other channels—for instance, tactics and strategy can be discussed on forums, or certain service-related announcements (posted by the customers, not the firm) can be displayed on various websites even using Google AdSense.

Most innovation outcomes in this site pertain to the techniques and devices deployed by the firm to facilitate the formation and cohesion of a community of customers. Firms provide a framework for those rich interactions among customers to emerge—examples here include dedicated forums, systems of achievements, extensive moderation, player councils and volunteers, contests, TV-style shows, as well as gatherings and festivals. Many of those techniques also serve the purposes of marketing and public relations, but their role in providing context and culture for the community of customers, and their interactions, is significant. The focus on those practices among creative firms is an innovation to many organizations, and represents a significant new site for resource allocation. A chief innovator in that field is CCP, which deploys a vast array of methods for structuring and shaping of users' interactions.

Content of Service and Its Genre

Content of a service is probably among the sites most affected by co-creation. For instance, many videogames are designed to allow a degree of emergent gameplay (Nardi, 2010), which relies on customers' coming up with new ways of interacting with the service. Customers are happily providing such content of service as writing, designs, art assets, quality testers and much more. Some activities of customers, such as organizing into guilds, clans and communities can also be seen as contributing to the content of those services, whch rely on social dynamics. Such manifestations of co-creation are relatively 'safe' for firms and do not disrupt internal NSD processes, as co-creating customers interact with the service artefacts and fellow customers and not with the firm itself. Firms in those instances control the degree of co-creation centrally by such tools as licensing agreements, secrecy and support shown to the co-creating customers. In the videogames industry cases studied above, customers provide ready-made assets, but also mods, improvements and extensive suggestions and feedback for the content of the service continuously and via different channels. Prime of those are forums and contests of various kinds. Customers can also vote on which features get incorporated into the service (i.e., through a process referred to as crowdvoting).

Service genre has a significant influence on the degree of co-creation. Genre denotes, among other things, the main mode of interaction between the customer and the service, and what the main premise of the service is, as well as what the customer's agency is in its context. Service platform has a similar strong effect on co-creation—proprietary interfaces tend to limit its scope (in the videogames industry that's consoles and Apple operating systems).[3]

User Interface With Product and User Capabilities

User capabilities (i.e., what customers' agency is in-service, what actions and interactions the customers can undertake) are defined throughout NSD (during the ideation and prototyping phase). They are a resultant force of technological choices made by the firm, as well as of the competences and skills of the studio staff. Strategic thinking also plays a role—sometimes in the videogames industry, as the result of using third-party software as the game engine, user capabilities must be limited and customers will not be permitted to manipulate the game code in any way. A company's fears of customers twisting and corrupting a particular IP and thus damaging its public image is another reason to limit user capabilities. Modding falls into this category.

Additional innovations are introduced by expansion of service experience to platforms different than the original; for creative services it often means to mobile platform. Those expansions are often the direct results of customer co-creation—who will create cheap and easy-to-make applications for mobile devices such as phones and tablets, allowing new dimensions and contexts of service experience. Firms also notice that and develop 'companion applications' of their own. Using either community- or firm-developed applications customers can engage with the service in new ways.

User interface is also an aspect of the service that is most readily co-created by the customers. This is the most visible element of the service experience. Customers have very strong opinions and preferences for the user interface that they like to use, and pressure the studio to take their wishes under consideration. In the videogames industry, we observe extensive manipulation of that interface, for instance in the case of *World of Warcraft* (described, for example, in Nardi, 2010; Davidovici-Nora, 2009; Taylor, 2008), where customers innovate not only new elements of user interface, but also introduce new ways of interacting with the service. Firms can then choose to either support those innovations, integrating them with the service, or attempt to stem customers' manipulation of the interface, due to prevention of loss of control over the service.

Summary

The majority of co-creation's outcomes in organizations pertains to the context of a firm and its functioning, as well as its market offerings, relationships with customers, and organizational culture. It is difficult to track the co-creation-resulting innovations when it comes to a service itself. This is because co-creation's impact on NSD in creative industries is largely co-located with hidden innovation, as well as due to the nebulous nature of the concept 'content' in the experiential services. Great many innovations introduced by co-creation also tend to be incremental improvements to existing services or parts of it, and the firms don't keep track of which idea originated externally, and which was sparked internally. Overall, it is safe to summarize that co-creation rarely results in radical innovations—and for other cases its outcomes on innovation are difficult to track (unless formal methods are used).

Still, the data confirms that customers provide firms with numerous ideas, and the firms benefit in their own creative practices. Those ideas are reconfigured, changed and developed before they reach implementation in NSD. They are very rarely integrated with the service in their original form (for instance, that happens during the contests or when community-made assets are purchased from online stores). Such direct sourcing of ideas and their assimilation occurs only in situation, where the intellectual property and copyright context can be clearly resolved, i.e., where the transfer of property is transparent and legally permissible.

Alternatively, customer inputs aren't used for their NSD value, but instead for their benefits to customer-firm relationship. In that scenario, a firm communicates extensively with its customers, informing them about NSD and other aspects of a service. The internal functioning and processes of the firm become part of the service experience, with the firm revealing some of its 'back-office' processes to customers, and inviting their idea-centric inputs (O'Hern et al., 2011). At the same time, the firm maintains tight control over the selection of those inputs (O'Hern and Rindfleisch, 2010).

The innovation outcomes are also explained by the dual nature of co-creation practice itself, as well as all of its inputs and outputs—namely, existing both as socio-cultural and market phenomena. Co-creation has the potential to affect actors other than the firm—especially the community of customers as well as third-party business partners—but when it comes to the organization itself, the eight sites outlined in this section capture all manifestations of co-creation's impact on innovation. Those sites are affected significantly by the customer inputs on one hand, and on the other by the organizational attempts to tap into customers' community as a resource (for either NSD or customer-firm relationship). The particular sites where innovation is affected by co-creation depend on a firm's unique competences for co-creation, as well as the role of co-creation in its organizational culture, as well as its funding arrangements. In various circumstances of these, the impact of co-creation on innovation in particular sites will also be different.

We observe how diverse co-creation approaches that firms adopt translate themselves into NSD and innovation outcomes. Those approaches hinge on a number of factors, such as the issues of control (O'Hern and Rindfleisch, 2010), the calculation of costs and benefits (Hoyer et al., 2010), service innovation methodology (Voss and Zomerdijk, 2007; den Hertog, 2000), stage in NSD (Piller et al., 2011), community profile (Burger-Helmchen and Cohendet, 2011), organizational culture (Malaby, 2009) and funding arrangements (Ordanini et al., 2011). Companies deploy the above approaches based on their organizational competences for co-creation and institutional arrangements, but also these competences develop and are established in the course of co-creation.

Table 4.5 below summarizes the organizational practices described in the cases and shows how these are categorized in terms of their function and meaning for co-creation. It brings together the observed practices of firms with their classification into three ideal types of co-creation. It also discusses the function of those practices, meaning the kind of effects that they trigger in a firm's assimilation of customer inputs.

Table 4.5 Table Listing Organizational Practices of Co-Creation

Organizational Practice of Co-Creation	Examples of Practices	Function in Co-Creation	Meaning for Co-Creation
Structured (illustrated by Case Alpha)	Inputs only from customers who crossed a crowdfunding threshold. Specific guidelines for what kind of customer inputs are accepted. Dedicated staff meetings for processing customer inputs. Targeted and individual methods of communication and iterating work with individual customers.	Adding order to co-creation— insertion into organizational routines. Minimizing disruptions stemming from co-creation. Visible to the customer community. Resolving potential IP issues. Making co-creation easier to adopt for organizations. Minimizing organizational changes stemming from the use of co-creation.	Relatively low degree of co-location with hidden innovation. Co-creation serving customer relationship gains. Co-creation format closest to crowdsourcing and classical open innovation practices (Chesbrough, 2011). Very often accompanies particular funding arrangements (the use of crowdfunding). Emphasis is on appropriation competence. Presence of top-down coordination in the company.
Semi-structured (illustrated by Case Beta)	Use of cross-disciplinary teams for discussing player inputs. Use of Scrum project management	Flexibility and emphasis on NSD inputs. High quality of customer inputs. Extensive	Optimal balance between co-creation for NSD inputs and customer relationship gains. Co-creation in

Organizational Practice of Co-Creation	Examples of Practices	Function in Co-Creation	Meaning for Co-Creation
	method and customers as its stakeholder. Dedicated employees for coordinating player inputs. Champions for customers' inputs. Use of player councils and volunteer programs. Prominent function of fan gatherings. Social interactions with customers.	integration with the internal practices and processes of the firm. Requires assimilation into business model and firm strategy. Gains to customer relationship tend to be a by-product of customers' involvement in NSD.	market niches. Organizational culture is of particular importance. Hidden innovation present to a moderate degree. High integration competence. Lateral coordination of NSD in organization among the teams.
Unstructured (illustrated by Case Gamma)	Individual employees as gatekeepers for customer inputs. Culture of respecting and working with the customers. Ongoing crowdfunding effort. Crowdfunding linked to business model, monetization of customer relationship by subscriptions. Visits from customers to the studio. No marketing budget. High visibility contests (formal co-creation elements).	Overlapping of co-creation with hidden innovation. Relative lack of structure to the practice, customer inputs occur 'under the radar' of formal recognition. Individual employees form co-creative relationships. Customer inputs are processed ad hoc in most part. Reliance on the skills of employees and their judgment of usefulness of customer inputs. Managing IP issues by	Significant gains to the customer relationship (positive word of mouth and increased willingness to pay). Excellent user involvement competence present. Organizational culture and funding arrangements very influential on this co-creation practice. Highly innovative model, unproven game development practice. Reliance on informal methods of co-creation.

(Continued)

Table 4.5 Continued

Organizational Practice of Co-Creation	Examples of Practices	Function in Co-Creation	Meaning for Co-Creation
		only formally accepting solution-centric inputs. Focus on marketing-related outcomes of co-creation. Geographically dispersed organizational structure of high individual autonomy; weak day-to-day project coordination.	

Notes

1. This chapter often refers to 'sites of innovation'—by them we mean the refined Olympian by Miles and Green model (2008) discussed in Chapter 1.
2. For competences the scale is from low, through moderate, to high.
3. Mobile and consoles attract more mainstream audiences, which are composed of more 'casual' players who have no interest in forming cognitive communities of customers (which are necessary for co-creation; Burger-Helmchen and Cohendet, 2011).

References

Aoyama, Y., and Izushi, H., (2008). User-led innovation and the video game industry. IRP Conference, London, May 22–23, 2008.

Bagozzi, R.P., and Dholakia, U.M., (2006). Open source software user communities: A study of participation in Linux user groups. *Management Science*, 52(7), pages 1099–1115.

Baldwin, C., Hienerth, C., and von Hippel, E., (2006). How user innovations become commercial products: A theoretical investigation and case study. *Research Policy*, 35(9), pages 1291–1313.

Banks, J., and Potts, J., (2010). Co-creating games: A co-evolutionary analysis. *New Media and Society*, 12(2), pages 252–270.

Benkler, Y., (2006). *The Wealth of Networks*. Yale: Yale University Press.

Bergstrom, K., Carter, M., Woodford, D., and Paul, C., (2013). Constructing the ideal EVE Online player. In Proceedings of DiGRA 2013: DeFragging Game Studies, Atlanta, USA.

Bethke, E., (2003). *Game Development and Production*. Plano, TX: Wordware Publishing, Inc.

Boellstorff, T., (2008). *Coming of Age in Second Life: An Anthropologist Explores the Virtually Human.* Princeton and Oxford: Princeton University Press.

Burger-Helmchen, T., and Cohendet, P., (2011). User communities and social software in the video game industry. *Long Range Planning*, 44, pages 317–343.

Castronova, E., (2005). *Synthetic Worlds: The Business and Culture of Online Games.* Chicago and London: The University of Chicago Press.

Chandra, Y., and Leenders, M.A., (2012). User innovation and entrepreneurship in the virtual world: A study of Second Life residents. *Technovation*, 32(7), pages 464–476.

Cheng, C.C., and Huizingh, E.K., (2014). When is open innovation beneficial? The role of strategic orientation. *Journal of Product Innovation Management*, 31(6), pages 1235–1253.

Chesbrough, H., (2011). Bringing open innovation to services. *MIT Sloan Management Review*, 52(2), pages 85–90.

Cohen, W.M., and Levinthal, D.A., (1990). Absorptive capacity: A new perspective on learning and innovation. *Administrative Science Quarterly*, Vol. 35, No. 1, pages 128–152.

Davidovici-Nora, M., (2009). The dynamics of co-creation in the video game industry: The case of World of Warcraft. *Communications & Strategies*, (73), pages 43–66.

den Hertog, P.D., (2000). Knowledge-intensive business services as co-producers of innovation. *International Journal of Innovation Management*, 4(4), pages 491–528.

Dibbell, J., (2006). *Play Money.* New York: Basic Books.

Dosi, G., and Nelson, R.R., (1994). An introduction to evolutionary theories in economics. *Journal of Evolutionary Economics*, 4(3), pages 153–172.

Ducheneaut, N., et al., (2007). The life and death of online gaming communities: A look at guilds in World of Warcraft. CHI 2007 Proceedings. April 28–May 3, 2007. San Jose, CA, USA.

Ebner, W., Leimeister, J.M., and Krcmar, H., (2009). Community engineering for innovations: The ideas competition as a method to nurture a virtual community for innovations. *R&D Management*, 39(4), pages 342–356.

Echeverri, P., and Skålén, P., (2011). Co-creation and co-destruction: A practice-theory based study of interactive value formation. *Marketing Theory*, 11(3), pages 351–373.

Edvardsson, B., Kristensson, P., Magnusson, P., and Sundström, E., (2012). Customer integration within service development—a review of methods and an analysis of insitu and exsitu contributions. *Technovation*, 32(7), pages 419–429.

Edvardsson, B., and Olsson, J., (1996). Key concepts for new service development. *Service Industries Journal*, 16(2), pages 140–164.

Edwards, M., Logue, D., and Schweitzer, J., (2015). Towards an understanding of open innovation in services: Beyond the firm and towards relational co-creation. In: Agarwal, R., Selen, W., Roos, G., and Green, R., (eds). *The Handbook of Service Innovation.* London: Springer London, pages 75–90.

Eisenhardt, K.M., (1989). Building theories from case study research. *Academy of Management Review*, 14(4), pages 532–550.

Enkel, E., Kausch, C., and Gassmann, O., (2005). Managing the risk of customer integration. *European Management Journal*, 23(2), pages 203–213.

Estelles-Arolas, E., and Gonzales-Ladron-de-Guevara, F., (2012). Towards an integrated crowdsourcing definition. *Journal of Information Science*, 38(2), pages 189–200.

Etgar, M., (2008). A descriptive model of the consumer co-production process. *Journal of the Academy of Marketing Science*, 36(1), pages 97–108.

Fang, E., (2008). Customer participation and the trade-off between new product innovativeness and speed to market. *Journal of Marketing*, 72(4), pages 90–101.

Feng, W., Brandt, D., and Saha, D., (2007). A long-term study of a popular MMORPG. In: *Proceedings of the 6th ACM SIGCOMM Workshop on Network and System Support for Games*. ACM Press, pages 19–24.

Fereday, J., and Muir-Cochrane, E., (2006). Demonstrating rigor using thematic analysis: A hybrid approach of inductive and deductive coding and theme development. *International Journal of Qualitative Methods*, 5(1), pages 80–92.

Fisher, D., and Smith, S., (2011). Co-creation is chaotic: What it means for marketing when no one has control. *Marketing Theory*, 11(3), pages 325–350.

Franke, N., and von Hippel, E., (2003). Satisfying heterogeneous user needs via innovation toolkits: The case of Apache security software. *Research Policy*, 32(7), pages 1199–1215.

Franke, N., and Shah, S., (2003). How communities support innovative activities: An exploration of assistance and sharing among end-users. *Research Policy*, 32, pages 157–178.

Franklin, M., Searle, N., Stoyanova, D., and Townley, B., (2013). Innovation in the application of digital tools for managing uncertainty: the case of UK independent film. *Creativity and Innovation Management*, 22(3), pages 320–333.

Frow, P., Payne, A., and Storbacka, K., (2011). Co-creation: A typology and conceptual framework. In: *Proceedings of ANZMAC* (November), pages 1–6.

Füller, J., (2010). Refining virtual co-creation from a consumer perspective. *California Management Review*, 52(2), pages 98–122.

Füller, J., and Matzler, K., (2007). Virtual product experience and customer participation—a chance for customer-centred, really new products. *Technovation*, 27(6), pages 378–387.

Füller, J., Matzler, K., and Hoppe, M., (2008). Brand community members as a source of innovation. *Journal of Product Innovation Management*, 25(6), pages 608–619.

Fynes, B., and Lally, A.M., (2008). Innovation in services: From service concepts to service experiences. In: Hefley, B. and Murphy, W., (eds). *Service Science, Management and Engineering: Education for the 21st Century*. New York: Springer Science & Business Media, pages 329–333.

Gangi, P.M., Wasko, M.M., and Hooker, R.E., (2010). Getting customers' ideas to work for you: Learning from Dell how to succeed with online user innovation communities. *MIS Quarterly Executive*, 9(4), pages 213–228.

Garcia-Lorenzo, L., (2004). (Re)producing the organization through narratives: The case of a multinational. *Intervention Research*, 1, pages 43–60.

Gebauer, J., Füller, J., and Pezzei, R., (2013). The dark and the bright side of co-creation: Triggers of member behaviour in online innovation communities. *Journal of Business Research*, 66, pages 1516–1527.

Gibbs, M.R., Carter, M., and Mori, J., (2013). Vile rat: Spontaneous shrines in EVE online. Paper presented at the EVE Online Workshop, Chania, Greece, May 14–17, 2013.

Gibbs, L., Kealy, M., Willis, K., Green, J., Welch, N., and Daly, J., (2007). What have sampling and data collection got to do with good qualitative research? *Australian and New Zealand Journal of Public Health*, 31(6), pages 540–544.

Grant, R.M., (2010). *Contemporary Strategy Analysis and Cases: Text and Cases*. New York: John Wiley & Sons.

Grantham, A., and Kaplinsky, R., (2005). Getting the measure of the electronic games industry: developers and the management of innovation. *International Journal of Innovation Management*, 9(2), pages 183–213.

Grimes, S.M., (2006). Online multiplayer games: A virtual space for intellectual property debates? *New Media & Society*, 8(6), pages 969–990.

Grönroos, C., (1994). From marketing mix to relationship marketing: Towards a paradigm shift in marketing. *Management Decision*, 32(2), pages 4–20.

Grönroos, C., (2011). Value co-creation in service logic: A critical analysis. *Marketing Theory*, 11(3), pages 279–301.

Grove, S.J., Fisk, R.P., and Bitner, M.J., (1992). Dramatizing the service experience: A managerial approach. *Advances in Services Marketing and Management*, 1, pages 91–121.

Gruner, K.E., and Homburg, C., (2000). Does customer interaction enhance new product success? *Journal of Business Research*, 49(1), pages 1–14.

Gummesson, E., (2002). Relationship marketing in the new economy. *Journal of Relationship Marketing*, 1(1), pages 37–57.

Gustafsson, A., Kristensson, P., and Witell, L., (2012). Customer co-creation in service innovation: A matter of communication? *Journal of Service Management*, 23(3), pages 311–327.

Haefliger, S., Jäger, P., and von Krogh, G., (2010). Under the radar: Industry entry by user entrepreneurs. *Research Policy*, 39(9), pages 1198–1213.

Hamari, J., Koivisto, J., and Sarsa, H., (2014). Does gamification work?—A literature review of empirical studies on gamification. In: *System Sciences (HICSS), 2014 47th Hawaii International Conference*, January, IEEE, pages 3025–3034.

Handke, C., (2004). Defining creative industries by comparing the creation of novelty. In the workshop Creative Industries—a measure of urban development, WIWIPOL and FOKUS, Vienna.

Hardt, M., and Negri, A., (2001). *Empire* (New ed). Cambridge, MA: Harvard University Press.

Hartley, J., (2008). *Television Truths*. Malden, MA: Wiley-Blackwell.

Hartley, J., Potts, J., Cunningham, S., Flew, T., Keane, M., and Banks, J., (2013). *Key Concepts in Creative Industries*. London: Sage.

Hartley, J., Potts, J., MacDonald, T., Erkunt, C., and Kufleitner, C., (2012). CCI creative city index. *Cultural Science Journal*, 5 (1–138).

Hartley, J., Sørensen, E., and Torfing, J., (2013). Collaborative innovation: A viable alternative to market competition and organizational entrepreneurship. *Public Administration Review*, 73(6), pages 821–830.

Harvard Law Review, (2012). Spare the mod: In support of total-conversion modified video games. *Harvard Law Review*, 125, pages 789–810.

Hau, Y.S., and Kim, Y.G., (2011). Why would online gamers share their innovation-conducive knowledge in the online game user community? Integrating individual motivations and social capital perspectives. *Computers in Human Behavior*, 27(2), pages 956–970.

Haythornthwaite, C., and Gruzd, A., (2007). A noun phrase analysis tool for mining online community conversations. Paper presented at the International Conference on Communications and Technologies, East Lansing, Michigan.

Hight, J., and Novak, J., (2008). *Game Development Essentials: Game Project Management*. Clifton Park, NY: Delmar.

Hills, M., (2002). *Fan Cultures*. London: Routledge.

Howe, J., (2008). *Crowdsourcing: Why the Power of the Crowd Is Driving the Future of Business*. New York: Crown Business.

Hoyer, W.D., Chandy, R., Dorotic, M., Krafft, M., and Singh, S.S., (2010). Consumer co-creation in new product development. *Journal of Service Research*, 13(3), pages 283–296.

Humphreys, S., (2005A). Productive users, intellectual property and governance: The challenges of computer games. *Media and Arts Law Review*, 10(4), pages 299–310.

Humphreys, S., (2005B). Productive players: Online computer games' challenge to conventional media forms. *Communication and Critical/Cultural Studies*, 2(1), pages 36–50.

Humphreys, S., (2007). You're in our world now: Ownership and access in the proprietary community of an MMOG. In: Sugumaran, V., (eds). *Intelligent Information Technologies: Concepts, Methodologies, Tools, and Applications*. Hershey, PA: Information Science Reference (IGI Global), pages 2058–2072.

Humphreys, S., Fitzgerald, B.F., Banks, J.A., and Suzor, N.P., (2005). Fan based production for computer games: User led innovation, the 'drift of value' and the negotiation of intellectual property rights. *Media International Australia Incorporating Culture and Policy: Quarterly Journal of Media Research and Resources*, Vol. 114, pages 16–29.

Ind, N., and Coates, N., (2013). The meanings of co-creation. *European Business Review*, 25(1), pages 86–95.

Irish, D., (2005). *The Game Producer's Handbook*. Boston, MA: Course Technology.

Jäger, P., Haefliger, S., and von Krogh, G., (2010). A directing audience: How specialized feedback in virtual community of consumption stimulates new media production. ETH Zurich Working Paper.

Jenkins, H., (2006). *Convergence Culture: Where Old and New Media Collide*. New York: New York University Press.

Jenkins, H., (2009). What happened before YouTube. In: Burgess, J. and Green, J., (eds). *YouTube: Online Video and the Politics of Participatory Culture*. London: Polity Press, pages 109–125.

Jensen, M.B., Johnson, B., Lorenz, E., and Lundvall, B.A., (2007). Forms of knowledge and modes of innovation. *Research Policy*, 36, pages 680–693.

Jeppesen, L.B., and Frederiksen, L., (2006). Why do users contribute to firm-hosted user communities? The case of computer-controlled music instruments. *Organization Science*, 17(1), pages 45–63.

Jeppesen, L.B., and Molin, M., (2003). Consumers as co-developers: Learning and innovation outside the firm. *Technology Analysis & Strategic Management*, 15(3), pages 363–383.

Jordan, T., (2008). *Hacking: Digital Media and Technological Determinism*. Cambridge: Polity Press.

Kasmire, J., Korhonen, J.M., and Nikolic, I., (2012). How radical is a radical innovation? An outline for a computational approach. *Energy Procedia*, 20, pages 346–353.

Keith, C., (2010). *Agile Game Development With Scrum*. Upper Saddle River, NJ: Addison-Wesley.

King, B., and Borland, J., (2014). *Dungeons and Dreamers*. Carnegie Mellon University: ETC Press.

Kline, S., Dyer-Witherford, N., and De Peuter, G., (2003). *Digital Play: The Interaction of Technology, Culture and Marketing.* Montreal: McGill-Queen's University Press.

Knight, F.H., (1921). *Risk, Uncertainty, and Profit.* Boston, MA: Hart, Schaffner & Marx and Houghton Mifflin Co.

Kohler, T., Füller, J., Matzler, K., and Stieger, D., (2011b). Co-creation in virtual worlds: The design of the user experience. *MIS Quarterly*, 35(3), pages 773–788.

Kohler, T., Füller, J., Stieger, D., and Matzler, K., (2011a). Avatar-based innovation: Consequences of the virtual co-creation experience. *Computers in Human Behaviour*, 27, pages 160–168.

Kohler, T., Matzler, K., and Füller, J., (2009). Avatar-based innovation: Using virtual worlds for real-world innovation. *Technovation*, 29(6), pages 395–407.

Koster, R., (2005). *A Theory of Fun for Game Design.* Sebastopol, CA: Paraglyph Press.

Kozinets, R.V., (2007). Inno-tribes: Star Trek as wikimedia. In: Cova, B., Kozinets, R., and Shankar, A., (eds). *Consumer Tribes.* New York: Routledge.

Kozinets, R.V., Hemetsberger, A., and Schau, H.J., (2008). The wisdom of consumer crowds collective innovation in the age of networked marketing. *Journal of Macromarketing*, 28(4), pages 339–354.

Kücklich, J., (2005). Precarious playbour: Modders and the digital games industry. *The Fibreculture Journal*, 5. http://five.fibreculturejournal.org.

Kuusisto, A., (2008). Customer roles in business service production-implications for involving the customer in service innovation. In: Kuusisto, A. and Päällysaho, S., (eds). *Customer Role in Service Production and Innovation—Looking for Directions for Future Research.* Lappeenranta University of Technology, Faculty of Technology Management Research Report.

Lakhani, K.R., and von Hippel, E., (2003). How open source software works: "Free" user-to-user assistance. *Research Policy*, 32(6), pages 923–943.

Lampel, J., Lant, T., and Shamsie, J., (2000). Balancing act: Learning from organizing practices in cultural industries. *Organization Science*, 11(3), pages 263–269.

Lehner, O.M., (2012). A literature review and research agenda for crowdfunding of social ventures. In: *2012 Research Cooloquium on Social Entrepreneurship*, 16–19.07, SAID Business School.

Lettl, C., (2007). User involvement competence for radical innovation. *Journal of Engineering and Technology Management*, 24, pages 53–75.

Lichtenthaler, U., and Lichtenthaler, E., (2009). A capability-based framework for open innovation: Complementing absorptive capacity. *Journal of Management Studies*, 46(8), pages 1315–1338.

Lusch, R.F., and Vargo, S.L., (2006). Service-dominant logic: Reactions, reflections and refinements. *Marketing Theory*, 6(3), pages 281–288.

Luthje, C., (2002). Characteristics of innovating users in a consumer goods field: An empirical study of sport-related product consumers. MIT Sloan Working Paper, No. 4331–02. Cambridge, MA, Massachusetts Institute of Technology.

Luthje, C., and Herstatt, C., (2004). The Lead User method: An outline of empirical findings and issues for future research. *R&D Management*, 34(5), pages 553–568.

Luthje, C., Herstatt, C., and von Hippel, E., (2006). User—innovators and "local" information: The case of mountain biking. *Research Policy*, 34(6), pages 951–965.

Lynn, G.S., and Akgun, A.E., (1998). Innovation strategies under uncertainty: A contingency approach for new product development. *Engineering Management Journal*, 10(3), pages 11–18.

Magnusson, P., Matthing, J., and Kristensson, P., (2003). Managing user involvement in service innovation. *Journal of Service Research*, 6(2), pages 111–24.

Magnusson, P.R., (2009). Exploring the contributions of involving ordinary users in ideation of technology-based services. *Journal of Product Innovation Management*, 26(5), pages 578–593.

Malaby, T.M., (2006). Coding control: Governance and contingency in the production of online worlds. *First Monday*, special issue no. 7(September).

Malaby, T.M., (2009). *Making Virtual Worlds: Linden Lab and Second Life*. Ithaca and London: Cornell University Press.

Marchand, A., and Hennig-Thurau, T., (2013). Value creation in the video game industry: Industry economics, consumer benefits, and research opportunities. *Journal of Interactive Marketing*, 27(3), pages 141–157.

Martins, E.C., and Terblanche, F., (2003). Building organisational culture that stimulates creativity and innovation. *European Journal of Innovation Management*, 6(1), pages 64–74.

Matthing, J., Sanden, B., and Edvardsson, B., (2004). New service development: Learning from and with customers. *International Journal of Service Industry Management*, 15(5), pages 479–98.

Miles, I., (1993). Services in the new industrial economy. *Futures*, 25(6), pages 653–672.

Miles, I., (2008). Patterns of innovation in service industries. *IBM Systems Journal*, 47(1), pages 115–128.

Miles, I., and Green, L., (2008). *Hidden Innovation in Creative Industries*. London: NESTA.

Mollick, E., (2012). The dynamics of crowdfunding: Determinants of success and failure. SSRN scholarly paper. Social Science Research Network, Rochester, NY.

Müller, K., Rammer, C., and Trüby, J., (2009). The role of creative industries in industrial innovation. *Innovation*, 11(2), pages 148–168.

Muniz, A.M., Jr., and O'Guinn, T.C., (2001). Brand community. *Journal of Consumer Research*, 27(4), pages 412–432.

Naranjo-Valencia, J.C., Jiménez-Jiménez, D., and Sanz-Valle, R., (2011). Innovation or imitation? The role of organizational culture. *Management Decision*, 49(1), pages 55–72.

Nardi, B.M., (2010). *My Life as a Night Elf Priest*. Ann Arbor: The University of Michigan Press and The University of Michigan Library.

Nardi, B.M., and Kallinikos, J., (2011). Technology, agency and community: The case of modding in World of Warcraft. In: Holmstrom, J., et al., (eds). *Industrial Informatics Design, Use and Innovation: Perspectives and Services*. New York: Innovation Science Reference and Hershey.

Nelson, R.R., (1991). Why do firms differ, and how does it matter? *Strategic Management Journal*, 12(1), pages 61–74.

Nelson, R.R., and Winter, S.G., (1982). The Schumpeterian tradeoff revisited. *The American Economic Review*, 72(1), pages 114–132.

Nenonen, S., and Storbacka, K., (2010). Business model design: Conceptualizing networked value co-creation. *International Journal of Quality and Service Sciences*, 2, pages 43–59.

O'Donnell, C., (2012). This is not a software industry. In: Zackariasson, P. and Wilson, T.L., (eds). *The Video Games Industry: Formation, Present State, and Future.* London and New York: Routledge.

O'Donnell, C., (2014). *Developer's Dilemma.* London, England: MIT Press.

OECD, (2007). *Annual Report.* Paris: OECD Publishing.

Ogawa, S., and Piller, F.T., (2006). Reducing the risks of new product development. *MIT Sloan Management Review,* 47(2), page 65.

O'Hern, M.S., and Rindfleisch, A., (2010). Customer co-creation: A typology and research Agenda. In: Malhotra, N.K., (ed). *Review of Marketing Research,* 6, pages 84–106, Bigley: Emerald Books.

O'Hern, M.S., Rindfleisch, A., Antia, K.D., and Schweidel, D.A., (2011). The impact of user-generated content on product innovation. SSRN. http://ssrn.com/abstract=1843250 or http://dx.doi.org/10.2139/ssrn.1843250

O'Mahony, S., and Ferraro, F., (2007). The emergence of governance in an open source community. *Academy of Management Journal,* 50(5), pages 1079–1106.

Ordanini, A., Miceli, L., Pizzetti, M., and Parasuraman, A., (2011). Crowd-funding: Transforming customers into investors through innovative service platforms. *Journal of Service Management,* 22(4), pages 443–470.

O'Reilly, T., (2005). Spreading the knowledge of innovators. What is web, 2.

Oskarsson, P.J., (2014). The council of stellar management. Implementation of deliberative, democratically elected, council in EVE. White Paper. http://web.ccpgamescdn.com/communityassets/pdf/csm/CSMSummary.pdf (accessed on 6.04.2014).

Päällysaho, S., (2008). Customer interaction in service innovations: A review of literature. In: Kuusisto, A. and Päällysaho, S., (ed). *Customer Role in Service Production and Innovation–Looking for Directions for Future Research.* Lappeenranta University of Technology, Faculty of Technology Management Research Report, 195.

Panourgias, N.S., Nandhakumar, J., and Scarbrough, H., (2014). Entanglements of creative agency and digital technology: A sociomaterial study of computer game development. *Technological Forecasting and Social Change,* 83, pages 111–126.

Paul, C., (2011). Don't play me: EVE online, new players and rhetoric. In: *Proceedings of the 6th International Conference on Foundations of Digital Games.* ACM Press, pages 262–264.

Pavitt, K., (1990). What we know about the strategic management of technology. *California Management Review,* 32(3), 17–26.

Payne, A., Storbacka, K., Frow, P., and Knox, S., (2009). Co-creating brands: Diagnosing and designing the relationship experience. *Journal of Business Research,* 62(3), pages 379–389.

Pearce, C., (2009). *Communities of Play: Emergent Cultures in Multiplayer Games and Virtual Worlds.* Cambridge, MA and London, England: MIT Press.

Peteraf, M.A., (1993). The cornerstones of competitive advantage: A resource-based view. *Strategic Management Journal,* 14(3), pages 179–191.

Piller, F., and Ihl, C., (2009). *Open Innovation With Customers: Foundations, Competences and International Trends.* RWTH Aachen University.

Piller, F., Ihl, C., and Vossen, A., (2011). A typology of customer co-creation in the innovation process. In: Hanekop, H. and Wittke, V., (eds). *New Forms of Collaborative Innovation and Production on the Internet: An Interdisciplinary Perspective.* University of Goettingen.

Pine, J., and Gilmore, J.H., (1998). Welcome to the experience economy. *Harvard Business Review,* (July–August), pages 97–105.

Pisano, G.P., and Verganti, R., (2008). Which kind of collaboration is right for you. *Harvard Business Review*, 86(12), pages 78–86.

Potts, J., (2009). Creative industries and innovation policy. *Innovation: Management, Policy and Practice*, 11(2), pages 138–147.

Potts, J., Hartley, J., Banks, J., Burgess, J., Cobcroft, R., Cunningham, S., and Montgomery, L., (2008). Consumer co-creation and situated creativity. *Industry and Innovation*, 15(5), pages 459–474.

Potts, J., Cunningham, S., Hartley, J., and Ormerod, P., (2008). Social network markets: A new definition of the creative industries. *Journal of Cultural Economics*, 32(3), pages 167–185.

Prahalad, C.K., and Hamel, G., (1994). Strategy as a field of study: Why search for a new paradigm? *Strategic Management Journal*, 15(S2), pages 5–16.

Prahalad, C.K., and Krishnan, M.S., (2008). *The New Age of Innovation. Driving Co-Created Value Through Global Networks*. New York: McGraw-Hill.

Prahalad, C.K., and Ramaswamy, V., (2004). Co-creation experiences: The next practice in value creation. *Journal of Interactive Marketing*, 18(3), pages 5–14.

Preston, P., Kerr, A., and Cawley, A., (2009). Innovation and knowledge in the digital media sector: An information economy approach. *Information, Communication & Society*, 12(7), pages 994–1014.

Raasch, C., and von Hippel, E., (2013). Innovation process benefits: The journey as reward. *MIT Sloan Review*, 55(1), pages 33–39.

Reissman, C., (2004). Narrative analysis. In: Lewis-Beck, M., Bryman, A., and Futing Liao, T., (eds). *Encyclopedia of Social Science Research Methods*. London: Sage, pages 705–709.

Ritzer, G., and Jurgenson, N., (2010). Production, consumption, prosumption: The nature of capitalism in the age of the digital 'prosumer'. *Journal of Consumer Culture*, 10(1), pages 13–36.

Roberts, D., Hughes, M., and Kertbo, K., (2014). Exploring consumers' motivations to engage in innovation through co-creation activities. *European Journal of Marketing*, 38(½), pages 147–169.

Robson, C., (2011). *Real World Research* (Third ed.). New York: John Wiley & Sons.

Rosenbloom, R.S., and Christensen, C.M., (1994). Technological discontinuities, organizational capabilities, and strategic commitments. *Industrial and Corporate Change*, 3(3), pages 655–685.

Rossignol, J., (2008). *This Gaming Life. Travels in Three Cities*. The University of Michigan Press and The University of Michigan Library.

Rowlands, T., (2012). *Video Game Worlds*. Walnut Creek, CA: Left Coast Press, Inc.

Saarijärvi, H., (2012). The mechanisms of value co-creation. *Journal of Strategic Marketing*, 20(5), pages 381–391.

Saarijärvi, H., Kannan, P.K., and Kuusela, H., (2013). Value co-creation: Theoretical approaches and practical implications. *European Business Review*, 25(1), pages 6–19.

Sakao, T., Panshef, V., and Dörsam, E., (2009). Addressing uncertainty of PSS for value-chain oriented service development. In: Sakao, T. and Lindahl, M., (eds). *Introduction to Product/Service-System Design*. London: Springer, pages 137–157.

Sanders, E.B.N., and Stappers, P.J., (2008). Co-creation and the new landscapes of design. *CoDesign*, 4(1), pages 5–18.

Santonen, T., and Lehtelä, M., (2010). Higher education student's motivation to participate in online mass innovation. *The XXI ISPIM Conference-The Dynamics of Innovation-Bilbao*, Spain, pages 6–9.

Saur-Amaral, I., (2012). Wisdom-of-the-crowds to enhance innovation: a conceptual framework. ISPIM Conference Proceedings 1–7. Barcelona, Spain, 17–20.06.2012.

Scarbrough, H., Panourgias, N.S., and Nandhakumar, J., (2015). Developing a relational view of the organizing role of objects: A study of the innovation process in computer games. *Organization Studies*, 36(2), 197–220.

Schau, H.J., Muniz, A.M., Jr., and Arnould, E.J., (2009). How brand community practices create value. *Journal of Marketing*, 73(5), pages 30–51.

Schell, J., (2008). *The Art of Game Design: A Book of Lenses*. Boca Raton, FL: CRC Press.

Schumpeter, J., (1950). *Capitalism, Socialism and Democracy* (Third ed.). New York: Harper and Brothers.

Sieg, J.H., Wallin, M.W., and Von Krogh, G., (2010). Managerial challenges in open innovation: A study of innovation intermediation in the chemical industry. *R&D Management*, 40(3), pages 281–291.

Sotamaa, O., (2004). Playing it my way? Mapping the modder agency. *In Internet Research Conference*, 5, pages 19–22.

Stoneman, P., (2007). *An Introduction to the Definition and Measurement of Soft Innovation*. London: NESTA.

Sundbo, J., and Toivonen, M., (eds). (2011). *User-Based Innovation in Services*. Cheltenham: Edward Elgar Publishing.

Surowiecki, J., (2004). *The Wisdom of Crowds*. New York: Anchor.

Tapscott, D., and Williams, A.D., (2008). *Wikinomics: How Mass Collaboration Changes Everything*. New York: Penguin.

Taylor, T.L., (2006a). Beyond management: Considering participatory design and governance in player culture. *First Monday*, special issue, 7(September). http://firstmonday.org/issues/issue11_9/taylor/index.html.

Taylor, T.L., (2006b). *Play Between Worlds: Exploring Online Game Culture*. Cambridge, MA: MIT Press.

Taylor, T.L., (2008). Does world of warcraft change everything? How a PvP server, multinational playerbase, and surveillance mod scene caused me pause. In: Corneliussen, H.G. and Rettberg, J.W., (eds). *Digital Culture, Play and Identity: A World of Warcraft Reader*. Cambridge, MA: MIT Press.

Teece, D.J., (2007). Explicating dynamic capabilities: The nature and microfoundations of (sustainable) enterprise performance. *Strategic Management Journal*, 28(13), pages1319–1350.

Teece, D.J., (2010). Business models, business strategy and innovation. *Long Range Planning*, 43(2), pages 172–194.

Teece, D.J., and Pisano, G., (1994). The dynamic capabilities of firms: An introduction. *Industrial and Corporate Change*, 3(3), pages 537–556.

Trott, P., (2005). *Innovation Management and New Product Development*. Harlow, Essex: Pearson Education.

Tschang, F.T., (2005). Videogames as interactive experiential products and their manner of development. *International Journal of Innovation Management*, 9(1), pages 103–131.

Tschang, F.T., (2007). Balancing the tensions between rationalization and creativity in the video games industry. *Organization Science*, 18(6), pages 989–1005.

Tushman, M.L., and Anderson, P., (1986). Technological discontinuities and organizational environments. *Administrative Science Quarterly*, 31(3), pages 439–465.

Utterback, J.M., (1994). *Mastering the Dynamics of Innovation*. Cambridge, MA: Harvard Business School Press.

Van de Ven, A.H., (1993). A community perspective on the emergence of innovations. *Journal of Engineering and Technology Management*, 10(1), pages 23–51.

Van der Graaf, S., (2009). Designing for mod development: User creativity as product development strategy on the firm-hosted 3D software platform. Ph.D Dissertation, LSE.

Van der Graaf, S., (2012). Get organized at work! A look inside the game design process of valve and linden lab. *Bulletin of Science, Technology & Society*, pages 1–9, 0270467612469079.

Van Dijck, J., (2009). Users like you? Theorizing agency in user-generated content. *Media, Culture and Society*, 31(1), pages 41–58.

Vargo, S.L., and Lusch, R.F., (2008). Service-dominant logic: Continuing the evolution. *Journal of the Academy of Marketing Science*, 36(1), pages 1–10.

Verhagen, T., Feldberg, F., van den Hooff, B., Meents, S., and Merikivi, J., (2011). Satisfaction with virtual worlds: An integrated model of experiential value. *Information & Management*, 48(6), pages 201–207.

Von Hippel, E., (1988). *The Sources of Innovation*. New York: Oxford University Press.

Von Hippel, E., (2005). *Democratizing Innovation*. Cambridge, MA: MIT Press.

Von Krogh, G., and von Hippel, E., (2006). The promise of research on open source software. *Management Science*, 52(7), pages 975–983.

Voss, C., and Zomerdijk, L., (2007). Innovation in experimental services—an empirical view. In: DTI (ed). *Innovation in Services*. London: DTI, pages 97–134.

Wexler, M.N., (2011). Reconfiguring the sociology of the crowd: Exploring crowdsourcing. *International Journal of Sociology and Social Policy*, 31, pages 6–20.

Zomerdijk, L.G., and de Vries, J., (2007). Structuring front office and back office work in service delivery systems: An empirical study of three design decisions. *International Journal of Operations & Production Management*, 27(1), pages 108–131.

5 Key Findings

To recap, the key findings presented above are as follows:

a. The outcomes of co-creation fall into two types: for relationship and for NSD. Firms can use co-creation for either one of these outcomes, or for both of them.
b. Two forms of co-creation are identifiable at a high level of organizational practice: informal (co-creation performed 'on the job', related to hidden innovation) and formal (co-creation mediated by the use of tools, formal channels, having a structure, and regulated in some way).
c. Firms are characterized by competences for co-creation—chief of which are user involvement and integration. Other competences include assimilation and disclosure.
d. Outcomes of co-creation are visible in eight sites of the firm, and those sites also constitute institutional/organizational conditions for it. They are organizational characteristics that both shape and are shaped by co-creation.
e. Organizational culture (explained as an organization's history, employees' attitude towards co-creation, and firm strategy) and funding arrangements (with particular attention to the use of crowdfunding) are the most important environmental catalysts for co-creation in a firm.

Co-creation is a multifaceted practice which is accompanied by numerous transformations to both how organizations function, as well as to how they structure and manage their relationship with customers. Finding a single prescriptive definition that would capture the main domains of co-creation is not possible. This is especially true given the hidden nature of co-creation and its co-location with 'under the radar' inputs to a firm's NSD.

Observing co-creation practice in the context of different firms sheds the light on how co-creation works in the industry as a whole. Co-creation in firms occurs as a set of practices, some of them visible, some formally articulated, some dependent on the strategic planning of the firm—and some not. Those practices stem from a firm's competences for co-creation, as well as from institutional arrangements of that company. Those practices escape categorization as formal routines, processes and prescriptive chains of events. The organizational context within which they occur is itself changing in response to them, making establishing any point of reference difficult. As co-creation is deployed, it affects the eight sites of a firm, progressively and iteratively changing its established routines and practices, and replacing them with the new ones. That's what Potts (2009) meant when he described co-creation as shifting the equilibrium of service development, leading to the establishing of new market and organizational practices. Studying prescriptive co-creation practices is made hard by the erosion of frames of references— what the firm routines are, what are the boundaries of the firm, who the customers are in the context of production, what are the roles of employees— which accompany co-creation practice.

Instead, it makes much more sense to talk about the degree of structure of any such co-creation practice. It allows us to find common elements among the otherwise highly heterogeneous landscape of co-creation across firms. We also use it to make sense of various assemblages of isolated practices within a particular firm which come together to form its co-creation practice.

Competences for co-creation serve a similar function. As particular practices of co-creation are difficult to pin-point, and may or may not exist in a given firm (co-creation can be a highly unstructured, ad hoc practice), it makes more sense analytically to focus on describing not those practices of co-creation, but on what determines them. Competences for co-creation affect whether a firm will engage in co-creation at all, and if so, what practice of co-creation will that be (as observed in the three cases—their practices vary in accordance to the strength of various competences that they have). Competences for co-creation therefore allow us to make sense of this highly elusive and chimeric phenomenon in firms.

Two Types of Co-Creation Outcomes: For Relationship and for NSD

Where applicable, the literature on co-creation focuses on the outcomes of co-creation for new service development. But an equally significant outcome of co-creation is its impact on relationship between the firm and its customers. This dimension has hardly been discussed in the literature in systematic way, largely ignored by chief contributors such as Hoyer et al. (2010), von Hippel (2007, 2005, 1988) and O'Hern et al. (2011). Co-creation should be framed in the context of a relationship between firms and not only communities, but with individual customers (Gummesson, 2002; Grönroos, 1994). In their discussions of co-creation in the videogames industry, Banks (2013) and Malaby (2009) point towards the significance of the relationship benefits stemming from successful co-creation. They make no attempt at framing it as a possible strategically planned outcome of co-creation. We need to make clear distinctions between the two types of co-creation's strategic outcomes.

Firms can and do engage with their customers in co-creation; and that they may do so not to obtain their inputs to NSD, but just to reinforce the customer community loyalty and affect for the brand and firm behind it. This is contrary to the established wisdom in the field, which focuses almost exclusively on co-creation's benefits for NPD or NSD (von Hippel, 2007, 2005; Hoyer et al., 2010; O'Hern and Rindfleisch, 2010).

Framed in such way, the actions of firms observed in Case Alpha (Obsidian Entertainment), as well as in Case Gamma (Cloud Imperium Games) make strategic sense. Obsidian Entertainment does not seek ideas from the community of customers other than to fulfil obligations stemming from promises made during crowdfunding campaigns. Those promises themselves were an effort to raise enthusiastic support from potential funders (i.e., to generate positive word of mouth and to increase backers' maximum willingness to pay; Gebauer et al., 2013).

The content of customer inputs pertains to mundane elements of the game, ones which are either entirely superfluous to the game experience itself, or ones which would be very easy to produce in-house by the firm employees. In fact, it is more resource-intensive from the organizational point of view to obtain those mundane inputs from the outside of the organization (due to the challenges associated with the management of an unruly community of customers, enforcing deadlines and appropriate formats of deliverables, providing codified guidance, etc.) as compared to simply developing them in-house. The explanation for choosing to do that from the perspective of firm strategy is exactly to produce relationship benefits from such exchanges. A similar dynamic is observed in Case Gamma, at Cloud Imperium Games— the firm is thoroughly engaged in crowdfunding and requires a continued support and 'buzz' among its customers, who generate positive word of mouth and increase the potential funders' maximum willingness to pay.

On the other hand, customer inputs can and do have real value for NSD in some cases and firms. Almost universally in the videogames industry for instance, customer inputs are welcomed by firms in functions such as quality assurance. Another such areas are the creation of non-critical art assets by the players (Case Alpha), or the writing of a game's underlying story minutiae by volunteers (Case Beta), as well as in community management and building (Case Beta). Those inputs are genuinely useful to the firm and constitute a quantifiable contribution to the service development effort (directly translated into labour-hours and reduced resource expenditure). Engaging in co-creation with customers is a viable method for a firm to obtain information about customers' need-related knowledge (von Hippel, 2007, 2005; Luthje et al., 2006; Lakhani and von Hippel, 2003), as well as to source high-quality elements of the game from their community (Dahlander and Magnusson, 2008; von Krogh and von Hippel, 2006).

Extensive communication between staff and customers serves to bolster the relationship between them, drawing customers into an 'open development' experience, where they can see how their anticipated service is being developed, as well as, to an extent, be a part of the process. A firm does not require the inputs from customers in many of its functions. Instead, they are accepted for the purposes of enhancing the relationship. Furthermore, such dynamic can be accompanied by the lack of a marketing budget and the reliance on the word of mouth (Gebauer et al., 2013) and market expansion (Whitla, 2009), benefits stemming exactly from co-creation for relationship (as observed in Case Gamma).

Firms can engage in co-creation to achieve either relationship, or both relationship and NSD, types of outcomes from co-creation. Some firms engage in co-creation overwhelmingly for relationship gains, while others are also interested in the benefits pertaining to NSD. Although not illustrated by the empirical evidence here, a firm engaging in co-creation purely for NSD benefits is also admissible, although rarely encountered in practice (due to the high value of positive WOM which is a by-product of a successful co-creation experience; Gebauer et al., 2013). Such form of co-creation would resemble a crowdsourcing approach (a firm's open call for contributions from a crowd, which does not need to be a community of customers; Saur-Amaral, 2012; Estelles-Arolas and Gonzales, 2012), or indeed would be something belonging to the realm of open source software development (where, in the absence of a corporate entity, WOM is not a supporting function to sales and expanding market reach; Dahlander and Magnusson, 2008; von Krogh and von Hippel, 2006).

Gustafsson et al. (2012), writing on the importance of communication between firm and customers, identified 'content' as one of four dimensions of that practice. They noted that the information transmitted during communication between customers and firms can focus on strengthening the relationship rather than improving NSD (due to the customers' difficulties in expressing their needs, in line with observations from von Hippel, 2005 and others). Gangi et al. (2010) noted various relationship and communication issues accompanying customers' involvement in co-creation as challenges to overcome. A challenge faced by many firms in creative industries is maintaining control over creative content while building better customer relationships through co-creation. In most cases it means navigating the narrow straits between von Hippel's (2007, 2005) user innovation (which means ceding a high degree of control over content to the customers) and co-production of services (which is common among experiential services in creative industries).

Two Forms of Co-Creation: Informal and Formal

A large proportion of exchanges between customers and a firm occur informally, under the radar of the official classification of 'community management', 'customer service' or 'marketing and public relations'. Such rich links that cross the boundary of the organization and are rooted in wider communities (geographic or focused around a particular field of interest) have been described by Cohendet and Simon (2007). They have also been hinted at by Naranjo-Valencia et al. (2011) in the discussion of ad hoc organizational culture (characterized by high flexibility and external focus) as promoting innovation.

Those exchanges exist independently of the other, more structured and officially recognized (and planned) forms of co-creation that take place in organizations—represented here by activities such as contests, votes or use of toolkits (described by Kohler et al., 2011a and b; von Hippel, 2005). The existing literature does not account for that dichotomy; it also does not account for the informal type of co-creation—save for its links to 'hidden innovation' described by Miles and Green (2008).

We investigated the impact of informal co-creation on organizations, and its role in relation to formal co-creation. This is an important for industrial practice—those two forms of co-creation have a different impact on NSD and are managed in different ways—for formal co-creation by top-down, managerial action and strategizing; and for informal co-creation by bottom-up forces of changing attitudes of employees, job responsibilities and fostering of interpersonal links between employees and customers. Empirical evidence suggests that the main body of co-creation occurs via informal co-creation practices, when the employees interact with the customers or are simply exposed to customers' ideas, internalizing and later reconfiguring those ideas (Bhalla, 2010). In Case Gamma in particular, the firm's employees on all levels of organization are encouraged to frequent forums where various features and aspects of the service are discussed in-depth by the customers, and to be active members of those forums. Feedback provided there by the customers, their suggestions and expressions of their needs (factual or perceived) seep into the minds of the employees, thus finding their way into the organization. Those ideas are introduced into the NSD resulting from those numerous and discrete interactions, that are difficult to track even for the employees involved in them. Hence the attempts to locate the origin of an idea that resulted from such informal co-creation within a service would be futile and, as the phenomenon of 'seeding an artist's mind' with ideas from various sources is relevant to all creative endeavours.

Therefore, the customers' inputs are in an overwhelming number of cases recombined by the employees, i.e., they are not assimilated in their original form. Instead, they circulate through the organization for some time, are gradually modified by the employees (for various reasons: for instance, to bring their quality up, or to change their technical characteristics such as programming language, sound sampling or number of polygons). This is not a practice that is planned or purposefully deployed by an organization—instead, that is the path that customers' inputs take in the context of a weak routine for processing of customers' inputs (Naranjo-Valencia et al., 2011).

Formal co-creation practices, on the other hand, are characterized by either a toolkit approach to user innovation (von Hippel, 2005) or by a dynamic native to crowdsourcing (Estelles-Arolas and Gonzales, 2012; Saur-Amaral,

2012) where an open call for submissions is made, with clear specifications and guidelines provided. In those cases, the firm formally invites its customers to participate in its service development process, although in the role and according to the rules set by the studio. Normally, formal co-creation is also accompanied by an internal routine or mechanism for processing of customers' inputs and thus assimilating them into firm's practices.

This is for instance observed at Case Beta, where dedicated employees, practices (bi-annual summits with selected customers, and analysis and codification of their feedback), as well as the time and place during daily team routine (daily stand-up meetings in Scrum project management) are designated to deal with the inputs form the customers. In Case Alpha we observe another aspect of formal co-creation: an organization preparing a call for submissions, together with providing the community with clear technical and artistic guidelines for submissions. In Case Gamma contests for customer inputs are launched, where the nature of the task is clearly described, and the process and criteria of judgment are broadcasted and fully transparent to the public.

Furthermore, one additional conclusion arising from firms' use of these two forms of co-creation is linked to the management of intellectual property risk. Current framings of intellectual property (copyright in particular in the context of software products and services) are unable to effectively account for and regulate IP arising from co-creation (Bach et al., 2008; Grimes, 2006; Humphreys et al., 2005a). Firms avoid a situation where the ownership of aspects of their service could be challenged by the customers who engaged in co-creation, seeking now to benefit financially from their inputs. Therefore, firms accept direct inputs from the customers only when they can clearly establish the rules for customers' involvement in NSD—for instance in contests, when using toolkits (if a customer uses a toolkit, which is a piece of proprietary software owned by the firm, they waive all rights to their creation's ownership) or in conditions of having signed an individual contract with the firm (most often an non-disclosure agreement; seen in the examples of player council or volunteer programs in Case Beta).

This result evidences the dynamic described by Cohendet and Simon (2007) and Amin and Cohendet (2004), who discussed the flows of knowledge and creativity between professionals in a community of specialists. It also updates and expands the findings of Grantham and Kaplinsky (2005), who discussed the innovation practices in the videogames industry. The community of specialists transcended the boundaries of the firm and was rooted in the wider local network of professionals. We make a twofold contribution to Cohendet and Simon's (2007) findings.

First of all, such community of specialists, where sharing of creativity and knowledge occurs, does not have to be geographically co-located, and can be formed by people from all over the world at the same time. Secondly, customers of a firm, and not only fellow professionals, can be involved in such a community. This is because customers can have professional skills comparable to those of a firm's employees (customers can be professionals in some other field, simply, or can be students or self-taught aficionados; Cook, 2008). We observe the blurring of the divide between professional and customer, or between a media producer and its consumer, confirming the observations of Jenkins (2006, 2009), Küklich (2005), Banks and Potts (2010), Hartley et al. (2013) and many others.

This finding also advances the observations of Burger-Helmchen and Cohendet (2011), Bhalla (2010) and von Hippel (2007, 2005), who note various forms of interaction between customers and a firm, but do not identify the dichotomy between formal and informal user involvement in the process. The use of social software and media described by the former falls into the realm of informal co-creation, while toolkits and company-run programs for lead users can be attributed to formal forms of co-creation.

Moreover, various customers have different skills and motivations to become involved in the NSD and innovation process (van Doorn et al., 2010; Ebner et al., 2009; Franke and Shah, 2003), and the opportunity to assign their involvement to either formal or informal co-creation sheds new light on the characteristics of those co-creating customers. Customers who engage in formal co-creation are likely to be characterized by more reward- and recognition-oriented motives, while customers engaging in informal co-creation are seeking more intrinsic and altruistic incentives such as sharing of knowledge, belonging to a community, or helping others. Literature on customer motivations for co-creation benefits from this evidence, for example, Füller (2010) and Roberts et al. (2014).

The Competences for Co-Creation

There are four competences that affect an organization's ability to engage in co-creation with its customers, as well as to subsequently integrate customers' inputs with the internal practices of the firm. We build on the work by Piller and Ihl (2009), Piller et al. (2011), Lichtenthaler and Lichtenthaler, 2009, Zahra and George (2002), as well as Lettl (2007). There is a clear link between those competences and a firm's ability to structure the co-creation experience for the customers (Gebauer et al., 2013), contributing to the work of Gangi et al. (2010), Kohler et al. (2009), Dahlander and Magnusson (2008), as well as Voss and Zomerdijk (2007).

Competences determine a firm's ability to structure and offer a co-creation experience to its customers, for which successful assimilation of customer inputs constitutes a *sine qua non* condition for a positive co-creation experience (Gebauer et al., 2013). The clearest examples of this are visible in Cases Beta and Gamma, where the firm treats co-creation as an extension of the service itself. In Case Beta, the unique selling point and capitalization on a market niche are constructed around customers' ability to both co-create the content of the service, as well as productively participate in NSD. In Case Gamma, experience of co-creation is currently the main offering of the firm, as the service itself is still in development. The success of such co-creation experiences hinges on the firm's ability to understand their customers, identify the best interaction patterns with them, as well as realistically and sustainably integrate their inputs with internal NSD practices.

We also bring the competences together in a single framework, demonstrating their importance and impact on organizations in co-creation. For instance, Dahlander and Magnusson's (2008) three themes of accessing, aligning and assimilating are unified with Gangi et al. (2010) user innovation community (UIC) challenges for a firm, and Piller et al.'s (2011) three competences for open innovation in firms are linked to Lettl's (2007) user involvement competence.

It is also demonstrated that organizations can structure co-creation experiences that have the potential to produce the two outcomes of co-creation (i.e., customer relationship outcome and NSD-input outcome). Those experiences are seen as the extension, and thus a part of, the service being offered by the firm (especially if that service is experiential in nature). This demonstrates that co-creation experiences take place not only in spaces specifically designated by the firm (as part of service offering), but instead they occur (or have the potential to occur) throughout all interactions between the firm and its customers. Literatures by Kohler et al. (2011a, b), Kohler et al. (2009), as well as Füller and Matzler (2007) and Füller et al. (2008) are expanded upon the most.

Eight Sites Within the Firm: Both the Conditions and Outcomes of Co-Creation

Organizations are characterized by structures that enable co-creation, but which are also reshaped by co-creation. This reshaping occurs via practical and process dynamics, and stems from the customers' gaining insight and access to back-office processes. Organizational structures, such as communication routines, coordination and project management processes, and team composition undergo change in response to the opportunities present in co-creation (Bengtsson and Ryzhkova (2015; Sundbo and Toivonen, 2011; Miles, 2008; den Hertog, 2000). Those changes are also linked to the phenomena of participatory culture outlined by Jenkins (2009, 2006), who discusses the customers' increased interest in influencing and shaping the development of 'cultural' services. By the means of rich and continuous communications between the customers and the firm, customers are given a direct line of influence into the back-office processes of the firm (Edvardsson et al., 2012; Voss and Zomerdijk, 2007; den Hertog, 2000). Firms capitalize on that trend as well, noticing both the customer relationship and NSD benefits stemming from it (for the latter, those can include co-creation of innovations, tapping into customers' need-related knowledge in experiential service development, etc.).

Across all three cases we observe a pattern within organizations that corresponds to both the impact that co-creation has on firms, as well as that which enables the functioning of co-creation in those organizations. This pattern is linked to the firm's opening up of its back-office processes and making them visible and accessible to the customers. In various firms this is done differently: devices vary from controlled, officially sanctioned practices to organic, free-flowing means of communication between the customers and the firm. With the increased knowledge of what is going on inside the studio, customers have the ability to contribute in new ways—for instance they know the technical specifications of what the firm is working on, or they know which employee is responsible for a given feature of the service and thus can contact him or her directly (Edvardsson et al., 2012). As we see in Case Gamma, customers can create their inputs to the exact specification of what the firm is working on at a given moment on their own accord, or—as it is demonstrated in Case Alpha—the firm can officially announce those specifications, thus further helping the customers in their co-creation efforts. The release of service design documents, as we see in inXile Entertainment (Case Alpha) is an example of exactly that—making available documents that so far have been the sole domain of the firm and have been so far considered confidential.

Internal communications are affected by the presence of a new actor—in Cases Beta and Gamma, new communication routines are established to account for the voice of the customers in NSD (Edvardsson et al., 2012). The content of the service is changing fundamentally as well, as the firms now attempt to integrate more room for 'emergence' (i.e., new patterns of interaction with the service innovated by the customers). Changes to service development practices, such as project management, are visible at firms: slack times are being planned into the task milestones in order to account for an unpredictable volume of customer inputs and the organizational resources required to assimilate them. The financing and revenue model is also affected (Nenonen and Storbacka, 2010)—in Cases Alpha and Gamma we observe customers funding the NSD effort, thus becoming the lifeline of the whole company. Consequently, some of the practices of the firm are rendered visible to entice customers to crowdfund by making them feel as members of the team.

The changes to organizations are also the factors enabling co-creation to occur in organizations. If it weren't for the room for emergent iteraction with a service, co-creation in that site would probably not happen. If there were no slack times in project management, integration of customer inputs would be much more difficult and unlikely. If customers were not informed about what the firm is working on and what are the technical specifications of its projects, they would not be able to contribute successfully to them. If a firm were unwilling to allow customers' insight into some of their internal practices, the crowdfunding approach of raising finance would not be as successful.

It is the eight sites of innovation that demarcate the institutional conditions and space within the organization for co-creation (Bhalla, 2010), and also where its influence is most visible and transformative of the existing firm structures (Kuusisto, 2008; Päällysaho, 2008). The transformation that occurs is pushing the firm deeper into organizational conditions of co-creating with customers, strengthening its ties to the community of customers, integrating customers' inputs more and more with its NSD (Sundbo and Toivonen, 2011). Co-creation becomes a defining feature of the firm's functioning and an important element of its business model and value proposition (Nenonen and Storbacka, 2010).

These observations contextualize and narrow down the typology of 15 sites of innovation in creative industries' firms proposed by Miles and Green (2008), validating them for the specific setting of co-creation. Empirical evidence illustrates the presence and impact of co-creation in various functions and departments of firms. The findings also confirm and expand on the observations of Edvardsson et al. (2012), den Hertog (2000) and Voss and Zomerdijk (2007) pertaining to the increasing influence of customers on back-office processes. We also link Miles and Green's (2008) phenomenon of hidden innovation to co-creation, and observation of co-creation's effect across organizations that result from informal, 'under the radar' co-creation. We map organizational and institutional circumstances in which co-creation takes place, as well as frame co-creation in firms as an element of business strategy. Co-creation has a transformative effect on some characteristics of a firm (captured as the eight sites) which relate to its management of innovation practices.

This is also related to a number of implications for practitioners. It allows for enhanced understanding of firms of the organizational conditions that need to be in place before successful co-creation can take place. Furthermore, it assists in the anticipation of the transformative outcomes of co-creation.

Catalysts for Co-Creation: Organizational Culture and Funding Arrangements

Co-creation in firms is not only determined by competences and the organizational conditions for co-creation. There are two more factors, which we refer to as 'institutional arrangements': organizational culture and funding arrangements. They significantly influence whether a firm decides to embark on a co-created project, and its characteristics. They form a palpable (and at times unarticulated within a company) force affecting co-creation in NSD.

The organizational culture consists of the following elements (Cheng and Huizingh, 2014; Grant, 2010): strategic orientation—which denotes the organization's attitude towards its customers as a creative and innovative resource; the history of the firm—what approaches to NSD have allowed it to succeed, what methods and practices are proven, what are the positive and negative NSD experiences of staff; and the attitude of employees—how willing they are to collaborate with the customers, how they perceive themselves in their professional roles, as well as what is their attitude towards customer community.

On the other hand, funding arrangements are related to crowdfunding. It is a form of social contract where future customers, in exchange for their donations, become participants and members of a defined community of 'backers' (Ordanini et al., 2011). Backers are synonymous to dedicated customers, who are characterized by their interest in the internal practices of the firm, as well as who seek a deeper level of involvement with the service than just consuming it. They wish to be better informed, as well as to be able to influence—in exchange for their trust and financial support—the development of the service. The impact of organizational culture (Naranjo-Valencia et al., 2011; Martins and Terblanche, 2003; Barney, 1986) on co-creation is visible in all three cases.

The impact of crowdfunding on NSD activities in firms has not yet been described in academic literature (the phenomenon of crowdfunding itself has been described by Ordanini et al., 2011, and others). Similarly, combining co-creation with crowdfunding in a single framework sheds new light on the proximity of those two phenomena and their common elements (which mostly reside in their impact on firm-customer relationships). This also relates to the role of firm strategy in shaping co-creation. It builds on Malaby (2009) about organizational culture in the videogame studio, as well as on Cheng and Huizingh (2014) on strategic orientation. It demonstrates how co-creation becomes a strategic choice for a firm. Co-creation is not something that happens 'by the way' in firms—it needs to be managed and integrated into a company's planning, as we see in all three case studies.

Integrating Framework

We propose an integrating framework to demonstrate, on the basis of the data, what the general conditions for co-creation's success or failure could be. Such framework functions most of all as an exploratory exercise, because in order to make it fully reliable much more research into various co-creation practices in different firms would be required. Moreover, as there are numerous permutations to the conditions accompanying co-creation in firms, this framework can be expanded and more detail added to it. Still, based on the patterns and tendencies observed, the following framework is put forward (Table 5.1):

Table 5.1 Integrating Framework Clarifying the Conditions of Co-Creation

Co-Creation Competences	Crowdfunding	Organizational Culture	In what broader conditions should it be deployed?
All competences strong	Yes	Culture cannot be negative to customer co-creation.	When a firm needs the funds to develop its services and has experience in dealing with customer communities. All forms of co-creation are useful here.

(Continued)

Table 5.1 Continued

Co-Creation Competences	Crowdfunding	Organizational Culture	*In what broader conditions should it be deployed?*
All competences strong	No	Organizational culture should be positive towards co-creation— customers are deeply integrated into a firm's functioning. Culture can't be negative.	When a firm wishes to integrate co-creation into its business model and when co-creation is its unique selling point. Use of player councils.
Emphasis on involvement and integration	Yes	Any organizational culture.	Must be formal co-creation, especially if the culture is less inclined towards co-creation. Use of contests and volunteer programs.
Emphasis on involvement and integration	No	Positive or neutral organizational culture.	Informal co-creation approaches are recommended, 'on the job' solutions. Target lead users (for inputs) and market influencers.
Emphasis on disclosure and appropriation	Yes	Any organizational culture.	Engage customers in late stages of NSD, quality assurance for instance. Formal and clearly defined co-creation channels: use of asset stores, for example, or release of design documents.
Emphasis on disclosure and appropriation	No	Positive or neutral culture.	Use informal methods of co-creation and tap into the lead users, although the community cannot be tapped as a marketing resource.
No competences for co-creation	Yes	Positive culture only.	High chance of failure and not delivering any service. Risk of big marketing failure.
No competences for co-creation	No	Positive culture only.	High chance of failure and severe delays and disruptions to NSD.

To reduce the number of possible permutations, user involvement and integration competences, as well as disclosure and appropriation competences, have been bundled together. This is because the findings demonstrate that user involvement and integration competence tend to co-occur in organizations strongly engaged in co-creation practices, while disclosure and appropriation competence tend to be second-order, supporting competences in the context of co-creation (but they still remain of consequence on co-creation practice, as reflected in Table 5.1 and in the case studies).

The above framework is designed to assist industry practitioners in deciding whether to engage in co-creation under particular circumstances. One challenge to its practical implementation will be the self-determination of the firms whether they have the required competences, as well as the ability to describe their own organizational culture in the context of co-creation. The concepts of co-creation competences have been outlined and clarified also in practical terms (illustrated by case narratives), thus being of assistance to practitioners also in that dimension. Furthermore, this framework is designed to function with other findings of this study—and with the description of cases in particular. Cases discuss, based on the real-world data, the examples of various permutations of competences and institutional arrangements, and show what kind of co-creation approaches worked for those firms.

As we focused on the firms engaged in co-creation, we lack the empirical insight into the scenarios described by the two bottom rows of Table 5.1— co-creation failures. As such, those represent only informed guesses about what would happen if co-creation were attempted by a firm with no competences for it (the probability of such scenario actually taking place is another matter altogether). Filling that gap could be an interesting avenue for future research.

Conclusions

We mapped the effects of co-creation on organizations, as well as accounted for the key factors shaping it in firms. We explored the entirety of organizations and offered an insight into the main determinants of co-creation in a firm's NSD, and united differing typologies and taxonomies of that phenomenon. We have studied 13 firms in the videogames industry, accounting for various organizational changes, practices and attitudes accompanying co-creation. We conducted detailed case studies of those firm's practices, using methods such as interviews, participant observation, and analysis of documents and cultural artefacts. We observed the online and offline interfaces between firms and their customers, as well as internal affairs of firms—their practices, communication routines and cultures. We have brought literatures from various schools together—innovation, co-creation, experiential services, crowdfunding, customer communities, as well as creative industries.

We accounted for co-creation in a holistic manner, expanding on the incomplete view of innovation with customers in management literature. Various institutional arrangements, as well as organizational characteristics come together to shape it. Processes beyond innovation and NSD have been demonstrated to be affected and changed by it. This work at its core demonstrates how co-creation is useful for generating innovations in NSD by bringing in customers' inputs, but also how it by itself is an innovation in the organizations' functioning.

Four competences influence a firm's propensity for and style of co-creation: user involvement, integration, disclosure and appropriation, as well as two institutional arrangements: organizational culture and funding arrangements. Together, these factors determine how likely the firms are to use co-creation in their strategy, as well as how successful they will be. The style of co-creation is also influenced by these factors—various configurations of competences, use of crowdfunding and organizational culture determine the form of co-creation. Furthermore, style of co-creation is also determined by the outcome of that practice desired by a firm—whether it seeks NSD inputs from customers, or customer relationship gains.

Firms are characterized by structured, semi-structured or unstructured co-creation practices. Those practices are in turn determined by the competences for co-creation that a particular firm holds. User involvement and integration competences tend to favour unstructured forms of co-creation, while assimilation and disclosure competence are linked to more structured practices of co-creation. Organizational culture and funding arrangements are also of consequence: crowdfunding shifts co-creation practice closer to structured characteristics, while organizational culture which favours interactions with customers pulls a firm towards more unstructured co-creation practices.

For each of the co-creation types customers' inputs contribute to a firm's co-creation practices in different ways. In the unstructured type, there is a heavy co-location of co-creation with hidden innovation. The semi-structured type displays a high integration of co-creation with the business model and overall firm strategy. The structured type is accompanied by the fewest organizational transformations and is most compatible with more traditional, 'closed innovation' approaches to NSD (where service consumers and producers are two separate groups).

Customer inputs contribute to a firm's NSD and innovation in both formal and informal ways. An important manifestation of co-creation takes place in the individual relationships and interactions between firms' employees and customers. Ideas seep into the firm's environment without official detection. On the other hand, firms do deploy formal means of co-creation as well—in many instances resembling crowdsourcing approaches. Those are planned and coordinated approaches often involving toolkits, guidelines, as well as legal agreements. These two forms of co-creation are accompanied by either structured, or ad hoc means of internally processing customer inputs by the firm (the integration competence). The way in which those inputs are assimilated determines how a firm's NSD and other characteristics (eight sites of the firm) will be transformed.

The effects of co-creation are manifested in eight sites of the organization. Those sites have been derived from a framework by Miles and Green (2008), who demonstrate that innovation in creative industries is not just limited to the 'content' of a service, but to the wider functioning of the firm. Customer inputs, despite being intended as contributions to NSD and improvements to the service, have a wider transformative impact on the entirety of an organization. This is because processing those inputs and their assimilation within, for example, organizational culture and professional identities of employees are significantly different from how firms have functioned thus far. Today, firms develop their services not only *for* their customers, but also *with* their customers' active presence in that process (also as sources of funding). Co-creation frames that widespread organizational transformation. By providing their inputs to NSD, the customers trigger profound organizational transformations, and all transformations of the firm affect its main function, which is innovation (Teece, 2007; Teece and Pisano, 1994; Cohen and Levinthal, 1990; Schumpeter, 1950).

Funding arrangements and organizational culture are equally transformed by the practice of co-creation in firms. Depending on the strength of various competences for co-creation, a firm's generation of value is altered. Organizational culture (whether it is inclined positively or negatively towards co-creating customers) catalyzes and reacts to those changes simultaneously.

Co-creation cannot be looked at as just occurring in the immediate context of NSD within firms—instead, its effects are seen across the whole organization. We addressed the weaknesses of existing knowledge on this challenge by linking together the concepts from various fields. We began to understand co-creation's influence on organizations, as this influence is holistic, dispersed, and at times difficult to pin-point with traditional concepts and metrics. We also expanded on the limited common sense and received wisdom statements about how co-creation should be used in firms, in order to inform industry practitioners.

The main practical goal for this research was to inform a firm's co-creation practice, and to enhance their understanding of its outcomes. At its core, we assisted industry practitioners in preparing their organizations and predicting the transformations accompanying co-creation. This research's outcomes are meant to inform strategic decision-making, as well as account for the influence of crowdfunding on the NSD.[1]

We proposed a structure for characterizing a firm's ability to co-create. Competences for co-creation, together with funding arrangements and organizational culture constitute tools that can be applied by managers to describe their company. They can then judge the appropriateness of co-creation in their business context and weigh its benefits against its costs.

Our research mapped a broad range of outcomes that co-creation may have on innovation within a firm, together with identifying the sites within an organization. Firms can anticipate the changes that co-creation will bring to their organizations. It helps firms to adjust organizational structures and culture to successfully co-create.

Many firms in creative industries are eager to embrace crowdfunding as 'the shot' at financial independence and as a marketing and PR tool. This work demonstrated how crowdfunding is linked to co-creation in the customer-firm relationship. Before using crowdfunding, organizations must understand its effects on the firm and its day-to-day functioning. We also advanced the practical understanding of the relationship with customers, highlighting the importance of individual employees' connections to the customers. We demonstrated that marketing work takes place in individual, day-to-day interactions of employees with customers. Similarly, the lack of such interactions, or their negative mood, have detrimental effects on a firm's service offerings.

Our study has practical implications for the customers. It sheds light on the firm's propensity for and style of co-creation; through that customers will understand better when their contribution has a chance of being looked at by firm employees and integrated with the service. This informs the works of communities of customers producing improvements to services.

Co-creation is problematic and disruptive to many studios, yet it becomes the customers' expectation for how a firm should be interacting with them. A firm's ability to expect its outcomes is an advantage in planning and strategizing. It eliminates a degree of uncertainty, as well as prevents potentially catastrophic effects of mismanaged or ill-executed co-creation (to firm-customer relationship, employees' esprit-de-corps, as well as to an organization's practices, planning, schedules and project management).

Co-creation, due to its potential in both socio-cultural as well as market spheres, will only increase in importance. We will observe that in creative industries and beyond. As organizations learn to share their findings, and as our understanding of co-creation advances (also as organizations shift their practices and commit to co-creation), it will be less of a mystery and risk, and more of a permanent element of 'doing business as usual'. Nevertheless, before reaching that stage, many firms will try co-creation and fail, inflicting serious damage on their business. Therefore, we must draw lessons from those failures, as well as successes, in order to map out and systematize this practice.

Note

1. Latin American and Asian videogames markets are unaccounted for in this work. Significant differences in the influence of organizational culture on co-creation, or different configurations of competences might exist in those settings. Considering the size and importance of those non-Western markets (Marchand and Hennig-Thurau, 2013; O'Donnell, 2012; Zackariasson and Wilson, 2012) and the increasing amount of creative service development there, accounting for them is instrumental for complete understanding of co-creation.

References

Amin, A., and Cohendet, P., (2004). *Architectures of Knowledge: Firms, Capabilities and Communities*. Oxford: Oxford University Press.

Bach, L., Cohendet, P., Penin, J., and Simon, L., (2008). IPR and "open creativity": The cases of videogames and of the music industry. The Creative Industries and Intellectual Property. DIME–London conference May 22–23, 2008.

Bagozzi, R.P., and Dholakia, U.M., (2006). Open source software user communities: A study of participation in Linux user groups. *Management Science*, 52(7), pages 1099–1115.

Baldwin, C., Hienerth, C., and von Hippel, E., (2006). How user innovations become commercial products: A theoretical investigation and case study. *Research Policy*, 35(9), pages 1291–1313.

Banks, J., and Potts, J., (2010). Co-creating games: A co-evolutionary analysis. *New Media and Society*, 12(2), pages 252–270.

Barney, J.B., (1986). Organizational culture: Can it be a source of sustained competitive advantage? *The Academy of Management Review*, 11(3), pages 656–665.

Bengtsson, L., and Ryzhkova, N., (2015). Managing online user co-creation in service innovation. In: Agarwal, R., Selen, W., Roos, G., and Green, R., (eds). *The Handbook of Service Innovation*. London: Springer, pages 575–589.

Benkler, Y., (2006). *The Wealth of Networks*. Yale: Yale University Press.

Bergstrom, K., Carter, M., Woodford, D., and Paul, C., (2013). Constructing the ideal EVE Online player. In Proceedings of DiGRA 2013: DeFragging Game Studies, Atlanta, USA.

Bethke, E., (2003). *Game Development and Production*. Plano, TX: Wordware Publishing, Inc.

Bhalla, G., (2010). *Collaboration and Co-Creation: New Platforms for Marketing and Innovation*. New York: Springer.

Burger-Helmchen, T., and Cohendet, P., (2011). User communities and social software in the video game industry. *Long Range Planning*, 44, pages 317–343.

Chathoth, P., Altinay, L., Harrington, R.J., Okumus, F., and Chan, E.S.W., (2013). Co-production versus co-creation: A process based continuum in the hotel service context. *International Journal of Hospitality Management*, 32, pages 11–20.

Cheng, C.C., and Huizingh, E.K., (2014). When is open innovation beneficial? The role of strategic orientation. *Journal of Product Innovation Management*, 31(6), pages 1235–1253.

Chesbrough, H., (2011). Bringing open innovation to services. *MIT Sloan Management Review*, 52(2), pages 85–90.

Christensen, J.F., Olesen, M.H., and Kjær, J.S., (2005). The industrial dynamics of open innovation: Evidence from the transformation of consumer electronics. *Research Policy*, 34(10), pages 1533–1549.

Cohen, W.M., and Levinthal, D.A., (1990). Absorptive capacity: A new perspective on learning and innovation. *Administrative Science Quarterly*, 35(1), pages 128–152.

den Hertog, P.D., (2000). Knowledge-intensive business services as co-producers of innovation. *International Journal of Innovation Management*, 4(04), pages 491–528.

Dibbell, J., (2006). *Play Money*. New York: Basic Books.

Dosi, G., and Nelson, R.R., (1994). An introduction to evolutionary theories in economics. *Journal of Evolutionary Economics*, 4(3), pages 153–172.

Ducheneaut, N., et al., (2007). The life and death of online gaming communities: A look at guilds in World of Warcraft. CHI 2007 Proceedings. April 28–May 3, 2007. San Jose, CA, USA.

Ebner, W., Leimeister, J.M., Krcmar, H., (2009). Community engineering for innovations: The ideas competition as a method to nurture a virtual community for innovations. *R&D Management*, 39(4), pages 342–356.

Echeverri, P., and Skålén, P., (2011). Co-creation and co-destruction: A practice-theory based study of interactive value formation. *Marketing Theory*, 11(3), pages 351–373.

Edvardsson, B., Kristensson, P., Magnusson, P., and Sundström, E., (2012). Customer integration within service development—a review of methods and an analysis of insitu and exsitu contributions. *Technovation*, 32(7), pages 419–429.

Edvardsson, B., and Olsson, J., (1996). Key concepts for new service development. *Service Industries Journal*, 16(2), pages 140–164.

Edwards, M., Logue, D., and Schweitzer, J., (2015). Towards an understanding of open innovation in services: Beyond the firm and towards relational co-creation. In: Agarwal, R., Selen, W., Roos, G., and Green, R., (eds). *The Handbook of Service Innovation*. London: Springer, pages 75–90.

Eisenhardt, K.M., (1989). Building theories from case study research. *Academy of Management Review*, 14(4), pages 532–550.

Enkel, E., Kausch, C., and Gassmann, O., (2005). Managing the risk of customer integration. *European Management Journal*, 23(2), pages 203–213.

Estelles-Arolas, E., and Gonzales-Ladron-de-Guevara, F., (2012). Towards an integrated crowdsourcing definition. *Journal of Information Science*, 38(2), pages 189–200.

Etgar, M., (2008). A descriptive model of the consumer co-production process. *Journal of the Academy of Marketing Science*, 36(1), pages 97–108.

Fang, E., (2008). Customer participation and the trade-off between new product innovativeness and speed to market. *Journal of Marketing*, 72(4), pages 90–101.

Feng, W., Brandt, D., and Saha, D., (2007). A long-term study of a popular MMORPG. In: *Proceedings of the 6th ACM SIGCOMM Workshop on Network and System Support for Games*. ACM Press, pages 19–24.

Fereday, J., and Muir-Cochrane, E., (2006). Demonstrating rigor using thematic analysis: A hybrid approach of inductive and deductive coding and theme development. *International Journal of Qualitative Methods*, 5(1), pages 80–92.

Fisher, D., and Smith, S., (2011). Co-creation is chaotic: What it means for marketing when no one has control. *Marketing Theory*, 11(3), pages 325–350.

Franke, N., and von Hippel, E., (2003). Satisfying heterogeneous user needs via innovation toolkits: The case of Apache security software. *Research Policy*, 32(7), pages 1199–1215.

Franke, N., and Shah, S., (2003). How communities support innovative activities: An exploration of assistance and sharing among end-users. *Research Policy*, 32, pages 157–178.

Franklin, M., Searle, N., Stoyanova, D., and Townley, B., (2013). Innovation in the application of digital tools for managing uncertainty: The case of UK independent film. *Creativity and Innovation Management*, 22(3), pages 320–333.

Frow, P., Payne, A., and Storbacka, K., (2011). Co-creation: A typology and conceptual framework. In: *Proceedings of ANZMAC* (November), pages 1–6.

Füller, J., (2010). Refining virtual co-creation from a consumer perspective. *California Management Review*, 52(2), pages 98–122.

Füller, J., and Matzler, K., (2007). Virtual product experience and customer participation—a chance for customer-centred, really new products. *Technovation*, 27(6), pages 378–387.

Füller, J., Matzler, K., and Hoppe, M., (2008). Brand community members as a source of innovation. Journal of Product Innovation Management, 25(6), pages 608–619.

Fynes, B., and Lally, A.M., (2008). Innovation in services: From service concepts to service experiences. In: Hefley, B. and Murphy, W., (eds). *Service Science, Management and Engineering: Education for the 21st Century*. New York: Springer Science & Business Media, pages 329–333.

Gangi, P.M., Wasko, M.M., and Hooker, R.E., (2010). Getting customers' ideas to work for you: Learning from Dell how to succeed with online user innovation communities. *MIS Quarterly Executive*, 9(4), pages 213–228.

Garcia-Lorenzo, L., (2004). (Re)producing the organization through narratives: The case of a multinational. *Intervention Research*, 1, pages 43–60.

Gebauer, J., Füller, J., and Pezzei, R., (2013). The dark and the bright side of co-creation: Triggers of member behaviour in online innovation communities. *Journal of Business Research*, 66, pages 1516–1527.

Gibbs, M.R., Carter, M., and Mori, J., (2013). Vile rat: Spontaneous shrines in EVE online. Paper presented at the EVE Online Workshop, Chania, Greece, May 14–17, 2013.

Gibbs, L., Kealy, M., Willis, K., Green, J., Welch, N., and Daly, J., (2007). What have sampling and data collection got to do with good qualitative research? *Australian and New Zealand Journal of Public Health*, 31(6), pages 540–544.

Grant, R.M., (2010). *Contemporary Strategy Analysis and Cases: Text and Cases*. New York: John Wiley & Sons.

Grantham, A., and Kaplinsky, R., (2005). Getting the measure of the electronic games industry: Developers and the management of innovation. *International Journal of Innovation Management*, 9(2), pages 183–213.

Grimes, S.M., (2006). Online multiplayer games: A virtual space for intellectual property debates? *New Media & Society*, 8(6), pages 969–990.

Grönroos, C., (1994). From marketing mix to relationship marketing: Towards a paradigm shift in marketing. *Management Decision*, 32(2), pages 4–20.

Grönroos, C., (2011). Value co-creation in service logic: A critical analysis. *Marketing Theory*, 11(3), pages 279–301.

Grove, S.J., Fisk, R.P., and Bitner, M.J., (1992). Dramatizing the service experience: A managerial approach. *Advances in Services Marketing and Management*, 1, pages 91–121.

Gruner, K.E., and Homburg, C., (2000). Does customer interaction enhance new product success? *Journal of Business Research*, 49(1), pages 1–14.

Gummesson, E., (2002). Relationship marketing in the new economy. *Journal of Relationship Marketing*, 1(1), pages 37–57.

Gustafsson, A., Kristensson, P., and Witell, L., (2012). Customer co-creation in service innovation: A matter of communication? *Journal of Service Management*, 23(3), pages 311–327.

Haefliger, S., Jäger, P., and von Krogh, G., (2010). Under the radar: Industry entry by user entrepreneurs. *Research Policy*, 39(9), pages 1198–1213.

Hamari, J., Koivisto, J., and Sarsa, H., (2014). Does gamification work?–A literature review of empirical studies on gamification. In: *System Sciences (HICSS), 2014 47th Hawaii International Conference*, January. IEEE, pages 3025–3034.

Handke, C., (2004). Defining creative industries by comparing the creation of novelty. In the workshop Creative Industries–a measure of urban development, WIWIPOL and FOKUS, Vienna.

Hardt, M., and Negri, A., (2001). *Empire* (New ed.). Cambridge, MA: Harvard University Press.

Hartley, J., (2008). *Television Truths*. Malden, MA: Wiley-Blackwell.

Hartley, J., Potts, J., Cunningham, S., Flew, T., Keane, M., and Banks, J., (2013). *Key Concepts in Creative Industries*. London: Sage.

Hartley, J., Potts, J., MacDonald, T., Erkunt, C., and Kufleitner, C., (2012). CCI creative city index. *Cultural Science Journal*, 5(1–138).

Hartley, J., Sørensen, E., and Torfing, J., (2013). Collaborative innovation: A viable alternative to market competition and organizational entrepreneurship. *Public Administration Review*, 73(6), pages 821–830.

Harvard Law Review, (2012). Spare the mod: In support of total-conversion modified video games. *Harvard Law Review*, 125, pages 789–810.

Hau, Y.S., and Kim, Y.G., (2011). Why would online gamers share their innovation-conducive knowledge in the online game user community? Integrating individual motivations and social capital perspectives. *Computers in Human Behavior*, 27(2), pages 956–970.

Haythornthwaite, C., and Gruzd, A., (2007). A noun phrase analysis tool for mining online community conversations. Paper presented at the International Conference on Communications and Technologies, East Lansing, Michigan.

Hight, J., and Novak, J., (2008). *Game Development Essentials: Game Project Management*. Clifton Park, NY: Delmar.

Hills, M., (2002). *Fan Cultures*. London: Routledge.

Howe, J., (2008). *Crowdsourcing: Why the Power of the Crowd Is Driving the Future of Business*. New York: Crown Business.

Hoyer, W.D., Chandy, R., Dorotic, M., Krafft, M., and Singh, S.S., (2010). Consumer co-creation in new product development. *Journal of Service Research*, 13(3), pages 283–296.

Humphreys, S., (2005a). Productive users, intellectual property and governance: The challenges of computer games. *Media and Arts Law Review*, 10(4), pages 299–310.

Humphreys, S., (2005b). Productive players: Online computer games' challenge to conventional media forms. *Communication and Critical/Cultural Studies*, 2(1), pages 36–50.

Humphreys, S., (2007). You're in our world now: Ownership and access in the proprietary community of an MMOG. In: Sugumaran, V., (eds). *Intelligent Information Technologies: Concepts, Methodologies, Tools, and Applications*. Hershey, PA: Information Science Reference (IGI Global), pages 2058–2072.

Humphreys, S., Fitzgerald, B.F., Banks, J.A., and Suzor, N.P., (2005). Fan based production for computer games: User led innovation, the 'drift of value' and the negotiation of intellectual property rights. *Media International Australia*

Incorporating Culture and Policy: Quarterly Journal of Media Research and Resources, 114, pages 16–29.

Ind, N., and Coates, N., (2013). The meanings of co-creation. *European Business Review*, 25(1), pages 86–95.

Irish, D., (2005). *The Game Producer's Handbook*. Boston, MA: Course Technology.

Jäger, P., Haefliger, S., and von Krogh, G., (2010). A directing audience: How specialized feedback in virtual community of consumption stimulates new media production. ETH Zurich Working Paper.

Jenkins, H., (2006). *Convergence Culture: Where Old and New Media Collide*. New York: New York University Press.

Jenkins, H., (2009). What happened before YouTube. In: Burgess, J. and Green, J., (eds). *YouTube: Online Video and the Politics of Participatory Culture*. London: Polity Press, pages 109–125.

Jensen, M.B., Johnson, B., Lorenz, E., and Lundvall, B.A., (2007). Forms of knowledge and modes of innovation. *Research Policy*, 36, pages 680–693.

Jeppesen, L.B., and Frederiksen, L., (2006). Why do users contribute to firm-hosted user communities? The case of computer-controlled music instruments. *Organization Science*, 17(1), pages 45–63.

Jeppesen, L.B., and Molin, M., (2003). Consumers as co-developers: Learning and innovation outside the firm. *Technology Analysis & Strategic Management*, 15(3), pages 363–383.

Jordan, T., (2008). *Hacking: Digital Media and Technological Determinism*. Cambridge: Polity Press.

Kasmire, J., Korhonen, J.M., and Nikolic, I., (2012). How radical is a radical innovation? An outline for a computational approach. *Energy Procedia*, 20, pages 346–353.

Keith, C., (2010). *Agile Game Development With Scrum*. Upper Saddle River, NJ: Addison-Wesley.

King, B., and Borland, J., (2014). *Dungeons and Dreamers*. Carnegie Mellon University: ETC Press.

Kline, S., Dyer-Witherford, N., and De Peuter, G., (2003). *Digital Play: The Interaction of Technology, Culture and Marketing*. Montreal: McGill-Queen's University Press.

Knight, F.H., (1921). *Risk, Uncertainty, and Profit*. Boston, MA: Hart, Schaffner & Marx and Houghton Mifflin Co.

Kohler, T., Füller, J., Matzler, K., and Stieger, D., (2011b). Co-creation in virtual worlds: The design of the user experience. *MIS Quarterly*, 35(3), pages 773–788.

Kohler, T., Füller, J., Stieger, D., and Matzler, K., (2011a). Avatar-based innovation: Consequences of the virtual co-creation experience. *Computers in Human Behaviour*, 27, pages 160–168.

Kohler, T., Matzler, K., and Füller, J., (2009). Avatar-based innovation: Using virtual worlds for real-world innovation. *Technovation*, 29(6), pages 395–407.

Koster, R., (2005). *A Theory of Fun for Game Design*. Sebastopol, CA: Paraglyph Press.

Kozinets, R.V., (2007). Inno-tribes: Star Trek as wikimedia. In: Cova, B., Kozinets, R., and Shankar, A., (eds). *Consumer Tribes*. New York: Routledge.

Kozinets, R.V., Hemetsberger, A., and Schau, H.J., (2008). The wisdom of consumer crowds collective innovation in the age of networked marketing. *Journal of Macromarketing*, 28(4), pages 339–354.

Kücklich, J., (2005). Precarious playbour: Modders and the digital games industry. *The Fibreculture Journal*, 5. http://five.fibreculturejournal.org.

Kuusisto, A., (2008). Customer roles in business service production-implications for involving the customer in service innovation. In: Kuusisto, A. and Päällysaho, S., (eds). *Customer Role in Service Production and Innovation–Looking for Directions for Future Research*. Lappeenranta University of Technology, Faculty of Technology Management Research Report.

Lakhani, K.R., and von Hippel, E., (2003). How open source software works: "Free" user-to-user assistance. *Research Policy*, 32(6), pages 923–943.

Lampel, J., Lant, T., and Shamsie, J., (2000). Balancing act: Learning from organizing practices in cultural industries. *Organization Science*, 11(3), pages 263–269.

Lehner, O.M., (2012). A literature review and research agenda for crowdfunding of social ventures. In: *2012 Research Cooloquium on Social Entrepreneurship*, 16–19.07, SAID Business School.

Lettl, C., (2007). User involvement competence for radical innovation. *Journal of Engineering and Technology Management*, 24, pages 53–75.

Lichtenthaler, U., and Lichtenthaler, E., (2009). A capability-based framework for open innovation: Complementing absorptive capacity. *Journal of Management Studies*, 46(8), pages 1315–1338.

Lusch, R.F., and Vargo, S.L., (2006). Service-dominant logic: Reactions, reflections and refinements. *Marketing Theory*, 6(3), pages 281–288.

Luthje, C., (2002). Characteristics of innovating users in a consumer goods field: An empirical study of sport-related product consumers. MIT Sloan Working Paper, No. 4331–02. Cambridge, MA, Massachusetts Institute of Technology.

Luthje, C., and Herstatt, C., (2004). The lead user method: An outline of empirical findings and issues for future research. *R&D Management*, 34(5), pages 553–568.

Luthje, C., Herstatt, C., and von Hippel, E., (2006). User–innovators and "local" information: The case of mountain biking. *Research Policy*, 34(6), pages 951–965.

Lynn, G.S., and Akgun, A.E., (1998). Innovation strategies under uncertainty: A contingency approach for new product development. *Engineering Management Journal*, 10(3), pages 11–18.

Magnusson, P., Matthing, J., and Kristensson, P., (2003). Managing user involvement in service innovation. *Journal of Service Research*, 6(2), pages 111–24.

Magnusson, P.R., (2009). Exploring the contributions of involving ordinary users in ideation of technology-based services. *Journal of Product Innovation Management*, 26(5), pages 578–593.

Malaby, T.M., (2006). Coding control: Governance and contingency in the production of online worlds. *First Monday*, special issue no. 7(September).

Malaby, T.M., (2009). *Making Virtual Worlds: Linden Lab and Second Life*. Ithaca and London: Cornell University Press.

Marchand, A., and Hennig-Thurau, T., (2013). Value creation in the video game industry: Industry economics, consumer benefits, and research opportunities. *Journal of Interactive Marketing*, 27(3), pages 141–157.

Martins, E.C., and Terblanche, F., (2003). Building organisational culture that stimulates creativity and innovation. *European Journal of Innovation Management*, 6(1), pages 64–74.

Matthing, J., Sanden, B., and Edvardsson, B., (2004). New service development: Learning from and with customers. *International Journal of Service Industry Management*, 15(5), pages 479–98.

Miles, I., (1993). Services in the new industrial economy. *Futures*, 25(6), pages 653–672.

Miles, I., (2008). Patterns of innovation in service industries. *IBM Systems Journal*, 47(1), pages 115–128.

Miles, I., and Green, L., (2008). *Hidden Innovation in Creative Industries*. London: NESTA.

Mollick, E., (2012). The dynamics of crowdfunding: Determinants of success and failure. SSRN scholarly paper. Social Science Research Network, Rochester, NY.

Müller, K., Rammer, C., and Trüby, J., (2009). The role of creative industries in industrial innovation. *Innovation*, 11(2), pages 148–168.

Muniz, A.M., Jr., and O'Guinn, T.C., (2001). Brand community. *Journal of Consumer Research*, 27(4), pages 412–432.

Naranjo-Valencia, J.C., Jiménez-Jiménez, D., and Sanz-Valle, R., (2011). Innovation or imitation? The role of organizational culture. *Management Decision*, 49(1), pages 55–72.

Nardi, B.M., (2010). *My Life as a Night Elf Priest*. Ann Arbor: The University of Michigan Press and The University of Michigan Library.

Nardi, B.M., and Kallinikos, J., (2011). Technology, agency and community: The case of modding in world of warcraft. In: Holmstrom, J., et al., (eds). *Industrial Informatics Design, Use and Innovation: Perspectives and Services*. New York: Innovation Science Reference. Hershey.

Nelson, R.R., (1991). Why do firms differ, and how does it matter? *Strategic Management Journal*, 12(1), pages 61–74.

Nelson, R.R., and Winter, S.G., (1982). The Schumpeterian tradeoff revisited. *The American Economic Review*, 71(1), pages 114–132.

Nenonen, S., and Storbacka, K., (2010). Business model design: Conceptualizing networked value co-creation. *International Journal of Quality and Service Sciences*, 2, pages 43–59.

O'Donnell, C., (2012). This is not a software industry. In: Zackariasson, P. and Wilson, T.L., (eds). *The Video Games Industry: Formation, Present State, and Future*. London and New York: Routledge.

O'Donnell, C., (2014). *Developer's Dilemma*. London, England: MIT Press.

OECD, (2007). *Annual Report*. Paris: OECD Publishing.

Ogawa, S., and Piller, F.T., (2006). Reducing the risks of new product development. *MIT Sloan Management Review*, 47(2), page 65.

O'Hern, M.S., and Rindfleisch, A., (2010). Customer co-creation: A typology and research Agenda. In: Malhotra, N.K., (ed) *Review of Marketing Research*, 6, pages 84–106, Bigley: Emerald Books.

O'Hern, M.S., Rindfleisch, A., Antia, K.D., and Schweidel, D.A., (2011). The impact of user-generated content on product innovation. SSRN. http://ssrn.com/abstract=1843250 or http://dx.doi.org/10.2139/ssrn.1843250

O'Mahony, S., and Ferraro, F., (2007). The emergence of governance in an open source community. *Academy of Management Journal*, 50(5), pages 1079–1106.

Ordanini, A., Miceli, L., Pizzetti, M., and Parasuraman, A., (2011). Crowd-funding: Transforming customers into investors through innovative service platforms. *Journal of Service Management*, 22(4), pages 443–470.

O'Reilly, T., (2005). Spreading the knowledge of innovators. What is web, 2.

Oskarsson, P.J., (2014). The council of stellar management: Implementation of deliberative, democratically elected, council in EVE. White Paper. http://web.

ccpgamescdn.com/communityassets/pdf/csm/CSMSummary.pdf (accessed on 6.04.2014).

Päällysaho, S., (2008). Customer interaction in service innovations: A review of literature. In: Kuusisto, A. and Päällysaho, S., (eds). *Customer Role in Service Production and Innovation–Looking for Directions for Future Research.* Lappeenranta University of Technology, Faculty of Technology Management Research Report, 195.

Panourgias, N.S., Nandhakumar, J., and Scarbrough, H., (2014). Entanglements of creative agency and digital technology: A sociomaterial study of computer game development. *Technological Forecasting and Social Change*, 83, pages 111–126.

Paul, C., (2011). Don't play me: EVE online, new players and rhetoric. In: *Proceedings of the 6th International Conference on Foundations of Digital Games.* ACM Press, pages 262–264.

Pavitt, K., (1990). What we know about the strategic management of technology. *California Management Review*, 32(3), pages 17–26.

Payne, A., Storbacka, K., Frow, P., and Knox, S., (2009). Co-creating brands: Diagnosing and designing the relationship experience. *Journal of Business Research*, 62(3), pages 379–389.

Pearce, C., (2009). *Communities of Play: Emergent Cultures in Multiplayer Games and Virtual Worlds.* Cambridge, MA and London, England: MIT Press.

Peteraf, M.A., (1993). The cornerstones of competitive advantage: A resource-based view. *Strategic Management Journal*, 14(3), pages 179–191.

Piller, F., and Ihl, C., (2009). *Open Innovation With Customers: Foundations, Competences and International Trends.* RWTH Aachen University.

Piller, F., Ihl, C., and Vossen, A., (2011). A typology of customer co-creation in the innovation process. In: Hanekop, H. and Wittke, V., (eds). *New Forms of Collaborative Innovation and Production on the Internet: An Interdisciplinary Perspective.* University of Goettingen.

Pine, J., and Gilmore, J.H., (1998). Welcome to the experience economy. *Harvard Business Review*, (July–August), pages 97–105.

Pisano, G.P., and Verganti, R., (2008). Which kind of collaboration is right for you. *Harvard Business Review*, 86(12), pages 78–86.

Potts, J., (2009). Creative industries and innovation policy. *Innovation: Management, Policy and Practice*, 11(2), pages 138–147.

Potts, J., Hartley, J., Banks, J., Burgess, J., Cobcroft, R., Cunningham, S., and Montgomery, L., (2008). Consumer co-creation and situated creativity. *Industry and Innovation*, 15(5), pages 459–474.

Potts, J., Cunningham, S., Hartley, J., and Ormerod, P., (2008). Social network markets: A new definition of the creative industries. *Journal of Cultural Economics*, 32(3), pages 167–185.

Prahalad, C.K., and Hamel, G., (1994). Strategy as a field of study: Why search for a new paradigm? *Strategic Management Journal*, 15(S2), pages 5–16.

Prahalad, C.K., and Krishnan, M.S., (2008). *The New Age of Innovation. Driving Co-Created Value Through Global Networks.* New York: McGraw-Hill.

Prahalad, C.K., and Ramaswamy, V., (2004). Co-creation experiences: The next practice in value creation. *Journal of Interactive Marketing*, 18(3), pages 5–14.

Preston, P., Kerr, A., and Cawley, A., (2009). Innovation and knowledge in the digital media sector: An information economy approach. *Information, Communication & Society*, 12(7), pages 994–1014.

Raasch, C., and von Hippel, E., (2013). Innovation process benefits: The journey as reward. *MIT Sloan Review*, 55(1), pages 33–39.

Reissman, C., (2004). Narrative analysis. In: Lewis-Beck, M., Bryman, A., and Futing Liao, T., (eds). *Encyclopedia of Social Science Research Methods*. London: Sage, pages 705–709.

Ritzer, G., and Jurgenson, N., (2010). Production, consumption, prosumption: The nature of capitalism in the age of the digital 'prosumer'. *Journal of Consumer Culture*, 10(1), pages 13–36.

Roberts, D., Hughes, M., and Kertbo, K., (2014). Exploring consumers' motivations to engage in innovation through co-creation activities. *European Journal of Marketing*, 38(½), pages 147–169.

Robson, C., (2011). *Real World Research* (Third ed.). New York: John Wiley & Sons.

Rosenbloom, R.S., and Christensen, C.M., (1994)., Technological discontinuties, organizational capabilities, and strategic commitments. *Industrial and Corporate Change*, 3(3), pages 655–685.

Rossignol, J., (2008). *This Gaming Life: Travels in Three Cities*. The University of Michigan Press and The University of Michigan Library.

Rowlands, T., (2012). *Video Game Worlds*. Walnut Creek, CA: Left Coast Press, Inc.

Saarijärvi, H., (2012). The mechanisms of value co-creation. *Journal of Strategic Marketing*, 20(5), pages 381–391.

Saarijärvi, H., Kannan, P.K., and Kuusela, H., (2013). Value co-creation: Theoretical approaches and practical implications. *European Business Review*, 25(1), pages 6–19.

Sakao, T., Panshef, V., and Dörsam, E., (2009). Addressing uncertainty of PSS for value-chain oriented service development. In: Sakao, T. and Lindahl, M., (eds). *Introduction to Product/Service-System Design*. London: Springer, pages 137–157.

Sanders, E.B.N., and Stappers, P.J., (2008). Co-creation and the new landscapes of design. *CoDesign*, 4(1), pages 5–18.

Santonen, T., and Lehtelä, M., (2010). Higher education student's motivation to participate in online mass innovation. *The XXI ISPIM Conference-The Dynamics of Innovation-Bilbao*, Spain, pages 6–9.

Saur-Amaral, I., (2012). Wisdom-of-the-crowds to enhance innovation: A conceptual framework. ISPIM Conference Proceedings 1–7. Barcelona, Spain, 17–20.06.2012.

Scarbrough, H., Panourgias, N.S., and Nandhakumar, J., (2015). Developing a relational view of the organizing role of objects: A study of the innovation process in computer games. *Organization Studies*, 36(2), pages 197–220.

Schau, H.J., Muniz, A.M. Jr., and Arnould, E.J., (2009). How brand community practices create value. *Journal of Marketing*, 73(5), pages 30–51.

Schell, J., (2008). *The Art of Game Design: A Book of Lenses*. Boca Raton, FL: CRC Press.

Schumpeter, J., (1950). *Capitalism, Socialism and Democracy* (Third ed.). New York: Harper and Brothers.

Sieg, J.H., Wallin, M.W., and Von Krogh, G., (2010). Managerial challenges in open innovation: A study of innovation intermediation in the chemical industry. *R&D Management*, 40(3), pages 281–291.

Sotamaa, O., (2004). Playing it my way? Mapping the modder agency. *In Internet Research Conference*, 5, pages 19–22.

Stoneman, P., (2007). *An Introduction to the Definition and Measurement of Soft Innovation*. London: NESTA.

Sundbo, J., and Toivonen, M., (eds). (2011). *User-Based Innovation in Services*. Cheltenham: Edward Elgar Publishing.

Surowiecki, J., (2004). *The Wisdom of Crowds*. New York: Anchor.

Tapscott, D., and Williams, A.D., (2008). *Wikinomics: How Mass Collaboration Changes Everything*. New York: Penguin.

Taylor, T.L., (2006). *Play Between Worlds: Exploring Online Game Culture*. Cambridge, MA: MIT Press.

Taylor, T.L., (2006). Beyond management: Considering participatory design and governance in player culture. *First Monday*, special issue, 7(September 2006). http://firstmonday.org/issues/issue11_9/taylor/index.html.

Taylor, T.L., (2008). Does world of warcraft change everything? How a PvP server, multinational playerbase, and surveillance mod scene caused me pause. In: Corneliussen, H.G. and Rettberg, J.W., (eds). *Digital Culture, Play and Identity: A World of Warcraft Reader*. Cambridge, MA: MIT Press.

Teece, D.J., (2007). Explicating dynamic capabilities: The nature and microfoundations of (sustainable) enterprise performance. *Strategic Management Journal*, 28(13), pages 1319–1350.

Teece, D.J., (2010). Business models, business strategy and innovation. *Long Range Planning*, 43(2), pages 172–194.

Teece, D., and Pisano, G., (1994). The dynamic capabilities of firms: An introduction. *Industrial and Corporate Change*, 3(3), pages 537–556.

Trott, P., (2005). *Innovation Management and New Product Development*. Harlow, Essex: Pearson Education.

Tschang, F.T., (2005). Videogames as interactive experiential products and their manner of development. *International Journal of Innovation Management*, 9(1), pages 103–131.

Tschang, F.T., (2007). Balancing the tensions between rationalization and creativity in the video games industry. *Organization Science*, 18(60, pages 989–1005.

Tushman, M.L., and Anderson, P., (1986). Technological discontinuities and organizational environments. *Administrative Science Quarterly*, 31(3), pages 439–465.

Utterback, J.M., (1994). *Mastering the Dynamics of Innovation*. Cambridge, MA: Harvard Business School Press.

Van de Ven, A.H., (1993). A community perspective on the emergence of innovations. *Journal of Engineering and Technology Management*, 10(1), pages 23–51.

Van Dijck, J., (2009). Users like you? Theorizing agency in user-generated content. *Media, Culture and Society*, 31(1), pages 41–58.

van Doorn, J., Lemon, K.N., Mittal, V., Nass, S., Pick, D., Pirner, P., and Verhoef, P., (2010). Customer engagement behavior: Theoretical foundations and research directions. *Journal of Service Research*, 13(3), pages 253–266.

Vargo, S.L., and Lusch, R.F., (2004). Evolving to a new dominant logic for marketing. *Journal of Marketing*, 68, pages 1–17.

Vargo, S.L., and Lusch, R.F., (2008). Service-dominant logic: Continuing the evolution. *Journal of the Academy of Marketing Science*, 36(1), pages 1–10.

Verhagen, T., Feldberg, F., van den Hooff, B., Meents, S., and Merikivi, J., (2011). Satisfaction with virtual worlds: An integrated model of experiential value. *Information & Management*, 48(6), pages 201–207.

Van der Graaf, S., (2009). Designing for mod development: User creativity as product development strategy on the firm-hosted 3D software platform. Ph.D Dissertation, LSE.

Van der Graaf, S., (2012). Get organized at work! A look inside the game design process of valve and linden lab. *Bulletin of Science, Technology & Society*, pages 1–9, 0270467612469079.

Von Hippel, E., (1988). *The Sources of Innovation*. New York: Oxford University Press.

Von Hippel, E., (2005). *Democratizing Innovation*. Cambridge, MA: MIT Press.

Von Hippel, E., (2007). Horizontal innovation networks—by and for users. *Industrial and Corporate Change*, 16(2), pages 293–315.

Von Krogh, G., and von Hippel, E., (2006). The promise of research on open source software. *Management Science*, 52(7), pages 975–983.

Voss, C., and Zomerdijk, L., (2007). Innovation in experimental services—an empirical view. In: DTI (ed). *Innovation in Services*. London: DTI, pages 97–134.

Yin, R.K., (2009). *Case Study Research. Design and Methods* (Fourth ed.). Thousand Oaks and New Delhi: Sage.

Zackariasson, P., and Wilson, T.L., (2012). *The Video Games Industry. Formation, Present State, and Future*. London and New York: Routledge.

Zahra, S.A., and George, G., (2002). Absorptive capacity: A review, reconceptualization, and extension. *Academy of Management Review*, 27(2), pages 185–203.

Index

For Product Safety Concerns and Information please contact our EU
representative GPSR@taylorandfrancis.com
Taylor & Francis Verlag GmbH, Kaufingerstraße 24, 80331 München, Germany